About the Cover

The cover reproduces a portion of "The Body's Sun," a mural located in the cardiology waiting room of St. Luke's Hospital in San Francisco. Lead artist for the mural was Christy Majano.

"The Body's Sun" © 2004 Precita Eyes Muralists, Christy Majano

Service Learning for Civic Engagement Series
Series Editor: Gerald Eisman

Available:

Race, Poverty, and Social Justice
Multidisciplinary Perspectives Through Service Learning
Edited by José Calderón

Gender Identity, Equity, and Violence
Multidisciplinary Perspectives Through Service Learning
Edited by Geraldine B. Stahly

Research, Advocacy, and Political Engagement
Multidisciplinary Perspectives Through Service Learning
Edited by Sally Cahill Tannenbaum

Forthcoming:

Social Responsibility and Sustainability
Multidisciplinary Perspectives Through Service Learning

PROMOTING HEALTH AND WELLNESS IN
UNDERSERVED COMMUNITIES

PROMOTING HEALTH AND WELLNESS IN UNDERSERVED COMMUNITIES

Multidisciplinary Perspectives
Through Service Learning

Edited by
Anabel Pelham and
Elizabeth Sills

Foreword by Robert A. Corrigan

Sty/us

STERLING, VIRGINIA

Sty/us

COPYRIGHT © 2009 BY STYLUS PUBLISHING, LLC.

Published by Stylus Publishing, LLC
22883 Quicksilver Drive
Sterling, Virginia 20166-2102

Library of Congress Cataloging-in-Publication-Data
Promoting health and wellness in underserved
communities : multidisciplinary perspectives through service
learning / edited by Anabel Pelham and Elizabeth Sills ;
foreword by Robert A. Corrigan.
p. cm.— (Service learning for civic engagement series)
Includes index.
ISBN 978-1-57922-240-6 (cloth : alk. paper)
ISBN 978-1-57922-241-3 (pbk. : alk. paper)
1. Health promotion.   2. Community health services.
3. Medically underserved areas.   I. Pelham, Anabel O.
II. Sills, Elizabeth, 1971–
RA427.8.P7654   2009
362.1—dc22
2009026912

ISBN: 978-1-57922-240-6 (cloth)
ISBN: 978-1-57922-241-3 (paper)

Printed in the United States of America

All first editions printed on acid free paper
that meets the American National Standards Institute
Z39-48 Standard.

Bulk Purchases

Quantity discounts are available for use in workshops
and for staff development.
Call 1-800-232-0223

First Edition, 2009

10   9   8   7   6   5   4   3   2   1

CONTENTS

ACKNOWLEDGMENTS

Whe would like to give special thanks to colleagues within and external to the California State University who serve on the advisory board for the monograph series. Debra David, Barbara Holland, Kathy O'Byrne, Seth Pollack, and Maureen Rubin continue to provide invaluable advice on the development of the current volumes and the dimensions the series will explore in the future.

This volume would not be possible without the stories of inspired work of the thousands of dedicated faculty and lecturers working in the California State University system.

This material is based upon work supported by the Corporation for National and Community Service under Learn and Serve America Grant No. 03LHHCA003. Opinions or points of view expressed in this document are those of the authors and do not necessarily reflect the official position of the Corporation or the Learn and Serve America Program.

FOREWORD

Perhaps once in a generation a movement comes along to redefine—even transform—higher education. I can point to the GI Bill of 1944, which opened the gates to a much broader population than had ever before enjoyed the opportunity to receive higher education. The civil rights struggle and the later antiwar movement galvanized students and faculty across the nation. Many of us participated directly in these movements; many more worked then, and in the years that followed, to overhaul what we perceived as an outmoded university curriculum as we struggled to open up the university to new ideas, new teaching strategies, and most of all, to underrepresented populations.

To this list, I would now add community service learning. I consider this movement in higher education as exciting as anything I have experienced as an educator. Service learning, and its central role in our goals of campuswide civic engagement and ethical education, may be the most significant development on our campuses since the curricular reforms of the 1960s. In fact, I believe that it will prove to be *the* higher education legacy of the early 21st century, and that it will have a lifelong impact on our students.

Since service learning began to take formal hold throughout the nation in the early 1990s, it has come to be seen as much more than community volunteerism linked with academic study. It is a vehicle for character and citizenship development—in short, for all that we most value in a liberal education. Through thoughtfully structured service-learning experiences, students can test and apply the values of a healthy democracy to some of the most complex and challenging issues of our time.

In recent years, higher education has begun more deliberately to pursue a historic mission: what I might call moral education—our responsibility both to our students and society. The Association of American Colleges and Universities terms this "core commitments," and calls on us to educate our students "for personal and social responsibility." This is the highest aim of liberal education. It is the culmination of our mission to service, to preparing our students with the skills and desire to contribute positively to our democratic society and to the greater world, to fostering a campus climate where speech is open, but where we can disagree—even passionately—without venom or hatred, and to ensuring that our students find in the class-room a safe and receptive environment in which to express, test, and challenge varying views.

A true liberal education encompasses far more than the breadth of knowledge and exposure to fields other than one's major that typically shape general education programs. That is certainly necessary, but liberal education transcends subject matter. Liberal education addresses both mind and heart. It is a set of experiences that give our students the tools they will need to think about complex issues and to deal with them as informed, ethical citizens. Liberal education helps our students deal with ambiguity and contradictions, helps them evaluate competing arguments and perspectives so that they will not have to fall back on the comfort—and distortion—of a binary, good/bad worldview.

Complexity characterizes our key social missions, as we seek to foster in our students respect and understanding of other cultures and viewpoints together with the skills they will need to move positively and effectively in a diverse and global society. I am most emphatically not talking about indoctrinating our students—presenting our values and asking them to take them as their own. Rather, I am talking about teaching our students *why* and *how* to think and reason about ethical and moral issues—not presenting them with answers, but developing their skills in finding their own way.

Liberal education prepares our students to act—and to do so in the context of values that take in the needs and concerns of others. Viewed in this context, the value of civically focused service learning is clear. It places our students in the arenas where ethics and efficacy need to join, where disciplinary boundaries are often irrelevant and integrative learning occurs naturally, and where students can gain a profound experience of their capacity—and responsibility—to effect positive change. As an antidote to cynicism and passivity, it is hard to top service learning.

Looking at the society into which they are graduating, our students might be excused for being cynical. From the front page to the business page to the sports section, headlines repeatedly reflect the ethical lapses of our society. This profound lack of integrity—the failure of a moral value system—is not restricted to one political party, to one religious group, to one ethnic group, or one gender group. It cuts across our society. In giving a final message to graduating students, I have asked them to seek one goal: to say no—say no to greed, say no to opportunism, say no to dishonesty, and decide that integrity—their own moral compasses—is what really matters.

If we accept that aim—and I believe we do—then service learning deserves a proud and prominent place in our curriculum. This series provides less a road map than a spur to creative course development for all faculty and administrators eager to adapt a powerful educational tool to a particular institution's nature, community, and student population.

Robert A. Corrigan
President, San Francisco State University
October 6, 2006

ABOUT THIS SERIES

Many service-learning practitioners are familiar with the comprehensive series of monographs on *Service-Learning in the Disciplines* produced and published by the American Association of Higher Education (AAHE) between 1997 and 2005. (The series is now published by Stylus Publishing, LLC.) Each volume of the series focused on a specific discipline—accounting, biology, composition, and so on—and provided a rich collection of exemplary practices in service learning as constituted around a disciplinary theme. Edward Zlotkowski (1997–2002), then senior associate at AAHE and series editor for the monographs, wrote that in "winning faculty support for this [service-learning] work" it was important to recognize that faculty "define themselves largely in terms of [their] academic disciplines," and so it was logical to design a series around disciplinary themes. The AAHE series became a primary reference for faculty who were considering adopting service-learning pedagogy, and the community of service-learning practitioners have much for which to thank the editors and contributors to those volumes. Other resources that were discipline specific—such as collections of syllabi—also helped to promote service learning to the level of the widespread acceptance it enjoys today on both the national and international stages.

Over the past few years, as the civic engagement movement has gained momentum, as educators have taken on the challenge of producing graduates who are engaged civically and politically in their communities, there has been a growing reexamination of service learning as the means for producing "civic learning" outcomes, that is, the combination of knowledge, skills, and disposition to make a difference in the civic life of our communities. The ubiquitous three-element Venn diagram—three interlocking circles representing enhanced academic learning, meaningful community service, and civic learning—that defines the field of service learning at its intersection (Howard, 2001), continues to do so, but there has been a marked redirection of emphasis from academic learning to civic. Nonetheless, as John Saltmarsh points out in his 2004 white paper for Campus Compact, *The Civic Purpose of Higher Education: A Focus on Civic Learning,* service learning is "the most potent method for achieving civic learning if civic learning outcomes are a part of curricular goals" (p. 7).

In parallel to this shift in emphasis, a second, related movement within higher education, *integrative learning,* has begun to take hold. As characterized by the American Association of Colleges and Universities (AACU) in partnership with the Carnegie Foundation for the Advancement of Teaching (Huber & Hutchings, 2004), integrative learning encompasses practices such as thematic first-year experiences, learning circles, interdisciplinary studies, capstone experiences, and other initiatives to foster students' ability to integrate concepts "across courses, over time, and between campus and community life" (p. 13). These two educational reform movements—civic engagement and integrative learning—provide the motivation for the creation of the current series, *Service Learning for Civic Engagement.* Each volume of the series will focus on a specific social issue—gender and power, race and immigration, community health, and so forth—and then solicit contributions from faculty *across* disciplines who can provide insight into how they have motivated their students to engage in learning that extends beyond the boundaries of disciplinary goals. In some cases chapter contributors will be faculty within the "obvious" discipline relevant to a particular issue (e.g., women's studies faculty utilize service learning in the pursuit of knowledge on gender issues), but each volume will include multiple chapters from other disciplines as well. As each volume illustrates, when faculty step outside the normal confines of disciplinary learning, they can provide profound, transformational experiences for their students. Thus, the volume on gender issues includes examples from philosophy, psychology, ethnic studies, and more, and the volume on social justice includes contributions from communications, engineering, nutrition science, and so on.

It is also our intention to design each book as a collective whole. Each volume illustrates an array of approaches to examining a community issue, and we hope that, by exploring examples across the disciplines, faculty will be inspired to develop their own concepts for courses that combine academic and civic learning.

Over the past 10 years, service learning has enjoyed tremendous support throughout the California State University (CSU), from which most of our contributors have been recruited. The 23 campuses of the CSU form the largest university system in the country, with 405,000 students enrolled each year. Through strategic efforts and targeted funding, the CSU has created a systemwide network of service-learning offices with a center on each campus, a coordinating office at the chancellor's office, statewide conferences and initiatives, and a wide variety of service-learning courses and community-based research. In 2005 alone more than 1,800 service-learning courses provided opportunities for 65,000 students to participate. California, now one of four states designated minority-majority (i.e., a state in which a majority of the population differs from the national majority) by the U.S. Census Bureau, is rich in ethnic diversity and is home to great cities as well as vast rural areas. Virtually every societal issue challenges Californians, and our universities have pledged to use our resources to develop innovative ways to address them. It is this mixture of diversity and innovation that has created an environment for the success of service learning in the CSU represented in this series.

Gerald S. Eisman
CSU Service-Learning Faculty Scholar
July 19, 2006

References

Howard, J. (2001). *Service learning course design workbook.* Ann Arbor, MI: OCSL Press.

Huber, M. T., & Hutchings, P. (2004). *Integrative learning: Mapping the terrain.* The Academy in Transition. Washington, DC: Association of American Colleges and Universities.

Saltmarsh, J. (2004). *The civic purpose of higher education: A focus on civic learning.* Unpublished white paper for Campus Compact.

Zlotkowski, E. (1997–2002). (Ed.). *AAHE series on service-learning in the disciplines.* Washington, DC: American Association for Higher Education.

Promoting Health and Wellness Activity/Methodology Table

Chapter	Discipline	Service Activity	Methodology	Applications	Type of Partner	Size of Class
Chapter 1: Acosta-Deprez and Sinay	Public health	Community-based research in various public health fields	Survey research Focus groups Needs assessment Fieldwork	Public health Health care administration Behavioral and environmental health Biostatistics Epidemiology	Public health departments, community-based organizations, and health care providers	30 students
Chapter 2: Rose	Sociology Gerontology Psychology	Lead weekly inter-generational discussion groups	Group process and techniques	Social sciences Social work Older-adult activities	Senior centers and retirement communities	15–20 students
Chapter 3: Landry and Davis	Nursing	Assist low-income seniors and the disabled in preparing for a disaster	Service learning and community-based research	Community/public health nursing and psychiatric/mental health nursing	In-home supportive services, residences for low-income disabled	50 students

(continues)

Promoting Health and Wellness Activity/Methodology Table
Continued

Chapter	Discipline	Service Activity	Methodology	Applications	Type of Partner	Size of Class
Chapter 4: Hammond	Interdisciplinary studies	School gardens and survey of school district wellness policies	Service leaning and community-based research	Education and public policy	Schools and school district	~15 students
Chapter 5: Gordon, Santos, and Weinstein	Interdisciplinary: nursing English as a Second Language (ESL) teacher education	Health education workshops, health screenings, coaching groups of adult ESL learners	Community-based research, curriculum design, collection of learner stories	Education, immigration studies, health professions	Community-based programs providing services to immigrant adults	3 courses: English 425: 40–50 students; English 724: 15 students; nursing practicum: 50 students
Chapter 6: Reimann and Rodríguez-Reimann	Public health psychology	Community mental health needs assessments	Mixed quantitative (survey) and qualitative (focus group/key stakeholder interview) methods	Public health Community mental health services Health care access policy	Community clinic system Faith-based organization	Varied with project (internships, research assistantships)

Chapter	Discipline	Service Activity	Methodology	Applications	Type of Partner	Size of Class
Chapter 7: Pinzon-Perez	Health sciences	Community theaters	Community-based research	Public health	Migrant Head Start	4–5 internships
Chapter 8: Gresham, Ingmanson, and Cheng	Public health	Tabletop exercise Emergency operations workshop Organized community events	Evaluative authentic engagement Critical pedagogy Pre- postanalysis	Government Epidemiology Homeland Security Disaster mitigation	Government agencies Community leaders Government policy makers	30–35 students
Chapter 9: Darrah and Plante	Anthropology	Research to (a) understand health in an underserved neighborhood and (b) improve an organization's use of its volunteers	Ethnographic interviewing Structured observation Qualitative data analysis	Health science Social sciences	Nonprofit health agency	25 students

(continues)

Promoting Health and Wellness Activity/Methodology Table
Continued

Chapter	Discipline	Service Activity	Methodology	Applications	Type of Partner	Size of Class
Chapter 10: Sills	Interdisciplinary: psychology nursing public health information technology	Interdisciplinary: health research, education and screenings; organized community events	Service learning Quantitative research with pre- and postanalysis Qualitative interviews with stakeholders	Health professions Health care administration Behavioral health Social sciences	Nonprofit health agency Universities/ schools Local health care providers	Varied internships and research assistantships
Chapter 11: Roe, Nance, Galang, Bingham, Blanco, Duhe, and Lee	Health sciences Community health Health promotion Public health	Health education booths at large, multicultural community health fairs	Community-based research Participant observation of health education activities and outreach Quantitative data analysis Qualitative analysis of student reflection papers	Community health School health Latino/Latina health Vietnamese health	Nonprofit health agency	110 students

Chapter	Discipline	Service Activity	Methodology	Applications	Type of Partner	Size of Class
Chapter 12: Freedman	Nutrition	Organization and participation in community events Teaching Social action projects Advocacy	Fieldwork Experiential Reflection (oral and written) Civic skills development Presentation skills	Education Public health Social sciences	Community-based organizations (CBOs) Schools Local and state governmental organizations	40–50 students
Chapter 13: Roldan	Information systems management	Information system development	Experiential	Community health	Health care services agency	40–60 students

CONTRIBUTORS

Veronica Acosta-Deprez (chapter 1) is professor of health science at California State University, Long Beach. (vacosta@csulb.edu)

Anna Bingham (chapter 11) is a wellness program coordinator in the Department of Orthopedics at Baylor University Medical Center in Dallas, Texas. (annabi@baylorhealth.edu)

German Blanco (chapter 11) is a community health educator for the Health Trust in Campbell, California. (germanb@healthtrust.org)

Susan Cheng (chapter 8) is environmental health and safety specialist with the Native American Alliance for Emergency Preparedness in San Diego. (wscheng@ucsd.edu)

Robert A. Corrigan (Foreword) is president of San Francisco State University. (president@sfsu.edu)

Charles N. Darrah (chapter 9) is professor of anthropology at San José State University. (darrahc@email.sjsu.edu)

Harvey Davis (chapter 3) is assistant professor of nursing at San Francisco State University. (hardavis@sfsu.edu)

Ryan Duhe (chapter 11) is a cardiovascular sales specialist with Abbott Labs in San José, California. (ryan.duhe@abbbott.com)

Gerald S. Eisman (series editor) is director of the Institute for Civic and Community Engagement at San Francisco State University. (geisman@sfsu.edu)

Marjorie Freedman (chapter 12) is assistant professor of nutrition at San José State University. (mrfphd@earthlink.net)

Alvin Galang (chapter 11) is currently a Training Specialist with the City of San José-Department of Parks, Recreation and Neighborhood Services. (alvingalang@comcast.net)

Daryl M. Gordon (chapter 5) is assistant professor of education at Adelphi University. (dgordon@adelphi.edu)

Louise Gresham (chapter 8) is assistant director of the global health and security initiative for the Nuclear Threat Initiative (NTI) in Washington, DC. (gresham@nti.org)

Debora Hammond (chapter 4) is professor of interdisciplinary studies at Sonoma State University. (hammond@sonoma.edu)

Sonja Ingmanson (chapter 8) is an environmental health specialist with the County of San Diego, Hazardous Materials Division. (sonja.ingmanson@ sdcounty.ca.gov)

Lynette Landry (chapter 3) is assistant professor of nursing at San Francisco State University. (llandry@sfsu.edu)

Kenneth Lee (chapter 11) is a marketing specialist for Heptagon, a microoptics company headquartered in Switzerland. (Ken.Lee@heptagon.fi)

Andrea Nance (chapter 11) is a staff nurse in the Pediatric Intensive Care Unit at Lucile Packard Children's Hospital at Stanford. (andrea_nance@ hotmail.com)

Anabel Pelham (volume editor) is professor of gerontology and director of the Institute on Gerontology at San Francisco State University. (apelham@ sfsu.edu)

Helda Pinzon-Perez (chapter 7) is associate professor of health science at California State University, Fresno. (hpinzonp@csufresno.edu)

Joachim O. F. Reimann (chapter 6) is research assistant professor of public health at San Diego State University. (jreimann@projects.sdsu.edu)

Dolores I. Rodríguez-Reimann (chapter 6) is research assistant professor of public health at San Diego State University. (Dreimann@projects.sdsu.edu)

Kathleen M. Roe (chapter 11) is chair of the health science department and professor of community health education at San José State University. (kathleen.roe@sjsu.edu)

Malu Roldan (chapter 13) is associate professor of management information systems at San José State University. (roldan_m@cob.sjsu.edu)

Madeleine Rose (chapter 2) is adjunct professor of sociology at Sonoma State University. (madeleine.rose@sonoma.edu)

Maricel G. Santos (chapter 5) is assistant professor of English at San Francisco State University. (mgsantos@sfsu.edu)

Elizabeth Sills (volume editor) is community benefit manager for Kaiser Permanente San José. (elizabeth.sills@kp.org)

Jonathan Sills (chapter 10) is a geriatric/rehabilitation psychology fellow at the Veterans Affairs Palo Alto Health Care System in Palo Alto, California. (jonathan.sills@va.gov)

Tony Sinay (chapter 1) is professor of health care administration at California State University, Long Beach. (tsinay@csulb.edu)

Katie Plante Smith (chapter 9) is community partnerships coordinator of the Health Trust in Campbell, California. (katies@healthtrust.org)

Gail Weinstein (chapter 5) is professor of English at San Francisco State University and director of the Center for Immigrant and Refugee Community Literacy Education. (gailw@sfsu.edu)

INTRODUCTION

Anabel Pelham and Elizabeth Sills

The health and well-being of individuals, families, communities, and the planet are all inter-connected. When we reflect upon the nature of our lives, few of us would argue that anything has more impact on the day-to-day quality of life than our personal health and well-being and that of our family and community. Our health status, experiences with accidents and diseases, life chances, even the nature of our death will be determined by the organization, delivery, and financing of health care. Access to and availability of health care have become touchstone issues in almost every household and in political debates across the United States.

The macro sociopolitical issues of health care that face our communities and nation will affect each of us multiple times at the micro level. How do we as educators and community caretakers teach this complex web of inter-connection between the micro and the macro? How do we convey that the health of the person washing your salad lettuce in a neighborhood café directly affects your well-being, and that the cleanliness of the irrigation water used on the farm where that lettuce grew may be even more vital? Further, how do we encourage the leaders of tomorrow, our students, to understand that mammoth social organizations are in the end only that, socially constructed, and that change is possible? Teaching students and ourselves about the power of the academy to hold to the principles of liberty, equality, and justice and to feel empowered to use higher knowledge and skills to tackle the complexity of social problems is at the very heart of service learning for civic engagement.

One of the exciting hallmarks of civic engagement pedagogy is that it is a uniquely American cultural enterprise we truly can be proud of. While our international colleagues are slowly opening the door of their academy, most of the current work on the development of knowledge and skills to serve the public good is homegrown with an "act locally" charm and tested evidence that these approaches work. This volume illustrates the can-do idealistic virtue of volunteerism and teamwork and the pioneering spirit of solving social problems with elegant examples of intergenerational and interdisciplinary practice. Each of the contributors shares cutting-edge academic creativity to offer models to employ community service learning to promote social change. Hope lives in each of these stories.

Section One: Models of Community Engagement

In "Reaffirming the Role of Service Learning in Public Health Curricula," Veronica Acosta-Deprez and Tony Sinay expand the dialogue and ask a fundamental question, What is the best way to teach public health practice? Embedded in that question is the larger pedagogical challenge for higher education: How do we organize the integration of theory and practice? How do we make higher education relevant and capture the imagination of our students? In addition to pure academics, today's students must learn teamwork, problem solving, communication skills, and leadership. Today's students will live and work in a diverse and global environment where social justice and human rights are close to the surface of every conflict.

Acosta-Deprez and Sinay offer a shorthand of models of service learning that apply to a multitude of higher education situations. These include service learning internships, service-learning projects as part of a course, an actual service-learning course, an extra credit option, and how to structure a college or departmental graduation requirement. Acosta-Deprez and Sinay go further by illustrating how to insert a service-learning component into a variety of public health courses. Biostatistics? Yes, indeed, data gathering for a regional health alliance. Managerial epidemiology? Students undertook service with the local health department to learn public health prevention models and behavioral interventions. Environmental health? Students were asked to conduct research for California's emergency preparedness plan and seek new ways of responding to environmental health problems. Social and behavioral science? Students took on the task of evaluating the effectiveness of the Arthritis Foundation's self-help course. Health care organizations and health care management? Students volunteered in a variety of community agencies doing survey research, data gathering, and taking field trips. Key to this course is the pre- and posttest of student attitudes and values. Health care policy? Students prepared a briefing of a policy testimony for state or federal law and presented it to local health care providers.

Acosta-Deprez and Sinay close the chapter with an invitation for a research agenda to explore the underpinnings of community service learning: specifically, the impact on the personal (moral) development of the student and the potential for improved quality of teaching and learning in the classroom.

In "Connections Across Generations: Dialogue Groups Bridge the Generation Gap," Madeleine Rose tackles the myths, stereotypes, and, nonsense about elders and an aging society by bringing students and older adults face-to-face in a learning circle of dialogue. Her course "Group Work With Older Adults" allows students and seniors to meet within the community for 12 sessions and collaborate on an agenda of mutual interest for discussion. The agenda is student- and senior-centered and evolves over time. These Connections Across Generations groups meet at senior centers and retirement and assisted-living communities.

As sociological literature has long demonstrated, one of the most effective tactics to reduce any kind of *ism*—racism, sexism, or ageism—is contact; that is, bringing together differing individuals and groups in a respectful and relaxed social setting. The operative concept here is *social* as Rose makes clear; these are not therapy or support groups. Rather, the groups are intergenerational and social. Current events topics may begin the discussions, but soon deeper meanings emerge as students learn about life course, human development, individual histories and struggles, and the realities of aging. Some gatherings take on a lighthearted note as students and seniors discuss music, fashion, relationships, and technology; learning is multidimensional. At the most personal level, Rose reports that students' fears about aging were lessened, and at the societal level, students became involved in local politics to save a senior center threatened by budget cuts.

The Connections Across Generations groups offer seniors an opportunity for one of their most valuable tools for reminiscing: generativity—that is, talking, sharing, and reflecting about the past to make sense of a lifetime of experiences and offering a legacy to future generations. The seniors also learn through intergenerational contacts about the reality of today's student youth. Hope for the future lives within these settings of valued new relationships.

Lynette Landry and Harvey Davis begin their chapter, "Preparing Future Nurses for a Life of Civic Engagement: The Disaster Preparedness for Vulnerable Populations Project," with a reminder of a significant paradigm shift that has taken place in nursing education from a hierarchical to a collaborative model in which the client or patient is viewed as a partner. Using this model, the School of Nursing at San Francisco State University joined with other units at the university in an effort initiated by the Institute for Civic and Community Engagement to help prepare the most vulnerable populations of the region for a disaster. Domestic and international catastrophes have taught city, regional, and national leaders painful lessons about not being prepared for human-made and natural disasters, and that the most vulnerable among us are the most likely to suffer the gravest consequences.

The concept was to develop a series of service-learning courses that would directly involve nursing students, their roles, and responsibilities in an emergency, focusing on the unique situations of elders and people with disabilities; the value of this project cannot be overestimated. In addition to the significant contributions of the nursing faculty to public health and safety, and their service to the city of San Francisco, some of the nursing students discovered an affinity for geriatric clients. This exposure alone might encourage them to consider choosing to study aging—that is, gerontology and geriatrics, one of the fastest-growing areas of need with perhaps the fewest practitioners.

In "Cultivating Healthy Habits: Food, Gardens, and Community-Based Learning," Debora Hammond explores the critical importance of diet and exercise in helping students at all levels of the educational system to develop positive health habits and contribute to improving the general health of the population. Through hands-on experience in school gardens and in other areas of the local food system, students begin to understand the connection between personal health, the health of the environment, and the overall health of society.

Hammond also documents service and community-based learning projects developed in connection with an upper-division seminar, The Global Food Web, and discusses collaborative research opportunities in connection with community food assessment initiatives being implemented throughout the United States. Taught in the Hutchins School of Liberal Studies at Sonoma State University, the course has proven to be particularly relevant for prospective teachers who have gained valuable experience in integrating food, agriculture, and school gardens into all aspects of the elementary school curriculum.

Section Two: Cross-Cultural Competencies

In "Immigrant Health Literacy: Reaching Across Language, Cultures, and Disciplines in Service," Daryl M. Gordon, Maricel G. Santos, and Gail Weinstein tackle one of the most complex and vexing issues of social policy around the world: immigration and the status and well-being of immigrants. Gordon, Santos, and Weinstein's work details the humane, innovative, and multifaceted mission of expanding the circle of dialogue to include non-English-speaking people.

This assignment is taken on at the most personal, one-to-one level of teaching communication. Their value-neutral approach focuses on facilitating adaptation and assisting non-English speakers to better manage the business of everyday life, including citizenship, multicultural relationships, English as a Second Language, and civic, family, workplace, and health literacy. In this post-9/11 reality, these faculty and students are in no small way molding the bricks of a foundation of goodwill and successful integration to support a multicultural democracy.

Perhaps no professional group stands closer to the cutting edge of affecting health disparities than nurses, and educating this unique class of providers about the special needs of immigrants will be key to achieving the goals of the U.S. Department of Health and Human Services in its federal health initiative titled Healthy People 2010. The bachelor's program in nursing science at Temple University in Philadelphia takes bold steps toward educating nurses on the special needs of immigrants by requiring a geriatric clinical practicum in the first semester of the senior year. This course is designed to prepare students to care for geriatric clients with chronic health problems. Students participate in three separate clinical experiences in an acute care unit, a hospice unit, and in a community agency. As part of their community experience, students work in teams to provide services to senior centers in a variety of Philadelphia's immigrant communities. Nursing students also conduct weekly workshops and design on-the-spot projects to respond to current needs. One of the unintended consequences of these projects has been the heightened self-esteem of and appreciation for bilingual students.

At San Francisco State University, faculty in the English department have demonstrated that community service learning can find expression in even in the most traditional disciplines: As the authors state on p. 67, "Pre-service English-language teachers . . . have an opportunity to participate in language learning settings that sensitize them to the realities of older immigrant learners and the role of the English language in the immigrants' lives."

San Francisco State faculty have formed multidisciplinary collaborations by cosponsoring and offering joint lectures on specialized modules within particular courses. It is important to note that this kind of alliance requires no structural change or exchange of extremely limited university resources. San Francisco State faculty are, however, proposing to take the collaboration one step further and are moving toward institutionalization by mounting an interdisciplinary certificate program in immigrant family, community, and health literacy.

As the university's visionary and energetic Gail Weinstein said, "When future health professionals and future language teachers collaborate, something extraordinary happens. As these future professionals grapple together with the role of language in immigrant access to health and wellness, their learning comes alive. Their excitement also keeps us learning, and helps us remember why we went into teaching in the first place" (personal communication, 2008).

In "Community-Based Health Needs Assessments With Culturally Distinct Populations," Joachim O. F. Reimann and Dolores I. Rodríguez-Reimann, introduce us to the subtle and nuanced challenge of conducting research, specifically needs assessment research, in underserved communities. Such research can be the catalyst for "policy, resource, and service changes" (Plescia, Koontz, & Laurent, 2001). How indeed do we develop culturally effective and respectful services if we know little about the intricate relationship between health care and culture? Approaching any unknown community with humility and respect is a good start, but how does one go from there to the culturally savvy skills of outreach and engagement?

This unique chapter offers guidance on how to educate students in the most current and best practices models of community-based research with the parallel and overarching dynamic of interpersonal considerations of working and being in a community. The authors offer lessons learned from Project Salaam, an evaluation of mental health needs among greater San Diego's Middle Eastern and East African communities, and Project Saud

Libra, which appraised mental health needs in Southern California's mostly rural Imperial Valley. Each project became a reality check on the complex relationship between the individual, or micro level, and culture, or macro level, of inquiry.

In "The Role of Community-Based Participatory Research, Civic Engagement, and Service Learning in Reducing Health Disparities: An Experience in Using Community Health Theaters," Helda Pinzon-Perez continues the humane dialogue and outreach to disadvantaged and minority groups. In a rural area of California, she introduces the inventive use of community theater for health education on breast cancer among Latino farm workers.

Using the qualitative methodology of community-based participatory research, Pinzon-Perez tapped into one of the most ancient forms of human communication: the oral tradition of theater. Community theater requires no literacy, is multicultural and multilingual, and offers the benefit of involving and empowering local people to educate themselves and others. With the collaboration of faculty and students of the Department of Health Science at California State University, Fresno, and Migrant Head Start, Pinzon-Perez courageously reached out to Latino males to take the lead in this community theater project. What happened next was magic as focus groups of Latino males took the lead in creating a script for a theater presentation. Dialogues created with student and faculty input became living health education strategies designed for the stage.

Outcomes of the project touched every person involved, and behaviors changed. Additionally, Pinzon-Perez reports that through the community service learning pedagogy, students developed skills in group organizing, conflict resolution, health needs assessment, program implementation, program evaluation, and community-based participatory research.

In "Teaching Public Health Security Through Community-Based and Case-Based Learning," Louise Gresham, Sonja Ingmanson, and Susan Cheng go global as they introduce us to the sobering challenge of public health security and expand our understanding of the link between public health and national security.

Gresham, Ingmanson, and Cheng illustrate in compelling ways how the master of science degree in public health with a specialization in global emergency management at San Diego State University has relevance to a variety of disciplines in the behavioral and social sciences and health and human services. They examine how ethics, epidemiology, law, and sociocultural values and realities intersect to affect the nation's national security. Students are engaged in community service using an "evaluative" framework—a method of applying adult learning theory in three learning situations: the Native American Alliance for Emergency Preparedness (NAAEP), the Red Cross, and the Smallpox Tabletop Exercise.

In the NAAEP exercise, students developed a clinic preparedness survey in collaboration with Native American and public health experts. In the Red Cross project, students served as volunteers in community service activities ranging from wildfire relief to assisting Hurricane Katrina evacuees. The case-based tabletop exercise consisted of three modules, each portraying a bioterrorism attack. Students were responsible for taking on emergency management roles to put theory into practice in scenarios of smallpox, plague, or anthrax outbreaks.

Natural disasters in the United States and abroad have made it clear to everyone that there is no substitute for higher education and hands-on experience when it comes to responding quickly and well to threats to life, public health, and well-being.

Section Three: Community Partnerships

The roles of collaboration and partnership are explored in a series of chapters from San José State University in which students and faculty reflect on and shape solutions in service to the community.

In "From Projects to Partnership: Using Ethnography to Engage Students," Charles N. Darrah and Katie Plante reflect on an ethnographic research methods course designed to help students develop skills as researchers while generating data that can inform real-world decision making. In their chapter, Darrah and Plante describe the organization of the course and its outcomes from the perspective of the instructor and the student assistant who was simultaneously enrolled in the class. Darrah and Plante are frank and pragmatic in their reflections, thereby providing us with the opportunity to judge the merits and limitations of the course's approach. As you will see, the story they tell goes beyond that of a single course and traces how adopting a project-based model of instruction can ultimately develop into a partnership between instructor and organization.

In "The Accidental Service Learner: The Role of Graduate Education in Community Service Learning," Jonathan Sills discusses his involvement as a doctoral student in clinical psychology in the development, implementation, and evaluation of a cardiovascular risk factor prevention program serving immigrant residents of Santa Clara County, California. This innovative community-university collaborative included stakeholders from San José State University; the Health Trust, a nonprofit hospital conversion foundation; and the AmeriCorps Bridging Borders project.

In describing the experience of undergraduate and graduate students working in a community-university health collaborative, Sills illustrates how service learning provides a unique opportunity for students to develop their professional identity while working in an interdisciplinary team environment. As Sills writes on p. 142, the collaborative "clearly demonstrated the value that a service-learning experience can bring to graduate studies." He concludes on pp. 147–148, "[It] continues to be a dynamic learning environment, allowing diverse stakeholders to explore the problems of and the potential solutions for the emerging health needs of community residents . . . [and] has provided a vehicle for hundreds of students to contribute to the delivery of care for underserved populations, and I am confident many have continued their pursuit beyond their classroom experience as I have."

In "The Economy of Abundance: Developing Service Learning on a Grand Scale in a Rapidly Changing Environment," Kathleen M. Roe and her student coauthors describe the initial 3 years of an ongoing service-learning experience in San José State University's health science department that emerged quickly and grew exponentially, challenging the traditional economy of scale so central to effective community-based learning.

Roe and her coauthors review the process through which faculty and students from an undergraduate community health promotion course became partners with the Health Trust, a local nonprofit hospital conversion foundation, to provide health education at a large community health fair. Despite unprecedented and unanticipated increases in course enrollment and the growing complexity of the event itself, the partnership endured and service learning, albeit on a grand scale, emerged as a critical component of the course and broader major curriculum. Roe and her coauthors candidly share with us the opportunities, worries, commitments, and results that began with Roe's "quest for a new way of teaching community-based analysis, a group of civic-minded students, and their idea to take our learning out of the classroom" (p. 158).

In "Using Service Learning to Teach Community Nutrition," Marjorie Freedman uses a service-learning model developed by the Center for Service Learning at San José State University. As part of a community nutrition class, seniors and graduate students majoring in nutrition had the opportunity to use their nutrition knowledge and life skills in a variety of community settings. Using critical thinking and communication skills, public problem solving, and civic involvement, 48 students participated in 32 local community and civic organizations (e.g., Boys and Girls Club, After School All Stars, YMCA, Pediatric Lifestyle Clinic, Second Harvest Food Bank, and the city of San José) providing services to individuals of diverse ethnicities, ages, and educational and socioeconomic backgrounds. Their work complemented classroom learning and resulted in richer educational experiences that provided, for some, their first service-learning experience and a glimpse at what they will likely encounter after graduation.

Freedman, who was a new tenure-track faculty member with little experience with service learning before designing and teaching this course, writes on p. 184:

> Unless we take the classroom into the community and train our students to translate academic knowledge into social and civic action, we have little hope of making any headway into solving the serious health issues facing Americans today and in the future. Our students are the future, and we must not only provide them with academic knowledge but also help them to hone their personal skills and develop their inner beliefs and self-esteem so they will be successful when they graduate from our institutions of higher learning.

In "Affecting Community Wellness With Technology and Cross-Disciplinary Collaboration," Malu Roldan discusses a wide-ranging collaboration that aimed to have an impact on community health programs while helping students build knowledge and skills in the use of leading-edge technologies, cross-disciplinary teamwork, and healthy practices. The collaboration brought together various departments at San José State University, community partners, and industry partners with a strong interest in encouraging innovations that significantly address community needs.

Although the outcomes for this project were quite encouraging and show there are benefits to incorporating service learning even when community involvement is not traditionally integral to a field of study, the collaboration was especially ambitious and required a level of support that proved unsustainable. Still, it lives on through its influence, which can be seen in the establishment of well-attended undergraduate- and graduate-level mobile software development courses in San José's computer engineering department; a strong appreciation and active interest in mobile technologies in a wide range of disciplines at the university, including health science; and a rich collaboration in technology innovation to address community needs involving SJSU faculty, Hewlett-Packard, Purdue University's Engineering Projects in Community Service program, local entrepreneurs, and the National Collegiate Inventors and Innovators Alliance.

Each of these invigorating chapters illustrates the amazing diversity, energy, creativity, and service orientation brought to California State University classrooms. Every day faculty members dedicate mind and heart to the mission of stirring up a magical alchemy of knowledge, practice, and service to turn students into citizens. Every day the university's faculty, their colleagues around the nation, and community partners inspire, lead, and sometimes push back the frontiers of ignorance to nurture one of the rarest and most precious elements of the human condition: virtue. Aristotle was correct on this point: Virtue has to be taught, lived by example, and ultimately we will be judged by history on how well we as a people looked after the well-being of our fragile and precious social justice and human rights. Think about this the next time you take a deep breath, and be well.

Reference

Plescia, M., Koontz, S., & Laurent, S. (2001). Community assessment in a vertically integrated health care system. *American Journal of Public Health, 91,* 811–814.

SECTION ONE

MODELS OF COMMUNITY ENGAGEMENT

REAFFIRMING THE ROLE OF SERVICE LEARNING IN PUBLIC HEALTH CURRICULA

Veronica Acosta-Deprez and Tony Sinay

T he purpose of this chapter is to (a) describe and explain the concept of service learning in public health education, (b) demonstrate service-learning models that can be adapted by public health education programs, and (c) describe selected public health courses with service-learning activities. This chapter promotes the idea of integrating service learning into the public health discipline.

Continuing changes in the health care system present new challenges for public health programs as their administrators search for innovative ways to educate students who will work in interdisciplinary teams and serve diverse populations. Increased community involvement in public health decision making stresses the importance of a new set of skills and competencies required by public health education. The Association of Schools of Public Health recognizes significant changes in the expectations of students, the demand of employers, and the needs of communities. Traditionally, local, state, and federal health departments and agencies employed public health graduates. However, according to deans of schools of public health, fewer than 25% of graduates have followed this path. Instead, graduates chose to work in community-based organizations, nonprofit agencies, businesses, the insurance industry, foundations, and high-tech operations (Clark & Weis, 2000). In its 1988 report, "The Future of Public Health," the Institute of Medicine (IOM), a component of the National Academy of Sciences, identified a gap between academic public health and practice and the contribution this gap made to the disarray in public health (Institute of Medicine, 1988). Two other studies outlined barriers to the involvement of academics in public health practice activities and the factors that often prevent public health practitioners from working more effectively with public health academicians. Ten specific barriers for academics and practitioners were cited, and if removed would improve the link between public health practice and schools of public health and would strengthen the education and the public health system in this country (Rowitz, 1995, 1999).

Increasingly, public health departments are adopting a collaborative approach to improve population-based health services and the status of community health. Similarly, community-based organizations are collaborating with a wide variety of institutions to enhance community capacity in the areas of service delivery, planning and policy development, surveillance and assessment, and education and outreach. Many health care organizations have begun to pursue collaborative approaches with community organizations to improve the health of populations, and managers of health care organizations view this commitment as an investment in their communities rather than an expense (Olden & Clement, 1998). All converging factors present opportunities to bring together community, providers, public health practitioners, and academics to improve community health and student education.

Since the 1988 Institute of Medicine report, a great deal of progress has been made to address this issue by the academic community, state and local public health agencies, foundations, and federal health service organizations. For instance, the Council on Linkages Between Academia and Public Health Practice was formed to improve the relevance of public health education to practice with support from a large number of national organizations such as the American Public Health Association, the Association of Schools of Public Health, the American College of Preventive Medicine, the Society for Public Health Education, the Health Resources and Services Administration, the Centers for Disease Control, the Association of University Programs in Health Administration, and many others. Although the council contributed to major improvements in public health education and subsequent practice, a great deal of work still needs to be done to strengthen the education of public health professionals. What is the best way to teach public health practice? What is the definition of practicum? Or, how much and what types of practical experiences need to be included in a curriculum to prepare a public health professional (Clark & Weiss, 2000; Conrad, 2000)?

One of the most effective approaches to the integration of theory with practice in public health is service learning, an emerging andragogy that incorporates aspects of experiential education, critical thinking, ways of knowing, and civic and social responsibility into the curriculum to further enhance public health education and practice. Service learning enhances traditional teaching and learning by bringing the practitioner's perspective into the classroom, thus increasing the likelihood that the realities of health practices are included in the curriculum.

Service learning is a philosophy of education and a method of teaching that bridges the classroom and the community by engaging learners in the application of theory to service (University of Kentucky, 1997). It has its theoretical roots in experiential learning and enhances the curriculum by allowing students to apply learning to real-life situations. It also combines learning and community service with explicit learning objectives, preparation, and reflection. Students engaged in service learning are not only expected to provide direct community service but also to learn about the context in which the service is provided—the connection between the service and their academic course work and their role as citizens (Sinay, 2000). Service learning benefits the student and the community by establishing a partnership that focuses on meeting the needs of the student as well as the needs of the community.

A public health curriculum can be described as an interdisciplinary education that targets the prevention and control of damaging conditions and diseases. According to the Council of Education for Public Health (CEPH), accredited programs or those seeking accreditation must contain five core areas of public health in the curriculum: biostatistics, epidemiology, behavioral and social sciences, environmental sciences, and health services administration (Council on Linkages Between Academia and Public Health Practice, 2001b). Core programs of 29 accredited public schools offer at least one course in each content area to comply with the CEPH requirements. Elementary Statistics, Public Health Statistics, or Introduction to Biostatistics courses fulfill the biostatistics requirement; Principles of Epidemiology, Fundamentals of Epidemiology, or Essentials of Modern Epidemiology courses provide sufficient content in epidemiology; and courses such as Sociomedical Sciences, Sociobehavioral Sciences, Health and Social Behavior, and Health Behavior and Education meet the requirements of social and behavioral sciences. Finally, the environmental health area is covered in a standard course in most programs accredited by the CEPH since it is one of the five core areas.

Except for these five core areas, curricula across accredited graduate schools of public health do not constitute a standardized generalist approach and do not provide a uniform foundation for practice (Clark & Weis, 2000). In addition to differences in the configuration of current public health programs, dramatic changes in the field of practice are challenging schools of public health to change core competencies and skills as well as fundamentals of practice. Special attention is being paid to quantitative and qualitative skills, organizational leadership, predictors of health and disease, and problem solving through teamwork in multidisciplinary and dynamic situations.

The scope of public health and the essence of public health practice to the field (or the desire to improve the link between practice and public health academia) suggests that public health programs are a natural fit for service-learning opportunities that promote population health improvement, analytic and systems thinking, effective communication, sensitivity to cultural and human diversity, community respect and partnership, human rights and social justice, quality learning, and continuous self-assessment and evaluation. Service learning is important in achieving these goals by enhancing classroom learning through the application of concepts, theories, methods, and techniques to service while promoting social responsibility, tolerance, and antiracism.

Several studies have shown that a large number of college outcome measures were favorably affected by service participation including civic responsibility, academic development, social awareness, and higher-degree aspirations. Public health programs could accomplish similar outcomes by integrating service learning into their curricula (Astin, Sax, & Avalos, 1999; Boss, 1994).

The remainder of this chapter includes the definition of service learning; its determinants, rationale, and outcome; models or strategies that use service learning in the curricula; examples of service-learning activities in public health courses; and the conclusion and future considerations.

Service Learning

Service Learning, Determinants, Rationale and Outcome

Participants in service-learning courses meet community needs while developing their abilities for critical thinking and group problem solving, and improve their commitment, values, and the skills needed for effective citizenship (Mintz & Liu, 1994). The core elements of service learning are (a) service activities that help meet community needs, (b) structured educational components that challenge participants to think critically about and learn from their experience, and (c) student reflection that educates all parties involved in the service-learning activity.

Service learning is similar to experiential education but is not the same. The focus of experiential learning is often on how it benefits students. Service learning, on the other hand, is reciprocally beneficial; the community receives meaningful service, and the student has meaningful learning experiences (Kendall & Associates, 1990). Service learning also differs from community service in that it incorporates specific learning goals for community service and includes structured reflection on the service in relationship to those goals. Community service is an umbrella term referring to all activities that meet needs in areas as diverse as human health and welfare, education, public safety, religion, and the environment (Anderson, 1999).

Service learning creates potential benefits beyond what service or learning can offer separately (Honnet & Poulsen, 1989). Determinants of good practice in combining service and learning include 10 major components. An effective service-learning program (a) engages people in responsible and challenging actions for the common good where society recognizes these tasks as important; (b) provides structured opportunities for people to reflect critically on their service experience through discussions with others and through individual reflection on moral questions and relevant issues, and to develop a better sense of social responsibility, advocacy, and active citizenship; (c) articulates clear service and learning goals for everyone involved with a clear sense of what is to be accomplished and what is to be learned; (d) allows community groups, government agencies, and private organizations to define what service tasks are needed and when and how these tasks should be performed; (e) clarifies the responsibilities of each person and organization involved in the service activities, such as students and teachers, community leaders, service supervisors, and sponsoring organizations; (f) matches service providers with service needs through a process that recognizes changing circumstances; (g) expects genuine, active, and sustained organizational commitment; (h) includes training, supervision, monitoring, support, recognition, and evaluation to meet service and learning goals; (i) ensures that time commitments for service and learning is flexible, appropriate, and in the best interests of all involved; and (j) is committed to program participation by and with diverse populations (Honnet & Poulsen, 1989).

All parties involved in service-learning projects—students, faculty and their departments, and the community—benefit from the experience. Students receive an enriched learning experience, developing skills beyond classroom knowledge. Through service learning, students obtain work experience and job contracts, develop critical thinking skills, improve their self-confidence, and become more active and assertive citizens. Faculty develop opportunities for interdisciplinary collaboration and involvement in action research which could yield new knowledge and scholarship and can sequentially lead to publications. Academic departments benefit from service learning through better recruitment of students and an improved public image.

Sax and Astin (1997) grouped student outcomes of service learning into three categories: civic responsibility; academic and life skills development that included persistence in college, interest in graduate study, critical thinking, and leadership skills; and a commitment to promoting racial understanding. Another study investigated the cognitive and moral development of service learners and found higher levels of moral reasoning and higher course grade averages among service learners than nonservice participants (Boss, 1994). The psychosocial development of service learners was studied by several other researchers who reported significant improvements in students' motivation to learn, greater determination than nonparticipants to effect social change, and more involvement in academic pursuits, religious activities, and campus clubs (Cohen & Kinsey, 1994; Markus, Howard, & King, 1993; Serow, 1990).

A 2-year (1996–1997) external evaluation of the Health Professions Schools in Service to the Nation program, which was conducted by a team at Portland State University (Gelmon et al. 1997), offered similar results. Clearly, service learning is having a positive impact on communities, learners, and faculty.

Models of Service Learning

The National and Community Service Act of 1990 (1991) described the term *service-learning* as a method by which students learn and develop through active participation in:

- Organized service experiences that meet real community needs;
- Integrated into the students' academic curriculum;
- Provides structured time called reflection for youth to think, talk, or write about what they did and saw during the service activity;
- Enables youth to utilize newly acquired skills and knowledge and apply them in real-life situations in their own communities; and
- Enhances what is taught in school by extending learning beyond the classroom and into the community and helps to foster the development of a sense of caring for others. (p. 17)

Any activity or program, then, must demonstrate volunteer activity, advanced planning, intentional learning goals by faculty, and student reflection on the service experience to qualify as service learning. As faculty structure service-learning courses, the following models should be considered.

Service-Learning Internships

Students must extensively plan the internship opportunity with faculty and interact with stakeholders and public health officials to complete the internship project. Students and/or internship supervisors identify potential projects such as community health and needs assessment surveys, and county or statewide program evaluations such as the State Children's Health Insurance Programs. Following the completion of volunteer activity, an internship seminar is offered at the department or college to allow students to reflect on and integrate their experience into their discipline.

The Institute for Public Health at San Diego University linked academic community and local public health agencies through program evaluation, providing the institute with opportunities to address its mission of teaching, research, and service. The institute, which is the formal locus for public health practice at the university, receives requests from community agencies to assess and eventually improve the effectiveness of service provided. Student projects (or their volunteer work) may include (a) studying the effectiveness of prevention case management models at the community health center, which reduces high-risk behaviors, (b) providing literature to domestic violence victims at shelters to increase the knowledge of community resources and of the dynamics of domestic violence, (c) collaborating with nonprofit social service agencies to increase the knowledge of risks of sexual activity and strategies to postpone it, and (d) encouraging churches to adopt formal smoking cessation policies and education (Willis & White, 2000).

Service Learning as Part of a Course

An existing course in the public health program can incorporate service-learning projects with learning objectives. Students engage in relevant service activity that is either previously determined by the instructor or identified by students through a central office if necessary. For example, students conduct research on a particular issue identified by a community agency as part of a research methods or biostatistics course. The research project is designed to address informational needs of the agency and the application of classroom theory to a practice setting. For example, students administer pre-and post-surveys following the completion of an arthritis self-help course (ASHC) to determine whether the course makes a significant difference on the participant's knowledge, physical health, mental health, or attitude. Student reflection may take place in the classroom following completion of the service-learning project. Another idea for student reflection is a service-learning day designated for the entire college if service learning is a part of each program.

In Introduction to Population-Based Health Programs, a course designed to facilitate practice/academic interaction and reduce many barriers identified in public health literature, students extensively research their chosen program's history, population, and finances, as well as its scientific and public health rationale. Students work in teams and present their findings to other students and faculty in the classroom. By understanding not just one but many different programs of a health department, students and faculty alike can enhance the breadth of their knowledge base (Nason & Capper, 2001).

Service-Learning Course

A service-learning component can be added to a public health curriculum by integrating components such as the theory of service learning, student preparation for service in the community, sources of community problems, partnerships, and collaboration and human interaction. Action research could also be a part of the course to understand local residents and neighborhoods that are often marginalized in community development and health services (Kahne & Westheimer, 1996). For example, a course titled Community Problem Solving or Minority and Immigrant Health Problems would allow students to work with agencies such as migrant clinics, federally qualified community health centers, or rural health clinics, enhancing the student's learning with a field application.

Extra Credit Option

Students receive extra credit for participation in a community service project related to the course. For example, students in a health care policy course may have the option of giving a presentation at a community organization, such as the local public health department, health care task force, or the economic development council of the region, to disseminate relevant information. Presentation topics may be predetermined by the instructor and/or the agency. This method offers students an opportunity to earn 10 points, for example.

College or Departmental Graduation Requirement

Students are asked to volunteer at community health organizations for about 10 to 20 hours a semester (or year) and to document their experience through journals, essays, lectures, presentations, and/or artistic activities. The success of this integration strategy depends on a central office that manages the volunteer activity (e.g., Collegiate Volunteers Office, The Citizenship and Service Learning Department or Volunteers Office within the university), which is responsible for updating placement sites annually, and takes on the role of coordinator between students and community organizations. Students who do not complete their service-learning activities are not allowed to graduate in this model.

Public Health Courses With a Service-Learning Component

In a typical graduate health program, academic preparation requires content in five core areas: biostatistics, epidemiology, environmental sciences, social and behavioral sciences, and health services administration. The content of these courses can be easily linked to the service activity in the form of competencies that support core functions of public health service (Council on Linkages Between Academia and Public Health Practice, 2001a).

Biostatistics. A biostatistics course with a service-learning component enhances the student's understanding of statistics and research methods, and provides a practical application of theories, methods, and concepts to local or national public health issues. Students work on predetermined research projects in teams of three or four. A typical statistics and research course includes content in definition and types of research, research design, hypothesis development, sampling, data collection and survey development, basic foundations of statistics and analysis, and research reporting. For example, in one of the author's classes, a group of students conducted an access-to-care survey during the 1998–1999 academic years, and the research team, with the leadership of a faculty member, was able to design a telephone survey questionnaire and collect data for statistical analysis. This effort led to a written report, which was needed by the regional health alliance for planning purposes. This access-to-care study was the second stage in the community health and needs assessment project in that region. Students not only learned about biostatistics content and survey research, but the project also helped the community understand access barriers in the area. The service-learning biostatistics course also developed core practice competencies in the areas of analytic and assessment skills. Service-learning objectives of the course included understanding rural, diverse, and minority populations and their health care needs, along with the realities of scarce resources and the difficulties of workforce development.

Another service-learning example involved a collaborative activity where community groups, major employers, and university officials met to discuss using the clinic for a community health center in an area where significant immigrant and minority groups were located. Students were asked to conduct focus group research and identify community health needs while interacting with diverse populations to learn about their cultural differences. This project enhanced competency development in the areas of program planning, cultural competency, and leadership (Council on Linkages Between Academia and Public Health Practice, 2001a).

Epidemiology. A managerial epidemiology course that integrated service-learning activities allowed students to learn basic public health concepts and, most importantly, prepared them to be successful administrators in a population-focused health care environment. As managed care becomes more central to the practice of health care administration, executives and public health practitioners need to understand the health status of populations, which makes epidemiology a core discipline pertinent to all branches of health care. In collaboration with the state public health department, students not only learn traditional public health promotion models but also behavioral interventions designed to reduce smoking, substance abuse, violence, and risky sexual behavior (Fos, Fine, & Zuniga, 1998). Some specific projects are related to smoking cessation, access to care, and community health assessment surveys that are often conducted by state and local health departments. In addition, students perform other tasks, such as data entry, data cleaning, and survey design. When they return from volunteer sites they reflect on their valuable experience, which serves to develop practice competencies related to basic public health science (Council on Linkages Between Academia and Public Health Practice, 2001b).

Environmental health. An environmental health course generally deals with the identification and management of physical, chemical, biological, and other hazards in the environment, and students discuss ways to prevent or minimize adverse health effects on populations and individuals from exposure. Students are asked to demonstrate the ability to evaluate the health of individuals and populations of concern and to be able to conduct a basic evaluation. Terrorist activities (bioterrorism) in the United States has forced staff at state public health departments to reassess their emergency preparedness plans and seek new ways of responding to environmental health problems. For example, administrators at our state's public health department asked us to identify public health resources, how these resources were coordinated among several constituencies, and, most importantly, the role of the health care workforce in emergency situations. Students were asked to conduct interviews, perform extensive literature reviews, become familiar with laws and regulations, and recognize the appropriate regulatory agency in these situations. Students contacted people at hospitals, clinics, and other relevant provider sites for interviews and collected input from the state's public health department, emergency management division. This is an invaluable experience for students to learn more about the public health system and its relationship to the health care delivery system and emergency management while improving their leadership and communication skills. In the end we hope to design a simulation model for the public health department for the overall coordination of these resources and services. Because of the comprehensive nature of the organizations involved, this project is designed to develop entry-level competencies related to systems thinking.

Social and behavioral sciences. This course provides an overview of major health behavior methods, theories, and applications and distinguishes between behaviors that foster and those that hinder well-being by investigating physical, social, emotional, and intellectual factors influencing health-related choices. The emphasis is on identifying behaviors that tend to promote or compromise health and recognizing the role of learning and affective experiences in shaping patterns of health behavior. Such a course employs a wide range of strategies for dealing with controversial health issues and disseminates health education information and providers' messages.

Staff from the Arthritis Foundation's local chapter conducted a program evaluation project to study the effectiveness of the ASHC course. The course manual documented the effectiveness of the ASHC from earlier studies using 4- and 8-month follow-up data; however, there were inconsistencies in findings from previous studies, and a statewide evaluation of the course was needed to assess the effectiveness of the program. This future project aims to collect data to assess the effectiveness of the course on the following six areas: (a) arthritis knowledge, (b) exercise, (c) psychosocial status, (d) medication, (e) diet and unproven remedies, and (f) saving joints and energy (functional ability). The pre- and postcourse design will be used to maximize data collection, which means the survey will be administered three times: (a) precourse survey, (b) postcourse survey, and (c) 4-month follow up. Students will be able to assist with survey development, data collection, and analysis. Service-learning goals in this project include understanding the elderly and their chronic health problems, providing health education in physical activity and wellness, and offering strategies to change lifestyles and the daily activities of the elderly. Students are expected to present their experience in the classroom, highlighting service and learning goals of the course that were achieved. The service-learning goals related to this project also serve to support core competencies related to the community dimensions of practice.

Health services administration. This course provides content in organizational behavior, organizational theory, and management of health care organizations. Although health administration programs often separate organizational theory/behavior from the management content, we kept them together for simplicity. Typical health care organization and management courses study clinical and nonclinical aspects of hospital departments and other provider systems, along with health care system issues such as cost containment, managed care, physician practice, and ambulatory care (Wolper, 1995).

By integrating service learning, the course exposes students to various theories of experiential learning, team building and collaborative learning, interpersonal communication, and conflict resolution. To prepare students to apply these concepts in service-learning projects, the course requires students to analyze their values and attitudes regarding community issues and to learn the methods of needs/strengths assessments so they may engage fully in community partnerships. A student survey is administered before and after the course to assess changes in students' perceptions and attitudes and the effectiveness of service on learning objectives.

As a part of this course students are involved in various volunteer activities that may range from administering patient, employee, or health maintenance organization satisfaction surveys to the preparation of monthly performance reports for departments where students performed their service activity. A central office at the university or college may help identify the need for volunteers in local organizations in advance so that those students can be easily assigned to volunteer sites early in the semester, but this is not the only way to achieve course objectives. Field trips preplanned by the faculty member to provider sites could achieve the same goals, allowing students to collect the necessary information needed by providers. Students design and administer these surveys and eventually analyze the collected data to make presentations.

Health care policy. Another course that should be considered for service-learning integration is health care policy, which requires students to prepare a briefing of a policy, testimony, state or federal law that may affect local health care providers. Students can introduce these regulatory changes to local providers such as rural hospitals or to long-term care facilities and home health agencies to assist them in adapting new policies. Presentations can take place at the provider site on a designated day, such as the day of the preceptors' luncheon or the external advisory committee meeting. A health care policy course and its service-learning component supports the student's ability to (a) collect, summarize, and interpret information relevant to an issue; (b) state policy options and write policy statements; and (c) articulate the health, fiscal, administrative, legal, social, and political implications of each policy option (Council on Linkages Between Academia and Public Health Practice, 2001c).

Conclusion

Service learning is a natural extension of public health practice, which includes a service activity, a structured educational component, and student reflection. A much needed link between public health practice and schools of public health to close the gap has developed in the past two decades. Service learning is an important component that bridges the gap between public health theory and practice. The focus of the chapter was on the integration of service learning into public health courses, such as biostatistics, epidemiology, environmental health, social sciences and behavior, health services administration, and health care policy.

Although past studies show that service learning develops social responsibility, racial understanding, and moral reasoning, and improves critical thinking, leadership skills, motivation to learn, and life skills development, empirical studies on the impact of service on students' educational personal development is limited (Astin, 1996; Astin et al., 1999; Boss, 1994; Sax & Astin, 1997; Schaffer, Mather & Gustafson, 2000). It is especially not known whether service learning increases the quality of learning/teaching in the classroom while achieving course objectives. Future research should focus on classroom outcomes of service learning following the integration of service learning into public health curricula.

The challenge of integrating service learning into public health programs evolves around two parties: the faculty and the administration. Faculty must be educated in service learning and experiential learning theories through workshops, conferences, and other continuing education methods. The administration's commitment is as important as the faculty's involvement in service learning, which provides much needed leadership in this effort. Perhaps a full commitment by the faculty and administration may require a language change in the program's mission, goals, and objectives. This way, full integration of service learning into the program would be accomplished.

Service learning is rapidly gaining acceptance on college campuses, but ongoing issues of institutionalization, faculty not previously inclined toward service learning, and the difficulty of finding quality practices challenges service-learning programs and strategies. In response to these challenges, Communities and Campuses in Partnership to Improve Health (CCPH) positioned itself to assume the role of facilitating the network of health professional schools, creating an infrastructure for further development of service-learning programs. The CCPH aims to promote understanding of service learning to improve community health and student education. This chapter provides examples on how service learning can be integrated into public health practice. It is hoped that examples provided herein will inform and help others working in the field about the many opportunities in which service-learning activities can be integrated into their courses. This will not only enrich public health education but will also promote social responsibility, personal efficacy, and community health.

References

Anderson, J. (1999). *Service Learning and Teacher Education.* Retrieved from http://www.ericdigests.org/1999–1/service.html

Astin, A. W. (1996). The role of service in higher education. *About Campus, 1*(1), 14–19.

Astin, A. W., Sax, L. J., & Avalos, J. (1999). Long-term effects of volunteerism during the undergraduate years. *Review of Higher Education, 22*(2), 187–202.

Boss, J. A. (1994). The effect of community service in the moral development of college ethics students. *Journal of Moral Education, 23*, 183–198.

Clark, N. M., & Weis, E. (2000). Mastering the new public health. *American Journal of Public Health, 90*(1), 208–211.

Cohen, J., & Kinsey, D. (1994). Doing good and scholarship: A service learning study. *Journalism Educator, 48*, 4–14.

Conrad, D. (2000). Bringing two worlds closer: A three-year review of council activities. *The Link, 14*(1), 1–4. Retrieved November 2009 from http://www.phf.org/link/thelink/vol14n1/twoworlds.pdf

Council on Linkages Between Academia and Public Health Practice. (2001a). *What is the Council on Linages Between Academia and Public Health Practice?* Retrieved November 2009 from http://www.phf.org/link/index.htm

Council on Linkages Between Academia and Public Health Practice. (2001b). *Council on Linkages: Core competencies for public health professionals.* Retrieved November 2009 from http://www.phf.org/link/corecompetencies.htm

Council on Linkages Between Academia and Public Health Practice. (2001c). *Council on Linkages: Objectives and Strategies.* Retrieved November 2009 from http://www.phf.org/link/objectives.htm

Fos, P. J., Fine, D. J., & Zuniga, M. A. (1998). Managerial epidemiology in the health administration curriculum. *Health Administration Education, 16*(1), 1–12.

Gelmon, S., Holland, B., Morris, B. A., et al. (1997). *Health professionals schools in service to the nation: Evaluation report 1996–1997.* Portland, OR: Portland State University.

Honnet, E. P., & Poulsen, S. J. (1989). *Principles of good practice for combining service and learning: A Wingspread special report.* Racine, WI: The Johnson Foundation. Retrieved from http://www.apa.org/ed/slce/principles

Institute of Medicine. (1988). *The future of public health.* Washington, DC: National Academy Press.

Kahne, J., & Westheimer, J. (1996). In the service of what? The politics of service learning. *Phi Delta Kappan, 77*(9), 592–599.

Kendall, J. C., & Associates. (Eds.). (1990). *Combining service and learning: A resource book for community and public service.* Raleigh, NC: National Society for Internships and Experiential Education.

Markus, G. B., Howard, J. P. F., & King, D. C. (1993). Integrating community service and classroom instruction enhances learning: Results from one experiment. *Educational Evaluation and Policy Analysis, 15*(4), 410–419.

Mintz, S., & Liu, G. (1994). *Service-learning: An overview.* Washington, DC: Corporation for National Community Service.

Nason, C. S., & Capper, S. A. (2001). *Bringing two worlds together: Graduate research in health practice.* Retrieved from http://www.phf.org/link/thelink/vol13n1/two worlds.pdf

National Community Service Act of 1990. (1991). *Definition of service-learning.* In R. Willits-Cairn & Jim Kielsmeier (Eds.), Growing Hope (p. 17). Minneapolis, MN: National Youth and Leadership Council.

Olden, P. C., & Clement, D. G. (1998). Well-being revisited: Improving the health of a population. *Journal of Healthcare Management, 43,* 36–50.

Rowitz, L. (1995). Ten academic barriers to public health practice. *Journal of Public Health Management and Practice, 1*(2), 83–85.

Rowitz, L. (1999). Barriers to academic and practice linkages. *Journal of Public Health Management and Practice, 5*(6), 99–101.

Sax, L. J., & Astin, A. (1997). The benefits of service: Evidence from undergraduates. *Educational Record, 78*(3/4), 25–32.

Schaffer, M., Mather, S., & Gustafson, V. (2000). Service learning: A strategy for conducting health needs of the homeless. *Journal of Health Care of the Poor and Underserved, 11,* 385–399

Serow, R. C. (1990). Volunteering and values: An analysis of students' participation in community service. *Journal of Research Development in Education, 23,* 198–203.

Sinay, T. (2000). Service learning in the undergraduate health administration curriculum: Theory and practice. *Journal of Health Administration Education, 18,* 357–373.

University of Kentucky. (1997). *Service learning handbook.* Lexington: University of Kentucky Press.

Willis, W., & White, G. (2000). Linking public health academia to public health practice through program evaluation. *Public Health Reports, 115,* 292–295.

Wolper, L. P. (1995). *Health care administration: Principles, practices, structure, and delivery.* Gaithersburg, MD: Aspen.

2

CONNECTIONS ACROSS GENERATIONS

Dialogue Groups Bridge the Generation Gap

Madeleine Rose

As educators we are faced with preparing students to live and work in an aging society. Yet, many young people fear getting old and they resent older adults. These fears and resentments are fueled by current social discourse that casts young and old as opposites, engaged in conflict over power and resources. A class at Sonoma State University (SSU) offers undergraduate students a unique opportunity to engage in a weekly dialogue with older adults. In the process, students confront and discard myths and stereotypes about aging, lessen their own fears, and find unexpected mentors and friends in the older adult population.

The course, Group Work With Older Adults, has been offered at SSU for the past 10 years. It is an interdisciplinary elective, cross-listed in sociology, psychology, and gerontology. Learning takes place in the classroom and in the community. (This course was started in 2000 with the support of a grant, obtained with Susan Hillier, from Generations Together, The

I would like to thank the Connections Across Generations participants and program directors at the Rohnert Park Senior Center, Petaluma Senior Center, Sunrise Assisted Living at the Chanate, and Friends House for their collaboration in creating this program. Students, faculty, and the dean of the School of Social Sciences at Sonoma State University have given enthusiastic support. My son, Justin Kornfein, also a teacher committed to service learning, produced a short, no budget video about the Connections program that helps me recruit students. My husband, Edward Berger, has been my unofficial and unwavering assistant in developing and sustaining the Connections program. We worked side by side writing and editing this chapter. I am deeply grateful to him for his deep understanding and assistance.

Association for Gerontology in Higher Education, and the Corporation for National Service.) The class meets weekly on campus and is conducted as a seminar. As part of the requirements, students go into the community to lead and participate in weekly dialogue groups with seniors. These groups, called Connections Across Generations, meet for 12 sessions at senior centers and retirement facilities. Each Connections group has about 10 seniors and 2 to 4 students. To encourage the trust and candor necessary for a meaningful dialogue, students are assigned to one site for the duration of the semester. Likewise, community participants select a group and are encouraged to attend as many of the 12 sessions as possible.

Open to undergraduate juniors and seniors, the course has no prerequisites. Most students are sociology or human development majors or gerontology minors. Few students enroll with a career interest in working with older adults; rather, they want an opportunity to do something experiential, and the class fulfills a requirement for their major or minor.

The course learning objectives are to

- recognize myths and stereotypes about older adults
- develop awareness of the psychological, social, and health challenges of aging
- deepen sensitivity to gender, cultural, and historical differences in aging
- become familiar with social controversies concerning older adults
- lessen personal fears about aging
- develop awareness of elders as a personal and societal resource
- develop skills facilitating groups for older adults
- become familiar with the phases of group development
- understand the benefits and risks of group participation for older adults
- deepen community involvement

Creating an Intergenerational Dialogue

What do college students and older adults talk about? Students and seniors collaborate to develop an agenda of mutual interest. At the beginning of the semester, the students and some of the seniors assume that the instructor will select the topics. Instead, each group of students and seniors is encouraged to develop an evolving agenda that reflects their background and interests.

Prior to each community session, the students get together with their cofacilitators to select a topic (if that has not been done), decide who will open and close the meeting, and brainstorm questions to deepen the discussion. The assigned readings, class discussions where students share ideas, and current events provide an ample source of topics.

Articles from a gerontology journal introduce students to key issues and controversies in aging and often generate discussion topics. For example, readings about ageism stimulate conversations about myths and stereotypes about aging and peoples' experiences being treated as an older person in this society. Readings about sexuality and aging lead to discussions comparing past and current dating practices and coping with the loss or unavailability of a partner because of dementia or other illness. Readings about Social Security and physician-assisted suicide inform students about these controversies and prepare them to talk about such issues with the seniors.

Current events can lead the groups toward a meaningful dialogue. During the spring 2006 semester, immigration policy was widely discussed because of the determination of two seniors. These Latino elders alerted their group to controversial proposed legislation they considered harmful to immigrants. They brought this issue to their group's attention prior to the well-publicized pro-immigrant demonstrations in California and throughout the nation. This led to a highly engaging and educational discussion in which the men shared their personal struggles coming to this country, their experience of discrimination, and their concerns about people who would be vulnerable as a result of the legislation. To prepare for this meeting, several seniors and students did research and brought information to the group about the legislation and its potential impact. Deeply affected and energized by their meaningful discussion, the student facilitators couldn't wait to tell their classmates. Subsequently, the other students successfully introduced this topic to their groups. In some cases, students revealed the hardships their families had endured as immigrants trying to survive in a country in which they could not fully participate.

The initial group discussions, when the students seek to know the background of the seniors, invite the older adults to reminisce about topics such as the lingering personal impact of life events and decisions. This is similar to what occurs in guided autobiography groups for older adults (Birren & Deutchman, 1991). Later topics usually focus on the present, such as views about changes in Medicare drug coverage or the use of e-mail and the Internet. Toward the end, groups often discuss concerns and hopes for the future. Generational differences and commonalities become evident, for example, in educational options, family life, and use of technology. The tone of the sessions ranges from serious, tearful conversations about losses to light-hearted bantering about generational differences in music, fashion, and communication devices. In analyzing the group sessions, students are encouraged to think about underlying themes common in groups of older adults (Toseland, 1995). For example, the theme "continuity with the past," is revealed in members' efforts to show how their past experiences and accomplishments continue to give their lives meaning. Likewise, members' interests in the students' lives and in current events reflect their efforts to understand the modern world.

The Connections Across Generations groups are what Toseland (1995) would describe as "social/recreational/educational" groups rather than therapy or support groups (pp. 138–139). Promoted as intergenerational discussion groups, they provide an opportunity for older adults to engage with peers in an activity that provides enjoyment and stimulates their growth and development. The groups do not aim to help members change their behavior as in therapy groups. Although the group discussions may include adapting to losses, the groups are not focused on helping members deal with shared stressful or traumatic life events as in support groups.

Collaborating With Community Partners

The Connections Across Generations groups exist only through the efforts of this service-learning course. The faculty instructor must engage and sustain successful relationships with community partners who host the groups each spring semester. The program has four community partners—two senior centers, a retirement community, and an assisted living facility. At each site a collaborative relationship has been developed with the activities director, and in some cases, with a group of seniors responsible for programming. Although the faculty instructor supervises the students and oversees the program, it is essential to have a liaison at each site to help with publicity, scheduling, and logistical problems.

Weeks before class begins, the instructor and the community partners join forces to advertise the Connections Across Generations program and to recruit participants. Newsletter articles and flyers announce the formation of upcoming groups, highlighting this unique opportunity to create a dialogue between older adults and college students. The program has established a niche in the local community, and many seniors are eager to participate. The groups draw a mixture of new and returning members, including "pioneers" who have been involved for the entire 10 years the program has been offered.

Student Recruitment and Course Organization

Before students enroll, it is important for them to be aware that the course involves service at a community site at scheduled times. Students sometimes mistakenly assume that the community service can be done at their convenience. To recruit students, it has been helpful to post flyers about the course and its unique requirements. Some students hesitate to enroll because they fear it will be depressing to be around older adults. To deal with this, I post pictures of previous groups of students and seniors, obviously enjoying each other. I have also made a short video about the program; the friendly images and voices of the community participants reassure prospective students that the older adults welcome them and that their time together will be fun as well as educational.

The first class session is devoted to clarifying course expectations and to ascertaining students' schedules in order to assign them to the community sites. Students come to the first class assuming it will be awhile before they go into the community and have a leadership role with the groups. Often they are taken aback when informed that they are scheduled to go into the community and meet the seniors the following week! Students express not only excitement but also anxiety. They have many questions about the nature of the groups and about their roles as students and group leaders. They feel intimidated by their lack of experience. When addressing students' concerns, it is instructive to point out that the community participants have parallel concerns in this early stage of group development and are asking themselves: What is this program about? What is expected of me? Will people like me when they get to know me? Will I like them? (Black, Kelly, & Rice, 2005).

The introductory meeting at each site dramatically reduces the students' anxiety. The faculty instructor conducts this meeting, clarifying the nature of the program and what is expected of the participants. I emphasize that the seniors are needed by the university to help students learn about aging through interaction with older adults. The students introduce themselves, and students and seniors share their expectations and hopes about participating. Collectively we brainstorm topics. By the end of the meeting, a sense of camaraderie and excitement is palpable—students and seniors are eager to learn about each other in their weekly groups. Later sessions (except for the culmination meeting) are conducted by the students; I rotate through the groups, role modeling or participating in the discussions as needed.

The class seminar is a combination of lecture, class discussion, problem solving, and role playing. Students provide updates about their group to obtain help addressing problems and to share successful topics and approaches. Group process issues that commonly arise include whether the groups should be closed or open to new members, dealing with group conflict, and coping with overly talkative group members. We discuss the assigned readings, exploring how these may be relevant to the groups.

Each semester the seniors visit the university. The visits were added after evaluating the program the first year and discovering that many seniors had never been to SSU. Thereafter, in place of one of the weekly group meetings, the seniors come to campus, hosted by their student leaders and me. Some of the older adults stride briskly, and others use canes, walkers, or wheelchairs. Students proudly show them a selected part of campus—the high-tech library, the Environmental Technology Center—or arrange for a presentation by a campus group such as Project Censored or by a faculty member. For a visit that occurred on Cinco de Mayo, an emeritus history professor gave a presentation about the famous Mexican muralists to an appreciative audience.

The groups conclude with a festive culmination meeting at each site that includes a potluck lunch. The formal part of this session, conducted by the instructor, provides an opportunity for the students and seniors to convey how their lives have been affected by their time together. There are poignant comments, laughter and tears, hugs and kisses, and photo taking. Often, seniors bring in favorite quotes and written advice for the students:

"Live simply, laugh often, and love deeply."
 "Always learn what is going on in the world. Read the newspapers at least for a few minutes daily. Do not encapsulate your thoughts in your mind. Communicate with others, as we are not isolated islands."

"In 1863, the then President of Mexico, Benito Juarez, while addressing the Mexican Congress, told them: 'Among nations as among friends, respect for the rights of others promotes peace.' These thoughts are as valid today."

" 'The future does not belong to those who are content with today, apathetic toward common problems, timid and fearful in the face of new ideas and bold projects. Rather, it will belong to those who can blend vision, reason, and courage in a personal commitment.' From a speech delivered by Robert F. Kennedy at SSU in 1962."

In a formal ceremony, each community participant receives a Certificate of Appreciation (with a gold university seal), acknowledging that through their involvement in the Connections Across Generations program, they have enhanced the education of SSU students. For the older adults, many of whom never had the chance to attend or complete college, this recognition by the university affirms they are valued members of the community.

Assessment

Students write weekly reflection papers in which they describe the content of each session: the topic selected, how it was chosen, the sensitizing questions that were asked to deepen discussion, and insights obtained. They also analyze the group's dynamics, including the tasks and challenges at this particular phase of group development. In addition, students write their reaction to the assigned reading in which they consider how the ideas might apply to their group. As a final evaluation, students complete a take-home essay exam. This encourages students to analyze their Connections group by identifying themes, phases of group development, and the benefits and risks of group participation. The exam also asks students to discuss how the course has helped them to better understand older adults and prepared them to live and work in an aging society. This outcome has been identified as a potential benefit of college students interacting with older adults (Henkin & Kingson, 1998–1999).

During the culmination meetings, I specifically elicit feedback from the community participants. The older adults convey what they have gained from their participation in the intergenerational dialogues, and they offer suggestions on how to improve the program. I also obtain feedback from the activities director at each site during visits midway in the semester and following the culmination gathering.

What Do Students Learn?

The course creates a multidimensional learning experience. Academic concepts are comprehended when they are transformed from abstract theory, research, and policy to real-life people and interactions. For example, the course begins with readings about ageism. As if on cue, at an introductory meeting a man spoke movingly about feeling invisible to young people. Readings about sexuality and aging took on new meaning when students learned that older adults could talk candidly about this taboo subject. The students found out that a group of widows could tearfully describe how they mourn and miss their husbands, and moments later confide that they share a crush on one unsuspecting man in their senior apartment complex. The students learned not to assume that everyone in their group was heterosexual when a group member confided that she had felt left out of a discussion about dating, because she was a lesbian and had felt unsafe "coming out" to the group. Readings about Social Security and Medicare were no longer dry policy issues when students learned that group members could not afford to take medications daily as prescribed, or feared that they would have to move out of their retirement facility because they could not afford rising fees.

As revealed in their reflection papers, students learn to recognize myths and stereotypes about aging and realize that these are hurtful and self-perpetuating. Contact with the older adults seems to lessen their personal fears about aging.

"They taught me that old age could be filled with new friends, learning, and even love. They have conquered so many obstacles, from childhood abuse, divorce, death of a spouse, to being homeless and living in a shelter. They have become role models for me about how to live and how to age."

"I learned that aging is not something that can be universally defined; it is not something that is experienced in the same way by all of our aging population. . . . I learned that growing old is not something we should necessarily fear, as old age can be more than sickness and death. . . . it has life."

"I came into this class scared, nervous, and worried that I couldn't handle working with older adults. I've learned much about what it is like to be an older adult in this society. I have also learned I can communicate with seniors, and I have loved discovering that we have so much in common. I am no longer afraid of growing old."

Students also confront the health, economic, and social and psychological challenges faced by older adults.

> "I have become more knowledgeable about what it means to feel invisible, to depend on Social Security, to not have enough money for medications, to miss a partner who died many years ago."

They were surprised to learn how much older adults care about the younger generation.

> "I thought that they would be more concerned about themselves. Instead, each week, they wanted to know more about us . . . our goals, classes, friends and families, what we do for fun, and what is stressful for us. They wanted to know our views about the death penalty and the war in Iraq."

> "They persuaded me to speak up and to not be afraid to give my opinion. They encouraged me to further my education and to make a difference in my community."

An unintended but welcome outcome has been that students are inspired to become politically aware and active. Students report registering to vote for the first time.

> "I couldn't face telling them that I wasn't registered. They care so much and are concerned about the apathy of young people. I felt I had a responsibility to them, as well as to myself, to vote."

> "I can't get away with saying 'I am too busy' or 'What difference does it make?' They are so conscientious about being informed and voting, it has rubbed off on me."

The self-selected community participants frequently include people with a history of social and political activism. They share with students their perspectives about social change and stir the students to reflect upon and reconsider their lack of civic engagement.

> "They were baffled by the idea that we can sit by and not do anything, while the lives of so many are being torn apart. They continually asked questions about whether we are lazy or have an overabundance of other

responsibilities, leaving us with an inability to take time out to even think about current events that plague us."

"My group showed me that most of them care about what is happening in the world, and that they would like it to be better for us. I also know that they would like us to take a role in creating positive change in the world."

A few years ago when one of the senior centers was threatened with a huge budget cut, the students were so upset they attended their first city council meeting to advocate on behalf of the seniors. Another group of students was aware that the older adults had been skeptical and apprehensive about the younger generation's ability to cope with drastic local and global political issues. Rising to the challenge, the students prepared a two-page handout, ostensibly for the seniors: "What Can I Do to Help Effect Change for the Good in Our Society?" It consisted of contact information about political representatives, as well as lists of social action groups. Not only did the handout please the seniors, but the students recognized that by learning how they could make their voices heard, they had changed their own lives.

"I believe we earned the respect of our members. We left them with a sense of hope that we will continue the work of building a just and caring society."

In addition to teaching students about aging, the course instructs them in the fundamentals of group work. As the Connections groups evolve, the phases of group development become clear. In the beginning phase students learn the importance of clarifying expectations and understanding peoples' desires and fears about talking candidly. In the middle phase they learn to deepen discussions and to foster constructive group norms. In the termination phase they learn to face the bittersweet feelings of saying good-bye. Significantly, they discover firsthand the value of groups for older adults, who long for connection not only with younger generations, but also with their peers and community.

How Do Community Participants Benefit?

While the course is designed to educate students, the Connections Across Generations groups are a benefit to the community participants. Reminiscing and talking about their past to interested young people and peers, older adults come to terms with how they have lived their lives. In interaction with the students and other participants, they compose a psychosocial legacy, actively determining what to pass on (Kivnick, 1996). The older adults identify additional benefits from the groups, which they report in the culmination session. They appreciate the intergenerational contact, which provides a window to understanding the younger generation. Parallel to the students, the older adults find the intergenerational contact challenges their stereotypes. These are comments the seniors made during the culmination meetings:

"I can better understand the problems and joys of my grandchildren."

"Sometimes I want to talk to my grandchildren about what's going on, the changes in the world. They don't want to talk in depth with me. This was a chance to talk seriously with the younger generation, to find out what's on their minds."

"It makes me not afraid to get old with students like this. It makes me hopeful that there are intelligent, caring, curious young people."

"I was surprised to find out that we have many things in common. Although there are different generations, many of our ideas, likes, and dislikes are the same."

They like making a contribution to the students' lives.

"I wanted to participate because I feel young people are undervalued. I wanted to show my respect for them."

"I brought in the articles to bring these issues [immigration and discrimination] to their attention. It could make a difference in their thinking and actions."

They are surprised the students become fond of them and consider them as role models and as being "cool." They often say the program is a highlight in their week.

"This program gives me something to look forward to. I think about it all week. I even changed doctors' appointments so I would not miss a meeting with the students."

A consequence of an effective group is the deepening of peer relationships. Even in settings where people see each other frequently, relationships can be superficial. As a result of these weekly, candid discussions, members report that they value getting to know their peers better. Friendships are formed that continue outside the group.

Community members welcome not only the intergenerational contact but also opportunities to learn more about students and peers from different backgrounds. The groups become a comfortable place to acknowledge similarities and differences in cultural backgrounds and to discuss how these affect peoples' lives. For example, there was considerable interest in learning more about the experiences of a student who grew up in Eritrea and in a senior who experienced World War II in London, as well as in the Latino elders mentioned earlier. While gay and lesbian participants may hesitate to disclose their sexual orientation until they feel safe, those who have "come out" represent another dimension of diversity that participants value.

> "I don't want to be in a group of six other women who are within six months of my age and who share my experiences and views. I like getting to know and understand people of different ages and backgrounds and perspectives."

Involvement with the university brings status to the seniors and to the community partner agencies. The seniors feel respected and valued by the professor who recruits them to help college students learn about aging. The Certificates of Appreciation represent a personal accomplishment. The senior centers and retirement communities are proud to proclaim that they are affiliated with the university.

Program Roots and Future Directions

The course was based on a model developed by Professors James Kelly and Susan Rice in the Department of Social Work at California State University, Long Beach. Following them, I taught the course for 5 years. In that course students learned group-work skills and went to a nearby retirement community, Leisure World Seal Beach, to facilitate support groups focused on coping with aging. When I said good-bye to the Leisure World participants in preparation for my moving north, they encouraged me to start a similar program at SSU. They emphasized the part of the program they liked best—the interactions between generations. Thus, when adapting the course to SSU, I reconceptualized the groups as *intergenerational dialogue groups* rather than support groups.

Initially, the SSU Connections Across Generations discussions were expected to focus on aging and the older adults' lives. It soon became apparent that the older adults were determined to learn about the students' lives and perspectives. Furthermore, group members felt gratified when they learned how to talk and listen to each other about controversial current events and issues. I now recognize and appreciate that being interested in the well-being of young adults and staying informed about current events are central to the life of many older adults. Consequently, the group dialogues began to reflect this expanded focus. I now encourage the students to enter openly into the dialogue, and to share perspectives on relevant social issues.

Currently, the course is an elective that teaches group-work skills as well as key issues about aging. The dialogue groups could be part of social gerontology or sociology of aging courses. There would be less emphasis on group-work skills; instead, the instructor could incorporate intergenerational group discussions into the course. This could be done by inviting elders into the class or scheduling some class meetings in the community. Another possibility would be to partner with an elder college, such as a lifelong learning institute based on the campus.

The class and the Connections Across Generations groups have a momentum of their own. Students who have taken the course volunteer to recruit new students. The community sites have a waiting list of participants. In a troubled world, the experience of lifting boundaries and talking and listening to people who would otherwise be strangers produces a joyful feeling of accomplishment and community.

References

Birren, J. & Deutchman, D. (1991). *Guiding autobiography groups for older adults: Exploring the fabric of life.* Baltimore: Johns Hopkins University Press.

Black, J., Kelly, J. & Rice, S. (2005). A model of group work in retirement communities. In B. Haight & F. Gibson (Eds.), *Working with older adults: Group process and techniques* (4th ed., pp. 273–285). Boston: Jones and Bartlett.

Henkin, N., & Kingson, E. (1998–1999). Advancing an intergenerational agenda for the twenty-first century. *Generations, 22*(4), 99–105.

Kivnick, H. (1996). Remembering and being remembered: The reciprocity of psychosocial legacy. *Generations, 20*(3), 49–53.

Toseland, R. (1995). *Group work with the elderly.* New York: Springer.

3

PREPARING FUTURE NURSES FOR A LIFE OF CIVIC ENGAGEMENT

The Disaster Preparedness for
Vulnerable Populations Project

Lynette Landry and Harvey Davis

So never lose an opportunity of urging a practical beginning, however small, for it is wonderful how often in such matters the mustard-seed germinates and roots itself.

Florence Nightingale

As nurse educators we strive to instill in our students a sense of social responsibility as an integral part of the development of nursing professionalism. Service to the community is one aspect of social responsibility, and nursing practice is based on a long tradition of such service. Nurse leaders in the late 1800s and early 1900s understood the need to be actively engaged in working with communities to advocate for change in social conditions that lead to adverse health outcomes especially in poor communities, urban and rural (Zerwekh, 1992). Modern community/public health nurses are likewise focused on advocating for and developing capacity in marginalized and disenfranchised communities.

This project is supported by Award No. 4123–06, awarded by the Department of Homeland Security (DHS), Office of Grants & Training (G&T). The opinions, findings, and conclusions or recommendations expressed in this program are those of the authors and do not necessarily reflect the views of the Department of Homeland Security.

The challenge then to nursing educators is to design a curriculum that includes civic learning outcomes, which Thomas Erhlich (1999) defines as "coming to an understanding of how a community functions, what problems it faces, the richness of its diversity, and the importance of individual commitments of time and energy in enhancing community" (p. 6). Traditional nursing education has all too often used a hierarchical model to train students to provide care to the client or patient. By hierarchical we mean that because nursing practice was long dominated by medicine, nursing students were taught to master skills and follow procedures dictated by physicians (Antrobus, 1997). Though patient education has always been an integral component of nursing practice, the plan of care and, therefore, the focus of education were dominated by health care professionals allowing for little input from patients and families.

Fortunately, over the last decade nursing education has experienced a paradigm shift away from the hierarchical model to a collaborative model that views the client or patient as a partner. This collaborative model has been built on the work of numerous nurse theorists and the integration of a feminist perspective in which the nurse is seen as doing *with* rather than doing *to*. From the feminist perspective, each individual is valued and respected (Allan, 1993). Using this perspective, it is the responsibility of nurses to work with patients, families, and communities to attain the health goals of the individual, family, or community. As this shift in thinking has occurred, nurse educators are exploring educational methods that can be used to assist students in developing the skills necessary to work collaboratively with clients or patients and other service providers.

A powerful mechanism for nurse educators to engage students in civic learning is community service learning (CSL; Nokes, Nickitas, Keida, & Neville, 2005). CSL is different from the traditional clinical practicums that nursing students are required to complete before graduation and licensure. As Fusco states, "Service learning programs are distinguished from other approaches to experiential education by their intention to equally benefit the provider and the recipient of the service as well as to ensure equal focus on both the service being provided and the learning that is occurring" (as cited by Carpenter, 1999, p. 7). CSL has been used to engage nursing students in advocacy and capacity development in a variety of communities, nationally and internationally. Childs, Sepples, and Moody (2003) describe how CSL was used to inform students about children living in poverty in their community. Students enrolled in this CSL course learned to work collaboratively with various health care providers as well as with other service providers, such as police, teachers, school administrators, and the clergy, to ensure that services were in place to meet the needs of the community being served. By participating in CSL, nursing students develop the skills needed to work collaboratively with individuals, families, and communities.

This year, the San Francisco State University Institute for Civic and Community Engagement (ICCE) initiated the Disaster Preparedness for Vulnerable Populations (DPVP) project to help prepare the most vulnerable populations of the region for a man-made or natural disaster. In the aftermath of Hurricane Katrina and the attacks of 9/11, cities throughout the nation became concerned about their ability to prepare communities, such as their poorest neighborhoods or disabled seniors, for a mass emergency. In San Francisco the imminent threat of a serious earthquake is never far from our consciousness, though other disasters such as a flu epidemic or terrorist attack are not far behind. In responding to a disaster nurses will have an important role to play.

Faculty from the nursing program, in conjunction with colleagues in disciplines as disparate as Asian American studies, engineering, psychology, Raza (Latino/Chicano) studies, and Teachers of English to Speakers of Other Languages (TESOL), participated in the DPVP program to develop a series of service-learning courses that would directly engage nursing students in helping to prepare for the future. While the engineering department addressed issues such as identifying weaknesses in the structural integrity of buildings, the psychology department addressed issues of crisis counseling in the immediate aftermath of a disaster, and the Raza studies, Asian American studies, and TESOL programs confronted cross-cultural issues of preparedness, nursing examined the roles and responsibilities nurses would face in an emergency.

In this chapter we discuss the development of two CSL courses that nursing faculty for community/public health nursing (CPHN) and psychiatric/mental health nursing (PMHN) collaboratively enhanced to facilitate a deeper understanding of nursing's role in advocacy and partnership with the community. Though CSL in nursing is not new, this CSL project was unique because the curriculum allowed two concurrent nursing courses to align themselves so that nursing students would be immersed in the project for the entire semester. Academic learning in the lecture and assessment skill acquisition in the practicums was essential. Understanding the root causes of biological, psychological, and social problems from an individual's needs to the aggregate level was important for the students to learn. It was also important to begin to stimulate values in them, such as advocacy, ethics, and social justice.

Course Development

CPHN and PMHN faculty developed courses that incorporated the CSL pedagogy. In developing the course curriculum, faculty decided to use a framework based on collaboration with students, other faculty, and the community partners to address disaster preparedness needs among seniors and the disabled in an urban setting. Senior nursing students concurrently take the CPHN and PMHN courses that were selected for this project. The CPHN didactic course and the PMHN didactic course have a corresponding clinical practicum students are required to take at the same time. Thus, the assignments for the courses (didactic and practicum) needed to be closely aligned. In addition, faculty who taught the didactic content had to collaborate on an ongoing basis to ensure that students were given the opportunity to reflect on the CSL experience and to reinforce content related to disaster preparedness.

The foci of the CPHN and the PMHN didactic courses have been vulnerable populations, such as the elderly, the disabled, the homeless, and the mentally ill. Students are given didactic content regarding the social, economic, and political contexts of these vulnerable populations. However, since there is little opportunity for students to interact with the elderly or the disabled, much of what is learned is theoretical, and students are unable to relate this learning to their professional goals and civic responsibilities.

To instill in students an understanding of the importance of advocacy and civic engagement to nursing practice, faculty decided that an overarching goal of this project was to lead them to a deeper understanding of the importance of advocating for vulnerable populations by providing students with the opportunity to work with the elderly, disabled, and those who may have cognitive difficulties or mental health problems in their home. In addition, faculty decided that the didactic content (specific to disaster preparedness) for the CSL would be taught in each course during the 3rd week of the semester to enhance the students' understanding of the nursing role in disaster preparedness prior to their first home visiting experience.

Community Public Health Didactic

Integration of disaster preparedness content into undergraduate nursing education is a recent development. Students were introduced to the role of nurses in response to a disaster. When a disaster occurs, nurses are called upon to meet the emergent needs of the victims. Thus, nursing students must be introduced to how to prepare for a disaster; what a disaster plan is; the role of nursing in the development and maintenance of the disaster plan; how to assist community members in preparing for a disaster; what to do when a disaster occurs, including triage, first aid, and transport of victims; and what the role of nursing is in recovery from a disaster.

Prior to this project, the didactic CPHN course included a 45-minute presentation on disaster preparedness and bioterrorism. CPHN faculty did not feel that 45 minutes was adequate to meet the learning needs of the students, so the lecture was expanded to 3 hours. In addition, disaster preparedness was integrated into other lectures specifically when vulnerable populations such as the homeless, elderly, mentally ill, or disabled were discussed.

During the 3 hours of disaster preparedness lectures, students were introduced to disaster planning and the components of a disaster plan, on the personal and community levels. As part of this portion of the lecture, students learned about disaster kits and their contents. Students were invited to share what they personally had done to prepare for a disaster to encourage dialogue about how the students could assist others in preparing for a disaster. At this point, the Vial of Life Program and the San Francisco Department of Public Health's Disaster Registry Program were introduced as community-level interventions that nurses can participate in to increase the likelihood that the needs of vulnerable populations will be met when a disaster occurs.

The disaster registry will make sure that those most vulnerable to the effects of a disaster are known to first responders so that aid can be dispatched in a timely manner. The vial of life is a plastic container where individuals put their critical information—medical history and medications as well as emergency contact information. The container is stored inside the person's refrigerator, which has a sticker on the outside indicating the vial's presence. Refrigerators survive earthquakes, so when first responders arrive at an emergency scene, they can quickly identify the specific health needs of a particular person should assistance be necessary.

Once a disaster occurs nurses are invaluable to help meet the health care requirements of the community, including triage and first aid. Nursing students have an awareness of how triage in a hospital emergency room is carried out, but triage in the event of a disaster is not the same. Students had time in the lecture to talk about triage during a disaster when nurses and physicians will not be able to save the most severely injured. Once students had an understanding of basic triage principles, they were introduced to the types of injuries that would be expected when a natural disaster occurred in San Francisco (most likely an earthquake). Finally, students were introduced to the role of nurses postdisaster, such as meeting the long-term physical and psychological needs of the victims and their families.

To help the students understand the unique living situations of the elderly, disabled, and mentally ill, faculty decided to have the students complete the Environmental Home Safety Assessment (Tanner, 2003) as part of their home visit. This assessment tool is designed to identify hazards in the home and to direct nursing interventions to reduce these hazards. Low-income populations may have few resources available to them to ensure a safe living environment; as a result their economic situation can result in an increased risk of injury. This tool was used to help students focus not just on the physical needs of the patient but also on environmental needs that may influence health status. A safe environment can reduce the risk of injury on a daily basis as well as when a disaster occurs. Students were encouraged to educate the clients about how to reduce the risk of injury from falling objects and other hazards during an earthquake.

Psychiatric Mental Health Didactic

It was important for students to understand crisis intervention techniques, particularly for vulnerable populations such as the elderly who may suffer from cognitive deficits as a result of normal aging or those who have a mental health disorder such as dementia or Alzheimer's disease. The intent was to have the students understand that the confusion and disorientation that may occur during a disaster would leave them overwhelmed and at risk. The students also would recognize that further assistance would be needed because their ability to respond appropriately would be seriously compromised.

Faculty felt it was important for the students to gain an understanding of the baseline cognitive abilities of the elderly, disabled, and mentally ill. The Mini-Mental Status Examination (MMSE), selected for use in screening the cognitive ability during home visits is a measure that assesses orientation to time and place, attention, immediate and recall memory, calculation, language, and constructional ability (Folstein, Folstein, & McHugh, 1975). Content for the MMSE was given by lecture and included how to administer and interpret the results. Assessment is the first step of the nursing process. Accuracy in assessment determines better planning and intervention.

Finally, a global overall view of the city's planning for a disaster was presented by a key member of the San Francisco Housing Authority who volunteered to speak to the class. The speaker, whose duties include the administration of all contracting and procurement services and management of warehouse operations, fleets, information systems, administrative services, telecommunications, and safety operations, described his role in the administration and the plans San Francisco has in place if a disaster occurs.

Learning Objectives

Faculty decided the objectives of this project were threefold. The primary objective was to meet the needs of the community being served in relation to disaster preparedness. The target population for the project was the more than 15,000 seniors and disabled people in San Francisco served by the San Francisco In-Home Supportive Services Public Authority (IHSS), a statewide publicly funded program that provides in-home care to eligible consumers, that is, clients who are able to live at home with sufficient nonprofessional support. The key services to these clients were to register them with the San Francisco Department of Public Health's Disaster Registry and to provide them with the vial of life. In addition, students gave each person basic disaster preparedness information, such as what to do in the case of an earthquake or fire.

In understanding why and how low-income seniors and the disabled are vulnerable to adverse health outcomes and at particular risk during a disaster, students are engaged in civic learning as described by Ehrlich (1999) and are made aware of the importance of civic engagement as a form of health advocacy as well as nursing assessment skills. So, the second objective of the project was to engage the students in civic learning. Prior to this experience, the students had not participated in clinical practicums outside the acute care setting. Many were unaware of how low-income seniors and disabled people live. Few had been to a single-room occupancy (SRO) residence or support-ive housing where many of the IHSS clients live. Thus, students were re-quired to make at least eight home visits in pairs to IHSS clients who had expressed an interest in participating in the project. IHSS clients who re-ceived home visits from the students lived in an SRO, supportive housing, or a private home or apartment, but all were low income.

The final objective was to provide a baseline assessment of the function-ality of the living environment and a brief cognitive assessment by having students complete, with each individual's permission, the Environmental Home Safety Assessment (Tanner, 2003) and the MMSE (Folstein et al., 1975).

In reviewing the literature on CSL, faculty involved in the development of these courses decided that a single evaluation method would be included to assess student learning. Nursing research focused on CSL as a learning modality has shown that reflection is an important aspect of the learning experience (Bailey, Carpenter, & Harrington, 2002; Reising, Allen, & Hall, 2006). Thus, students were required to do reflective journaling involving a series of questions to help guide their reflection on their experiences (see Ap-pendix A).

The faculty in the didactic and practicum courses instructed students on what reflective journaling was and how it would be used to assess their learn-ing. The students also developed portfolios to further demonstrate learning.

Outreach

In collaboration with IHSS and the ICCE, letters were mailed to IHSS re-cipients in San Francisco describing the project and asking if they would be interested and willing to have a student visit them at home to assist them in completing the required forms for the disaster registry and the vial of life. A graduate student assistant was given a list of IHSS participants who indicated their interest, and the student made follow-up phone calls and set up times for the nursing students to make the home visits. Since the response rate to the mailer was very low (> 5%), a member of the ICCE team contacted social workers employed at various SROs in San Francisco to see if there would be an opportunity to canvass all the residents. It was decided that the best way to engage the SRO residents would be a health fair. Clinical faculty and students developed health fairs for five SROs, which included teaching people about disaster preparedness, providing assistance in completing the forms for the registry and the vial, nutrition education, and blood pressure screening.

Assessment

Journals and student portfolios were collected by the practicum faculty at the end of each 7-week practicum. Since students were engaged in this project throughout the semester, journals and portfolios were evaluated twice. This enabled the students to build on their work throughout the semester and incorporate feedback into subsequent journal entries.

What became apparent during the first review of the journals was that students did not fully understand what reflective journaling was. Though reflective questions were explicitly outlined in the course syllabi, most students failed to answer any of the questions. Rather, the majority of students provided a description of the events that occurred during the home visits. However, some journal entries were very insightful. The important themes that emerged from the journal entries included "concern," "isolation and loneliness," "neglect and marginalization," "increased awareness of vulnerable populations," "new sense of civic engagement," and "bio-psycho-social diversity" to mention just a few.

To encourage reflection about the service-learning experience, the faculty teaching the didactic classes during the second half of the semester fostered discussion about the importance of reflection as a learning tool. For subsequent semesters of this project, time will be allotted during each lecture to reflect on the experiences students are having. By providing more opportunities for reflection, students will become more engaged in the project and develop a deeper understanding of the nursing role in advocacy and working with communities to improve the health status of all members of the community.

Since the project was developed by two faculty members who were not engaged in the practicum portion of the project, practicum faculty attended an orientation session on the project and the learning goal and objectives at the beginning of the semester. In retrospect, the practicum faculty should have been more actively involved in developing rubrics to evaluate student learning. There was confusion on the part of practicum faculty on how to engage students in reflective learning. In subsequent semesters, more time will be spent with practicum faculty to facilitate expertise in the use of reflective learning strategies. Additionally, practicum faculty will be given a rubric that will make evaluation of the reflective journals and portfolios clearer and more consistent across groups.

Overall this project was successful; students learned about their community and the vulnerable populations they will be caring for as nurses. They had the opportunity to work with community members in preparing for a disaster. About 300 IHSS recipients were assisted in filling out the forms for the San Francisco Department of Public Health's Disaster Registry and had their information collected for the vial of life. In addition, many of the students have indicated they understand the importance of civic engagement and advocacy and see these activities as integral to their nursing career.

Appendix A

Reflective Journal Guidelines

You are required to hand in a journal entry for every clinical day during which you visit IHSS clients in their homes for a total of 4 journal entries—2 during your community health clinical placement and 2 during psychiatric nursing clinical placement. The purpose of writing journals is to provide an opportunity for reflection. Listed below are some questions you can answer, but if you find other things to reflect on, that is fine. Please *do not* just write about what you did or the activities you participated in (this *is not* a chronology of your activities); you will not receive credit. Your journal entries need to be reflective. There is no minimum or maximum length for the journal entries but they must be typed, double spaced, and handed in as part of your portfolio. Please refer to due dates listed above regarding when your portfolio is due to your clinical faculty.

Potential questions for you to answer:
   a. What have you learned about the population or group that you are serving?
   b. What have you learned about the specific needs of the population or person you are working with? How are their needs being met? How are they not being met?
   c. What are some of the broader social issues that affect this group, person, or population?

d. How do the theories covered in class relate to your experience, or those of whom you are serving? Are any theories applicable? Why or why not?

e. What are you learning about yourself through this experience?

f. What have you learned about the influence of your community, your society, the agency on the developmental needs of the population that you are serving?

g. In what ways did this service-learning experience connect to the course content of either N444 or N446?

h. How would you describe the community's perception of you or the program you are working with?

i. If you were in charge of the project/initiative/program, what would you do differently?

j. What has made your experience successful? What has made it difficult?

k. What does the word "volunteer" mean to you? How do you feel about the service you are doing?

l. How does this service relate to the nursing profession? Or your career goals?

References

Allan, H. T. (1993). Feminism: a concept analysis. *Journal of Advanced Nursing, 18,* 1547–1553.

Antrobus, S. (1997). Developing the nurse as a knowledge worker in health: Learning the artistry of practice. *Journal of Advanced Nursing, 25,* 829–835.

Bailey, P. A., Carpenter, D. R., & Harrington, P. (2002). Theoretical foundations of service-learning in nursing education. *Journal of Nursing Education, 41*(10), 433–438.

Carpenter, D. R. (1999). The concept of service-learning. In P. A. Bailey, D. R. Carpenter, & P. A. Harrington (Eds.), *Integrating community service learning into nursing education.* New York: Springer.

Childs, J. C., Sepples, S. B., & Moody, K. A. (2003). Mentoring youths: A service-learning course within a college of nursing. *Journal of Nursing Education, 42*(4), 182–185.

Erlich, T. (1999). Civic and moral learning. *About Campus, 4*(4), 4–9.

Folstein, M. F., Folstein, S. E., & McHugh, P. R. (1975). Mini-mental state: A practical method for grading the cognitive state of patients for the clinician. *Journal of Psychiatric Research, 12*(3),189–198.

Nokes, K. M., Nickitas, D. M., Keida, R., & Neville, S. (2005). Does service-learning increase cultural competency, critical thinking and civic engagement? *Journal of Nursing Education, 44*(2), 65–70.

Reising, D. L., Allen, P. N., & Hall, S. G. (2006). Student and community outcomes in service-learning: Part 1, student perceptions. *Journal of Nursing Education, 45*(12), 512–515.

Tanner, E. K. (2003). Home health care. Assessing home safety in homebound older adults. *Geriatric Nursing, 24*(4), 250–254.

Zerwekh, J. (1992). Public health nursing legacy: Historical practical wisdom. *Nursing and Health Care, 13*(2), 84–91.

4

CULTIVATING HEALTHY HABITS

Food, Gardens, and Community-Based Learning

Debora Hammond

T
he Hutchins School of Liberal Studies at Sonoma State University offers an interdisciplinary, seminar-based curriculum. Long a leader in the learning community movement (fostering interdisciplinary and dialogue-based learning), the Hutchins School is currently taking the learning community concept one step further, integrating service and community-based learning projects into the curriculum. In addition to an integrated 48-unit general education program (which meets all the general education requirements except mathematics), the Hutchins School offers two options for upper-division majors: one specifically tailored for students planning a career in elementary education, the other providing a more flexible option for students who appreciate the pedagogical orientation of the Hutchins School, which allows them to tailor their major around their specific areas of interest and career goals.

Upper-division core seminars provide an opportunity for integration across the disciplines around a particular topic or theme. The focus on food in the Global Food Web seminar lends itself to a discussion of (a) economics, specifically with regard to the increasingly industrialized and globalized food economy; (b) scientific and ecological dimensions in relation to land and water use, soil depletion, climate change, genetic engineering, and so on; (c) health and nutrition, particularly in connection with concerns about the increasing rates of obesity and diabetes among children; and (d) psychological/spiritual dimensions of food, including eating disorders as well as the relationship of humans to the land. In addition, it offers a variety of opportunities for community service and research projects relating to the local food economy.

The interdisciplinary nature of the Hutchins curriculum is well suited for prospective elementary teachers who make up roughly two thirds of our upper-division population. The food theme is particularly relevant to the needs of these students as there are numerous opportunities for community involvement in the local schools, such as working on school gardens and farm-to-school projects that use locally grown produce in school lunches. Thanks to the efforts of Alice Waters (chef, author, and owner of Chez Panisse Restaurant who has funded numerous school garden projects), Delaine Easton (former California state superintendent of education), and the Center for Ecoliteracy in Berkeley, among others, the San Francisco Bay Area is experiencing a flowering of garden-based curricula in the elementary schools and a rapidly growing farm-to-school movement. These initiatives serve to foster nutritional awareness among young children, improve the quality of food in school lunches, build stronger relationships between educational institutions and the local community, and provide support for small family farms.

This general idea is spreading to other institutions as well, providing exciting opportunities for service and research for our students who are not planning to teach. Hospitals, county agencies, and restaurants are also beginning to work with local farmers, helping to strengthen the local economy and build stronger ties at the community level. One of my students, who was working as an assistant manager at a chain restaurant in the area, did some research on produce that could be purchased locally and convinced his manager to implement significant changes in this area.

With regard to research, there is a great deal of interest in the idea of community food security. A growing underclass in the United States does not have adequate access to food. In addition, as fossil fuel becomes increasingly scarce and costly, it will become more and more critical for local communities to meet more of their own needs. Initiatives at the federal and state levels support community food assessments, which is an area that provides limitless opportunities for community-based research and interdisciplinary collaboration.

Following a brief description and outline of the course, this chapter documents service and research projects emerging from the first three sessions of the Global Food Web seminar (fall 2004, spring 2005, and spring 2006) and discusses opportunities for developing partnerships with other departments, other campuses, and community organizations in creating knowledge and building community around one of the most basic of human needs.

Motivation for Teaching the Course

Prior to the development of the Global Food Web seminar, I had been teaching two upper-division seminars that informed my thinking on this new one. One was Health and Healing, which encompassed economic, environmental, scientific, and psychological dimensions of health and healing, integrating Eastern and Western perspectives and exploring emerging views on the nature of the mind/body connection. As in the food course, a key theme in the health course was the relationship between individual, environmental, and social health. Along these lines, I have been very much inspired by the work of Len Duhl (1995), professor of public health at the University of California, Berkeley. In *The Social Entrepreneurship of Change*, he outlines Six Characteristics of a Healthy City:

1. Healthy cities/communities have a sense of history to which their citizens relate and upon which their commonly held values are grounded.
2. Healthy cities are multidimensional . . . and have a complex and interactive economy.
3. Healthy cities strive for decentralization of power and citizen participation in making decisions about policy.
4. Healthy cities are represented by leadership that focuses on the whole of a city and can visualize both parts and "wholes" simultaneously.
5. Healthy cities can adapt to change, cope with breakdown, repair themselves, and learn both from their own experience and that of other cities.
6. Healthy cities are those that support and maintain their infrastructures.

A similar orientation informed the second course, Oikos, from the Greek root of economics and ecology, meaning household or home. The course focused on the theme of sustainability, exploring the relationship between economics and ecology (nature's economy), beginning with nature writing on the theme of home. Paul Hawken (1994) cites Aristotle's distinction between the concept of *oikonomia*, defined as "the management of the household so as to increase its value to all members of the household over the long run," and the concept of *chrematistics*, which he defines as "a branch of political economy relating to the manipulation of property and wealth so as to maximize short-term monetary exchange value to the owner" (pp. 58–59). It is becoming increasingly apparent that the forces driving our economic system are operating according to the goals of the latter definition and not necessarily serving to foster healthy and sustainable communities.

In the Oikos course I began to integrate community-based research projects and, later, more active involvement in service learning. When I first began teaching the course, students were asked to do group projects on issues relating to energy, water, land use, and climate change in the local region. Later, after participating in the Engaged Department Institute (cosponsored by the California State University and Campus Compact in San Francisco, May 28–31, 2002), I worked with our community partner (Sustainable Sonoma County) and other local organizations to develop opportunities for more active participation in the community. Students worked in a variety of contexts, but perhaps the most successful projects involved working with programs in environmental education and community gardens.

Between February and November 2003, I worked with a team of faculty (from environmental studies and planning, geography, and philosophy) and community representatives, including a member of the local city council, to host a series of five public forums on climate change. I was responsible for the session on reducing greenhouse gases, which highlighted the efforts of local organizers who were working in collaboration with the International Center for Local Environmental Initiatives to get Sonoma County (as well as all nine of its cities) to commit to reducing greenhouse gas emissions. On the day before the event, I happened to hear Helena Norberg-Hodge, founder of the International Society for Ecology and Culture, on the radio, arguing that the single greatest thing we could do to reduce greenhouse gases would be to rebuild the local food system. Thus, the Global Food Web was born, initiated in the fall of 2004.

In the fall of 2003, I attended a workshop on the farm-to-school movement facilitated by the Center for Ecoliteracy in Berkeley and as a result was invited to participate in a meeting of the Fertile Crescent Network, a consortium of farmers, representatives from a variety of county agencies, school food service directors and garden coordinators, and others from the extended San Francisco Bay Area interested in furthering partnerships between schools and local farms. At this meeting, I became acquainted with the garden coordinator from Valley Vista Elementary School in Petaluma, which has done an exceptional job of integrating the school garden into the elementary curriculum, developing lessons specific to each grade level that address standards across the subject areas. In addition, I met a representative from Food Matters in Sonoma County who has been working to establish a food policy council in the county. Like the Fertile Crescent group, Food Matters brings together farmers, food service directors, county health officials, school garden coordinators, educators, and others to facilitate greater collaboration on issues of access to healthy food for all. All these associations provided excellent contacts for service-learning placements for the students in my course.

Learning Objectives, Outcomes, Assessment, and Methodology

The course objectives as noted in the syllabus are as follows:

1. To explore the political and economic factors underlying current systems of food production and distribution in the local economy, in the United States, and in the global economy.
2. To gain familiarity with recent policy and other initiatives seeking to address issues relating to community food security and access to healthy food, particularly in relation to education.
3. To understand the ecology of our food system, in the broadest sense possible.
4. To learn about the chemistry of the basic elements in our food system.
5. To reflect on the meaning of food in our day-to-day lives and to explore the various dimensions of our relationships, both individual and collective, with the food we eat, specifically with how the food we eat affects our health and the health of the environment.

Specifically in relation to community-based learning, the focus on food provides numerous opportunities for engagement in the local community, which empowers the students to make substantial contributions while also learning valuable skills relevant in their own life as well as in their chosen career. Outcomes include a greater awareness of the role of nutrition in health and the tools to share this knowledge with schoolchildren and colleagues in other fields. Within the context of the seminar, student learning is assessed on the basis of student writing and participation in the seminar. Students submit weekly reflections on the progress of community-based projects, and the final assignment in the course is a presentation to the class and a written evaluation of what the student learned through the project, tying the project to the academic content of the course.

Course Content

I have used a variety of texts and reader articles in this course. The constant has been Paul Fleischman's (2004) *Seedfolks*. Great for beginning the semester, it is a delightful story of a community garden cultivated in an empty lot in Cleveland, Ohio. The first two times I taught the course, I used Frances Moore Lappé and Anna Lappé's (2003) *Hope's Edge: The Next Diet for a Small Planet*, which provides inspiring accounts of food-related initiatives from all corners of the world, and Charles Eisenstein's (2003) *The Yoga of Eating: Transcending Diets and Dogma to Nourish the Natural Self*. Currently I am using Michael Pollan's (2006) *The Omnivore's Dilemma: A Natural History of Four Meals*, a comprehensive and beautifully written overview of the dynamics of our industrial food system that challenges students to consider where their food comes from and the impact it has in its journey from seed to table. In addition, a classic that I have excerpted passages from in the past but have decided to include in its entirety in the current course is Harold McGee's (2004) *On Food and Cooking: The Science and Lore of the Kitchen*, an informative account of the history and chemistry of the foods we eat, from milk, eggs, meat, vegetables, fruit, seeds, and nuts, to fermented beverages, spices, and additives. It is a particularly valuable resource for students who plan to teach. An excellent collection of articles published in cooperation with Earth Ministry that I have included in the course is Michael Schut's (2002) *Food and Faith: Justice, Joy and Daily Bread*. Coming from a faith-based perspective, it illustrates the potential for the topic of food to bridge the seemingly insurmountable ideological divisions in our culture.

Course topics and relevant sources include:

School gardens and farm-to-school initiatives. The Lappés' (2003) book includes a section on this topic. Excellent resources are the Life Lab Science Program's (1997) *Getting Started: A Guide for Creating School Gardens as Outdoor Classrooms*, along with other relevant resources available on its Web site at http://www.ecoliteracy.org); the California Department of Education's (2005) *Taking Action for Healthy School Environments: Linking Education, Activity, and Food in California Secondary Schools*; Azuma and Fisher's (2001) *Healthy Farms, Healthy Kids: Evaluating the Barriers and Opportunities for Farm-To-School Programs*; and Siedenburg and Pothukuchi's (2002) *What's Cooking in Your Food System: A Guide to Community Food Assessment.* See also Federico's (2001) "Teaching About Food Systems" in the summer issue of *Green Teacher.*

Diet, nutrition and food fads. Eisenstein's (2003) *Yoga of Eating* is a good text for addressing this topic. The introduction in Arthur Agatston's (2005) *The South Beach Diet* provides an interesting history of dietary fads. Also relevant in this section are discussions of the evolution of the food pyramid and official nutritional recommendations. With regard to nutrition, McGee's (2004) book provides a good foundation in his overview of the basic chemistry of carbohydrates, proteins, and fats, as well as the relationship between the health of the soil and the quality of the food.

Fast food, slow food, and the American way of eating. Eric Schlosser's (2001) *Fast Food Nation* does an excellent job of documenting the fast-food industry, and I have often included excerpts from his book in a reader. Pollan's (2006) book addresses this to a certain extent, although he does not focus as extensively on the fast-food industry (and of course students love Morgan Spurloc's [2004] *Supersize Me*). Wendell Berry's (1986) *The Unsettling of America: Culture and Agriculture* is also an excellent source for a more philosophical perspective on this topic, particularly the chapter "The Agricultural Crisis as a Crisis of Culture." The Schut (2002) volume also includes a couple of Berry's articles along with a number of others that are relevant to this section. In the past, I have invited representatives from the Slow Food organization to talk to the class about the implications of this movement, which offers an alternative vision for a more sustainable food system.

Vegetarianism. An abundance of resources exist on this topic, although I make it clear to my students from the beginning that I am not trying to convince them to become vegetarians; I myself am not a strict vegetarian, and I think the important point here is to get the students to reflect on where their food comes from and what processes are involved in its production and distribution. I have used selections from John Robbins's (1998) *Diet for a New America*, which makes a strong argument for vegetarianism, while Pollan's (2006) book makes a good case for introducing more humane practices in animal husbandry as an integral part of a truly sustainable food system. Articles in the Schut (2002) reader document the appalling conditions for humans and animals in slaughterhouses, as well as the more intimate (and humorous) relationships between humans and animals on the farm. In fact, the Schut collection provides a thoughtful balance of perspectives on a wide variety of topics.

Agroecology and soil. I gathered some of the material for this section from the California Foundation for Agriculture in the Classroom, which provides excellent materials and workshops for teachers. In addition, I have used a great collection of articles from an issue of *Whole Earth* titled "Celebrating Soil" (Warshall, 1999). Pollan's (2006) book is also a thoughtful elaboration on some general agroecological principles. Clearly this course is not the place for a comprehensive overview of this topic, but it gives the students enough of a foundation for further inquiry (and perhaps hands-on exploration with their own future students).

Genetic engineering. This is a particularly challenging and controversial topic, and I try to provide a balanced view of the issues and concerns on both sides of the debate. Once again, Schut (2002) does a good job of providing different perspectives, although he leans strongly toward a critical stance. In the past I have invited local farmers, organic and conventional, to the seminar to talk about the challenges they face in making a living off the land.

Reclaiming the local food economy. Along with Wendell Berry's (1986) work, the best resources I have found on this topic are two studies published by the International Society for Ecology and Culture: *Bringing the Food Economy Home: The Social, Ecological and Economic Benefits of Local Food* (Norberg-Hodge, Merrifield, & Gorelick, 2000) and *Ripe for Change: Thinking California's Food Economy* (Mamen, Gorelick, Norberg-Hodge, & Deumling, 2004).

Readings on the history and current state of local agriculture. Drawing from a variety of local publications, I have compiled a series of writings that address issues in San Francisco's North Bay community, including the Sonoma

County Agricultural Commissioner's Crop Report (1999) *Looking Back to the Future: The Last 100 Years in Sonoma County Agriculture*, and a study from the Redwood Empire Food Bank (2003), *Understanding the Economics of Hunger in Sonoma County: A Study of Emergency Food Recipients*.

Civic Engagement and Community-Based Learning

Within this context, then, students have been involved in a variety of service-learning projects in the community. During the first two semesters, the majority of students worked in some capacity with school gardens. Some were able to procure donated materials to start new gardens in schools that previously had none, building raised beds and getting the schoolchildren involved in preparing the soil, planting the seedlings, and maintaining the site. Most sophisticated projects at sites with long-established gardens included working with the schoolchildren at different levels in projects tailored to meet specific standards for different subjects including mathematics, biology, history, and literature.

There was some flexibility in the nature of the project, depending upon the seminar students' schedules. One student surveyed the food being served in school lunches, while another surveyed school gardens in elementary schools in one of the local districts. The student who was employed as an assistant manager at a local chain restaurant worked with his manager to purchase locally grown produce wherever possible. Another worked with Oxfam (an international organization devoted to fighting poverty and injustice; see http://www.oxfam.org) to organize a hunger awareness dinner for a statewide event. Some chose to work at the local food bank or with other similar programs.

Time for reflection on the students' experience was set aside throughout the semester, and the assignment culminated in an oral presentation to the class along with a written reflection on the experience drawing on course readings to assess what they had learned. The presentations were amazingly creative; some students put together excellent handouts on topics such as starting a garden or getting rid of pests naturally. It was clear that in most cases they found the experience to be informative, inspiring, and enjoyable. A couple of students plan to devote their careers to fostering school gardens. Others were inspired to explore the policy aspect of the food system and become more actively involved in local initiatives. Many felt that food and farming is a topic the majority of the population is woefully uninformed on and were inspired to work toward bringing about change in one way or another.

In the 3rd year, I changed the focus of the project somewhat in response to conversations with the Sonoma County superintendent of schools, Carl Wong, who has been very supportive of the school garden and farm-to-school initiatives. In response to my question about how my students might support the county, he suggested a survey of school districts to assess the impact of the federal mandate for all districts to have in place a wellness policy for the 2006–2007 academic year. Students were expected to get copies of the policy and the administrative regulations, and to talk with superintendents, principals, teachers, and/or students to find out what impact, if any, the new policies might have. Of course, it is early to see any substantial changes, but this project will establish an initial baseline to measure similar assessments in the future.

Future Directions

My goal in future seminars is to engage the students in a comprehensive food assessment project, building on the work of the Community Food Security Coalition, which has worked with a number of communities to facilitate community-based participatory inquiry. This kind of project would be ongoing over several years and could link the school garden and farm-to-school movements with broader social justice concerns relating to food access and with environmental concerns relating to sustainable agriculture. In addition, it could engage students and faculty from a broad range of disciplines, including environmental studies, geography, economics, public policy studies, and education, among others.

References

Agatston, A. (2005). *The South Beach Diet.* New York: St. Martin's.

Azuma, A., & Fisher, A. (2001). *Healthy farms, healthy kids: Evaluating the barriers and opportunities for farm-to-school programs.* Portland, OR: Community Food Security Coalition.

Berry, W. (1986). *The unsettling of America: Culture and agriculture.* San Francisco: Sierra Club Books.

Duhl, L. J. (1995). *The social entrepreneurship of change.* New York: Pace University Press.

Eisenstein, C. (2003). *The yoga of eating: Transcending diets and dogma to nourish the natural self.* Lanham, MD: New Trends Publishing.

Federico, C. (2001). Teaching about food systems. *Green Teacher: Education for Planet Earth, 65,* 6–11.

Fleischman, P. (2004). *Seedfolks.* New York: HarperTrophy.

Hawken, P. (1994). *The ecology of commerce.* New York: Collins.

Lappé, F. M., & Lappé, A. (2003). *Hope's edge: The next diet for a small planet.* New York: Tarcher.

Life Lab Science Program. (1997). *Getting started: A guide for creating school gardens as outdoor classrooms.* Berkeley, CA: Center for Ecoliteracy.

Mamen, K., Gorelick, S., Norberg-Hodge, H., & Deumling, D. (2004). *Ripe for change: Thinking California's food economy.* Berkeley, CA: International Society for Ecology and Culture.

McGee, H. (2004). *On food and cooking: The science and lore of the kitchen.* New York: Scribner.

Norberg-Hodge, H., Merrifield, T., & Gorelick, S. (2000). *Bringing the food economy home: The social, ecological and economic benefits of local food.* Berkeley, CA: International Society for Ecology and Culture.

O'Malley, E. (Ed.). (2005). *Taking action for healthy school environments: Linking education, activity, and food in California secondary schools.* Sacramento, CA: California Department of Education, Nutrition Services Division.

Pollan, M. (2006). *The omnivore's dilemma.* New York: Penguin.

Redwood Empire Food Bank. (2003). *Understanding the economics of hunger in Sonoma County: A study of emergency food recipients.* Santa Rosa, CA: Redwood Empire Food Bank.

Robbins, J. (1998). *Diet for a new America: How your food choices affect your health, happiness, and the future of life on earth.* Novato, CA: H. J. Kramer.

Schlosser, E. (2001). *Fast food nation.* New York: Harper Perennial.

Schut, M. (Ed.). (2002). *Food and faith: Justice, joy and daily bread.* Denver, CO: Morehouse Group.

Siedenburg, K., & Pothukuchi, K. (2002). *What's cooking in your food system? A guide to community food assessment.* Portland, OR: Community Food Security Coalition.

Sonoma County Agricultural Commissioner's Crop Report. (1999). *Looking back to the future: The last 100 years in Sonoma County agriculture.* Santa Rosa, CA: Sonoma County Agricultural Commissioner.

Spurlock, M. (Producer/Writer/Director). (2004). *Supersize me* [Motion picture]. United States: Samuel Goldwyn Films.

Warshall, P. (Ed.). (1999, spring). Celebrating soil. *Whole Earth Catalog,* 203–216.

SECTION TWO

CROSS-CULTURAL
COMPETENCIES

5

IMMIGRANT HEALTH LITERACY

Reaching Across Languages, Cultures, and Disciplines in Service

Daryl M. Gordon, Maricel G. Santos, and Gail Weinstein

I tried to call [to make a doctor's appointment] but it is all automated. Nobody is there. "If you want . . . press 1 . . . press 2." I do not understand and get frustrated. I don't understand. I'm sorry; I should go back to my country. It is very difficult to live here even with the amount of English I understand. What about those who do not understand at all?

Responding to Health Inequalities Through Community Service Learning

Older immigrants living in the United States, especially those with limited English proficiency, experience many difficulties in obtaining health care. The quotation above exemplifies the aggravation and sense of defeat a Chinese immigrant experienced in simply trying to make an appointment with the doctor.

This individual was a participant in a focus group that assessed the health communication and literacy needs of older immigrants. Findings from these focus groups informed the service-learning activities of Project

We would like to thank the many community partners, university faculty, Project SHINE coaches, and most especially the many immigrant elders throughout Philadelphia, San Francisco, and San José whose hard work and reflections provide the inspiration for this chapter.

SHINE (Students Helping in the Naturalization of Elders), a national service-learning initiative that builds partnerships between colleges and community-based organizations to engage college students in service to older immigrants. Students from a range of disciplines participate in tutoring activities to improve the health communication skills of older immigrants, while health professions students and faculty develop health education workshops customized to the needs of older immigrants. Bilingual/bicultural students play a particularly important role, using their cultural and linguistic resources to translate health information into the native language of older immigrants and help them access health care services.

The main objectives of SHINE service learning are to

- promote intercultural and intergenerational understanding within diverse communities;
- improve the ability of older immigrants to access health care, exercise their rights, and perform their responsibilities as family and community members;
- increase the academic knowledge, personal growth, and civic engagement of college students;
- enhance the ability of faculty members to create stronger links between community service and academic course work;
- build the capacity of community colleges and universities to develop sustainable, mutually beneficial partnerships with immigrant communities. (Gordon, Yoshida, Hikoyeda, & David, 2006)

In this community service-learning initiative students and faculty at our universities have come to better understand the experiences of immigrant elders in health care, as well as strengthen our belief that community partnerships represent one vehicle for creating hope and change.

Immigrant Health Literacy and Health Care Access

While the sources of health disparities are complex, cultural and linguistic barriers for patients with limited English proficiency have been identified as primary factors. One study found that over 60% of patients who were non-native speakers of English lacked the literacy skills adequate to function in health care settings (Williams et al., 2005). A report by the Institute of Medicine (2004) indicates that ethnic minorities are less likely than White patients to receive needed medical services including clinically necessary procedures.

The difficulties immigrants experience accessing health care are of urgent concern, given the steep increase in the foreign-born population. Between 1990 and 2000, the foreign-born population in the United States increased by 57%, from 19 million to 31 million. Of the foreign-born population in 2002, 20% or 6 million people are over the age of 55. Asian and Latino elders will be the fastest-growing sectors of this population. By 2050, the Latino elderly population is projected to grow from 2 million to 13 million, while the population of Asian elders will expand from 660,000 to 5.7 million during the same period. As the population of ethnic minority elders increases, their need for health and educational services become ever more pressing (Federal Interagency Forum on Aging-Related Statistics, 2008; U.S. Census Bureau, 2002).

The English-language and literacy barriers in medical contexts faced by older immigrant adults in particular may have potentially serious consequences. The 2003 National Adult Literacy Survey found that adults over the age of 65 have weaker health literacy skills than their younger counterparts (Kutner, Greenberg, Jin, & Paulsen, 2006; Rudd, Kirsch, & Yamamoto, 2004). These low-scoring performances indicate that many elderly adults in the United States would have difficulty with the following health literacy tasks:

- reading and interpreting dosage charts on prescription labels,
- calculating maximum dosage amounts for a given time period (e.g., maximum number of tablets per 24-hour period),
- determining eligibility based on a chart of health benefits,
- completing a medical history form,
- locating information in a nutrition article (Gorospe, 2006).

In a review of the literature on the health care of elderly immigrants in the United States, Gorospe (2006) cited several key issues that present ongoing challenges, including:

- the differences in health status among immigrant elders, with immigrants who arrive as elders exhibiting poorer health overall than immigrants who have aged in the United States;
- the acculturation stressors associated with immigrating to a new country as an elder;
- immigrant elders' limited access to adequate health care services because of cost and ineligibility;
- the lack of culturally appropriate practices in providing services to immigrant elders.

Our own work as part of Project SHINE has also highlighted the specific health concerns of immigrant elders. In 2003 Daryl Gordon was part of a research team that investigated the health communication and access needs of older immigrants and refugees to guide the development of English as a Second Language (ESL) health education materials to help immigrant elders communicate with health care providers.

This investigation involved focus groups and follow-up interviews with over 100 older immigrants from seven ethnolinguistic groups in Philadelphia and San José.[1] Participants were asked to discuss their experiences accessing health care in the United States and their interest in learning about topics related to health problems and communication in health care settings. Additional insights were gathered from providers in health care, senior services, immigrant services, and adult education who work with older immigrants.

The immigrants who participated in the focus groups and interviews told poignant stories illustrating their struggles related to health literacy and communication. Some elders waited to seek medical care until health problems developed into emergencies because they were unable to read or understand insurance information to ascertain if they had coverage. Many could not understand what a doctor said to them during an office visit, had no access to competent bilingual interpreters, and were not able to ask for clarification. Breakdown in communication was the source of many health care–related mishaps reported by the elders. (Appendix A offers a list of online resources related to immigrant health care access.)

There is a critical need for collaboration among stakeholders to address these health inequities, as emphasized by the U.S. Department of Health and Human Services (DHHS, 2005) in its federal health initiative Healthy People 2010:

Healthy People 2010 offers a simple but powerful idea: Give our country clear health objectives in a way that allows *diverse groups to combine their efforts and work together as a team* [emphasis added]. Healthy People 2010 is the basis for coordinated public health action on the national, state, and local levels and has been used as a teaching tool for the next generation of public health leaders.

The need for community-based collaboration is further underscored by the Department's contention that "community partnerships, particularly when they reach out to nontraditional partners, can be among the most effective tools for improving health in communities" (DHHS, 2000). Similarly, the Institute of Medicine (2004) also calls for collaboration among agencies to address health inequities among vulnerable populations.

These calls for collaboration raise critical questions about the kind of knowledge, attitudes, and skills required to develop and maintain productive partnerships that address health inequities in linguistic and ethnic minority communities in general and among immigrant elders specifically. Are university students who intend to work in health care settings, educational programs, and other community-based organizations willing and able to contribute to building partnerships? Do they possess the knowledge, attitudes, and skills that help create and maintain productive partnerships that address health inequities? We contend that the cultivation of this knowledge base in our university students cannot be left to chance. We cannot presume that this knowledge will be cultivated when "participatory programs and experiential learning are still not the norm in either health or adult education settings" (Rudd, 2002).

Overcoming the particular challenges experienced by older immigrants requires the assistance and support of a range of professionals. Health care providers, ESL instructors, senior service providers, and staff of community-based organizations can play important roles in helping elder immigrants better access the care they need. Health professional schools and teacher training programs have a long tradition of engaging students in practicum experiences as part of their professional development.

Service learning, "an educational methodology that combines community service with explicit learning objectives, preparation, and high level reflective activities" (Gelmon, Holland, Seifer, Shinnamon, & Connors, 1998, p. 97) has great potential to contribute to the preparation of future educators and health care professionals. Integration of service learning into health professions, Teaching English to Speakers of Other Languages (TESOL), social work, and gerontology can help prepare future professionals to confront the health communication and literacy challenges that contribute to health inequities. Students who participate in service-learning opportunities such as SHINE represent one subset of logical leaders of such partnerships because they will likely have gained hands-on experience in problem solving, team building, and interacting directly with immigrant elders and other community partners.

Community Service-Learning Activities

This section describes two types of community service-learning activities in which students provide services to help adult immigrants address challenges in accessing health care in the United States. Two SHINE service activities that benefit older immigrants are described. The first focuses on a nursing course in which students design and conduct health workshops for immigrant audiences. The second concerns a course for preservice teachers in a TESOL program. Students in this program work as language coaches in ESL, citizenship, literacy, and health literacy classes. Both groups of students gained professional skills, experience in cross-cultural communication, and a greater appreciation of the challenges of immigrant communities through their service experiences. Service activities from two separate academic disciplines are presented to demonstrate the opportunities for cross-discipline collaboration to provide more comprehensive service to the community. In the following section, we show how conversations and coordination among faculty in these disciplines have led to a more systemic collaboration with resulting new structures and institutional changes.

Health Professions as a Point of Entry: Nursing Students in the Community

Students in Temple University's nursing program combine knowledge of physical, biological, and social sciences with interpersonal and problem-solving skills to prepare them for their career as nurses. The department is committed to providing students with quality clinical experiences in a variety of settings, celebrating the diversity of the students, and working with under-served communities.

Students completing their bachelor of science in nursing are required to take the Geriatric Clinical Practicum in the first semester of their senior year. This course is designed to prepare students to care for geriatric clients with chronic health problems. Students in the course have multiple opportunities to apply theory and principles of practices, plan interventions, and refine critical thinking and therapeutic communication. Course objectives include students' being able to apply appropriate research findings, manage care of culturally diverse geriatric clients, and design teaching plans for this group.

Students participate in three separate clinical experiences in an acute care unit, a hospice unit, and in a community setting. As part of their community experience, students work in teams to provide services to senior centers in a variety of Philadelphia's immigrant communities, including Norris Square Senior Center in the Latino community, the Asian Pacific Senior Resource Center at Coffee Cup in the Chinese community, Golden Slipper Senior Center in the Russian/Eastern European community, and University Square in the Korean community. Student teams, under the direction of a faculty supervisor, began by researching the history of the immigrant community and collecting demographic data and health statistics about the community. Teams interviewed immigrant elders and service providers to identify health resources and barriers to health care in the community. Based on this needs assessment, students designed health screenings and education programs in collaboration with faculty mentors and community providers. Bilingual interpretation was provided by nursing students or senior center staff members.

At Norris Square Senior Center, diabetes and hypertension were identified as primary health problems in the Latino population. Students conducted a blood pressure screening and began an exercise class in which elders perform gentle exercises while seated in chairs. Students also conducted diabetic screenings and offered an educational workshop on diabetes using a food pyramid in Spanish and providing meal-planning suggestions based on foods familiar to the Latino participants.

Students also responded to the challenges elders experienced communicating with health care providers. Students developed bilingual emergency cards and assisted elders in completing them. These laminated, pocket-size cards provide emergency information including doctors' phone numbers, prescriptions, and body parts in English and Spanish. To increase elders' safety in an emergency situation, students assisted elders in completing forms specifying their first language that were filed with the local police station. In the event of an emergency, police would have language information on file to immediately obtain bilingual interpretation services.

Teams of students offered weekly workshops at the same senior center over the 6-week period of their practicum course, which allowed them to foster regular interactions with older immigrants, learn about the communication and health challenges they experienced, and develop appropriate interventions. Because students from this course provided service to the same senior centers over 3 years, students have been able to benefit from the needs assessment conducted by students in previous years. This helps new students to more quickly design projects that respond to the needs of their group. Each year students update previously collected health statistics, contributing to a fuller and more accurate knowledge base of the health needs in immigrant communities.

Faculty members observed that students who participated in service developed a better appreciation of how cultural and linguistic differences affect health care access. Preparation of a more culturally competent future workforce is a priority of the National Standards on Culturally and Linguistically Appropriate Services (CLAS) developed by DHHS (2001), which proposes that staff at all levels of health care organizations "receive on-going education and training in culturally and linguistically appropriate service delivery." The Institute of Medicine (2004) recommends that "cross-cultural curricula should be integrated early into the training of future health care providers" (p. 241). Involvement in this service-learning initiative helps institutions comply with the CLAS standards and better prepare their students for the workforce.

Outcomes for Health Professions Students

The successful implementation of service-learning activities with older immigrants in the Temple nursing course influenced the integration of service-learning activities into health professions courses in eight colleges and universities in the SHINE consortium. Health professions students from 40 courses, including nursing, gerontology, occupational therapy, medical interpreting, nutrition, and pharmacology, have provided services for immigrant elders. Students from a wide range of health professions disciplines have developed a better appreciation of the challenges older immigrants face accessing health care and acknowledged the importance of bilingual interpreters. One Temple nursing student commented in a reflection paper that

> The [service] experience provided us with the opportunity to teach a skill to those who may not completely understand us. In health care, it is inevitable that we will encounter clients of varying levels of cognition as well as those who do not speak English. In each case it is important to know how to effectively communicate to make the relationship successful. [The service experience] gave us a taste of what it is like to interact with those with limited understanding as well as the skill to problem solve and come up with ways to compensate for the deficit in communication.

For students who were unfamiliar with the elder's culture and language, the service opportunity made them realize the challenges health professionals and immigrants may experience in communicating across a language barrier:

> This project helps me to appreciate the difficulties that healthcare professionals face when dealing with this population, as well as the difficulties that this population has when dealing with healthcare professionals. It is a process that requires a lot of patience—something that I have acquired more of through this experience. (Emory University nursing student)

> I learned first-hand the impact of language barriers. I have seen videos and read articles about the importance of cultural diversity, but this event was first-hand experience with it. It was a great feeling to see the shine in people's eyes when what I was saying "clicked." (Utica College occupational therapy student)

Students gained skills in working effectively with a bilingual interpreter to communicate with patients who are not native speakers of English:

> The session nurtured my personal goal of being able to work with the translator, and cater to the needs of people of different cultures while incorporating cultural sensitivity. Overall, this clinical was a great example of partnering with the community and providing them with tools to help themselves in the future. (Emory University nursing student)

In the absence of effective bilingual interpretation, students came to appreciate the importance of simple, clear messages in health education:

I learned that people from other countries don't have the same knowledge about healthcare. It surprised me a little bit. It helped because I realized I talk fast or complex even though I thought I was being simple. (Utica College occupational therapy student)

Faculty members observed significant impacts on bilingual nursing students who acted as interpreters for many of the health education workshops. The role of interpreter necessitated that students assume a leadership role among their classmates, so their native language ability was perceived as an asset by their peers. Prior to the initiative, faculty members reported that monolingual English-speaking students were more likely to perceive their bilingual peers as merely "English learners" who were often reticent to participate in classroom discussions and group work in class. However, over the course of the initiative, it became clear to all that the bilingual students possessed critical interpretation skills that were essential to the success of the collaboration. In addition, the bilingual students reported feeling more confident in their abilities as future health care professionals.

Language as Point of Entry: Innovative ESL Teacher Training

Students in San Francisco State University's (SFSU) master's program in TESOL (MATESOL) engage in theoretical training as well as practical experiences to prepare for careers in English-language teaching. According to the program's Web site, "the majority of graduates have become classroom teachers of English as a Second Language (ESL) in this country and of English as a Foreign Language (EFL) abroad. Many have gone on to become ESL/EFL materials specialists, curriculum designers and administrators" (see http://www.sfsu.edu/~matesol/program.html#1).

While English-language teacher training programs across the nation have traditionally focused on preparing teachers to teach in either K–12 or higher education ESL/EFL settings, administrators of SFSU's MATESOL program recognized the importance of addressing community-based adult ESL concerns by developing two faculty positions in this area. In the San Francisco Bay Area, the need for high-quality teacher training in adult ESL takes on particular urgency in light of the diversity of the community. In San Francisco County, a natural learning laboratory for addressing immigrant-related issues, nearly 45% of the 745,000 residents over the age of 5 speak a language other than English in their home (U.S. Census Bureau, 2002).

For this reason, several opportunities in the MATESOL program have been created to prepare teachers to address the needs of adult immigrants, with Project SHINE as the most prominent service-learning option. SFSU has created partnerships with community organizations that support immigrant adults in their roles as parents, workers, citizens, and consumers of health care services.

Adult immigrants need information and tools to maintain wellness, access and navigate health care systems, and integrate their home country's ways of managing wellness with the U.S. health care systems (Rudd, 2002; Rudd et al., 2005; Schillinger & Chen, 2004; Singleton, 2002). As language instruction shifts to the focus on how immigrants must use language in their lives, the intersection of English and health management will become more central to the preparation of teachers who can best meet their learners' needs.

Getting Their Feet Wet: Exploring Language in Context in an Undergraduate Sociolinguistics Course

From the beginning of their studies, preservice English-language teachers in the MATESOL program have an opportunity to participate in language learning settings that sensitize them to the realities of older immigrant learners and the role of the English language in the immigrants' lives. The academic content of English 425 Language in Context, an upper-division course in sociolinguistics, focuses on themes such as language variation, bilingualism, and meaning in linguistic choice. Students may choose as a final project option to participate in SHINE, acting as a language coach for individuals or small groups of immigrant learners. Students' service placements are in a range of classes with a focus on citizenship preparation, beginning literacy instruction, or general ESL at City College of San Francisco, a large community college system serving more than 20,000 ESL learners each year throughout the city.

The service-learning dynamic in this course challenges MATESOL students to contemplate connections between their growing knowledge about sociolinguistic concepts and their own sense of social responsibility. In this way we address the question, How can sociolinguistic knowledge be used toward solving social problems that affect immigrant communities? When students examine the relationship between language and power, they are able to reflect on their interactions with the adult ESL learners who often struggle to learn English, the language of power in the United States. For example, when our MATESOL students asked the learners about their English learning goals related to health care, one 57-year-old immigrant from China explained, "Because new immigrants are struggling with new languages and cultures, we have limited information about health. . . . we have to learn to survive by ourselves. So if there's an emergency, we have no choice but to find a Chinese doctor." This learner's response, translated from Chinese, provides MATESOL students with a powerful example of how language use is tied to access to health information. In addition, by reflecting on comments such as this one, MATESOL students are able to understand that many adult ESL learners are acutely aware of the health disparities that affect them as nonnative speakers of English. In this way, the service-learning experience enables MATESOL students to see adult ESL learners' "own sociolinguistic knowledge as a valuable classroom resource" (Jacobson, 2003).

Going Deeper: Exploring ESL in the Community at the Graduate Level

Once SFSU students have had an opportunity to be immersed in the adult ESL field, to coach and to reflect on what they've seen, they may pursue opportunities to take their experience further through more structured study and training. In the graduate-level course Teaching ESL in the Community, one of the major learning objectives is for students to examine the role of language and literacy skills in everyday contexts immigrants participate in (e.g., family, work, community, health care). In addition, students are asked to reflect on their own hopes and responsibilities as adult ESL teachers. Like the undergraduate course Language in Context, described on p. xx, participants write reflection papers that integrate their observations with their readings. However, in the graduate-level course, students are also asked to complete an additional final project focused on examining the learning needs of the immigrant learners they have come to know. Projects may take several forms, such as an issues paper (i.e., on elders and language learning), a research project (i.e., on the most prevalent health concerns of a particular group), development of a curricular or training module, design of ESL teaching and health resource materials, or the collection and analysis of narratives based on immigrant experiences in health care.

Additional health content classes, such as ESL for Health Literacy, have been added to the menu of choices for graduate student coaches. In this adult ESL course, health professionals from diverse backgrounds prepare to reenter the health field using their new language, and MATESOL students learn about health issues as they develop their professional language teaching skills.

One of the most powerful projects that students take on is the collection and analysis of learner narratives, which is one vehicle for coaches to develop an understanding of immigrant elders' lives outside the classroom. The following is from an immigrant elder who struggles with several health issues:

> I have been in the United States for 7 years. My most serious concern is my diabetes, because I am afraid to lose my legs. A couple of years back, the doctor gave me a physical, and my blood test showed the diabetes. I thought I was going to die. I'm not disciplined, and I don't like to follow diets or exercise. I'm supposed to walk for exercise, but because I have bone spurs it is very difficult for me. I want you to know that I'm very heavy, and because I have problems with my metabolism, it's hard for me to lose weight. I try to take my pills, and they are many. I try to keep it under control, but I have trouble.

This narrative offers coaches critical insight into the health challenges faced by immigrant elders. Narratives such as this provide insights into immigrant elders' personal struggles that are rarely highlighted in current policy and research on chronic disease among immigrant elderly (see Centers for Disease Control and Prevention & the Merck Company Foundation, 2007). Through an online course, Learner-Centered Teaching With Accountability, students use narratives to develop a language learning unit to address learners' most pressing needs. Student authors, in collaboration with health education students, use the language and ideas in the learner narrative to generate vocabulary exercises, grammar tasks, and language awareness exercises. In the process of listening to learners and collecting and writing material, preservice teachers develop professional skills of curriculum development, lesson planning, and task design, and experience the excitement of creating their own learner-centered curricular module. Perhaps more significant, however, is the potential impact of graduate students' curriculum efforts on the creation of materials specifically geared toward the language and health concerns of immigrant elders.

Community service-learning experiences with a focus on health and health issues provide an opportunity for students to develop their evolving skills as English language teachers while learning from the immigrants they will ultimately serve. Through serving in a community context, these future ESL teachers have an opportunity to better understand the English-language needs of immigrant adults and the contexts of their English-language use outside the classroom.

Outcomes for Students in the Language Professions

In all courses with a community service-learning component, participants engage in a variety of reflection activities, individual and collective. One such activity is to keep a log of observations of the classroom and of specific learners, successes and excitement about their work, challenges they face and how they address them, and questions that emerge from their service experiences.

These logs provide the basis for a midterm summary and final reflection paper about the coaching experience. This form of structured reflection enables participants to organize their own experiences and present them collectively by synthesizing their work within consistent categories.

At the end of their service-learning experience, Project SHINE coaches attend a final reflection/celebration with other coaches, current ESL teachers, and immigrant learners to talk about and reflect on their SHINE experiences. In the December 2006 final reflection, coaches described the rewards of their community service, which prove to be important cognitive and affective outcomes:

I learned how to communicate with older learners.
I know myself better.
I gained confidence.
I [felt that I] gained teaching experience because the teacher let me teach a
    small group of students.
[I helped] 4 out of 5 students pass the citizenship test.
[It was rewarding to see] how much the students appreciated me.
[It was great] knowing that I made a difference.

The reflection is also when MATESOL students are reminded of the connection between the ESL classroom and life in the community, a critical part of the graduate students' service-learning experience as well as their teacher training overall. In this way, Project SHINE has become an important mechanism for the TESOL program to prime teacher candidates so they make their classrooms sensitive to the demands of their learners' life outside the classroom, something that is often lacking in novice teachers.

Wrigley (2001) notes that novice teachers often do not take advantage of *teachable moments* in the classroom. Through experiences such as Project SHINE, teachers are poised to keep their ear to the ground and are able to anticipate ways language learning and real-life issues such as health can come together. Coauthor Maricel Santos observed a former SHINE coach teach an ESL lesson on treating everyday ailments. During the class, an immigrant learner pointed out that the textbook had failed to include herbal medicine as a possible remedy for treating a cold, a remark that prompted other learners to mention alternative remedies that reflected home cultures (e.g., "eat rice," "acupuncture"). The coach-now-teacher effectively made an on-the-spot change in her lesson plan to allow the learners to share culturally based beliefs about the "best" way to treat illness as well as talk about the difficulty of sharing these beliefs with doctors in the United States. The teacher's ability to make the most of a teachable moment enabled her immigrant learners to share personal issues and work together to come up with solutions, a skill we hope the SHINE experience fosters in our MATESOL coaches. As one SFSU coach put it, the personal and the professional rewards so far are very exciting:

> This experience has convinced me that I definitely want to work in the immigrant community. For me, this was an "aha" experience! On a personal note, I've come to see my own grandmother with new eyes.

Collaboration Between Health and Language Professionals

The significant impact these initiatives have had on faculty and students, and more important on immigrant learners, affirms our commitment to community service in professional training programs. These initiatives represent genuine opportunities to effect positive change in the way immigrant elders are able to navigate the U.S. health care system and the way that future nurses and ESL teachers perceive the link between language, literacy, and health outcomes. At the same time, these initiatives present new challenges regarding the need for students and faculty to reconsider conventional disciplinary boundaries at the university. Our experience has shown that one way to address health inequities is to encourage health professionals to focus not just on knowledge about health care but on language and literacy issues and, likewise, to encourage ESL professionals to focus not only on language education but on those health care activities that are a struggle for many immigrant elders. How then do we foster this kind of cross-disciplinary collaboration that develops a sustainable foundation for the success of the initiatives described here? In this section, we examine the possibilities for approaching health issues through cross-disciplinary collaborations.

Moving Toward Collaboration

The simplest way to begin a collaborative process is through informal channels that require little structural change. At SFSU, faculty in TESOL found areas of common interest with colleagues in health education and agreed informally to create a 2-week unit on health literacy their respective students will complete simultaneously. Specifically, students and faculty in English 724 Teaching ESL in the Community came together with students in Health Education 310 Health in Society for a 2-week module. Faculty gave joint lectures and assigned the same set of readings, including an article on the role of language and literacy in health care, one on cross-cultural communication in medical practice, and a study that highlighted the immigrant experience in health care. The two classes came together for two sessions to discuss the readings and engage in problem-based learning activities; students were asked to work in cross-disciplinary groups to come up with solutions to real-life problems experienced by immigrants in the health care system. This move toward collaboration took little more than some planning and discussion among the faculty and the willingness to build a bridge in a small subset of their curricula.

Institutionalizing Collaboration

A next logical step in the process of increasing collaboration is to institutionalize collaborative relationships. At SFSU, we are proposing an interdisciplinary certificate program in Immigrant Family, Community, and Health Literacies. The certificate represents an innovative preservice and in-service professional development program with a focus on improved linguistic and social outcomes for immigrants. Through this certificate program students from a variety of disciplines (e.g., health, adult ESL, business, technology) have the opportunity to strengthen the knowledge base gained in their home degree program by engaging in focused interdisciplinary exploration of the influence of language, literacies, and culture in a particular context immigrants participate in (e.g., home, work, community, or health).

The key features of the certificate program in Immigrant Family, Community, and Health Literacies include

- an orientation course designed to help students from a variety of backgrounds and disciplines examine the influence of language, literacies, and culture in everyday settings immigrants participate in (e.g., health care);
- flexibility in the combination of courses and interdisciplinary focus that students can use toward certification;
- emphasis on networking and collaboration between preservice and inservice professionals;
- a capstone community service-learning project whose purpose is to focus and integrate the student's course work, interdisciplinary thinking, and civic engagement;
- hosting an annual community forum featuring student presentations on their service-learning projects, and commentators from the SFSU faculty as well as the local community.

Students are expected to work toward certification at the interface of a variety of different disciplines (e.g., TESOL and health). In this way, the certificate program provides a flexible and integrated structure that enables faculty and students to reach outside traditional disciplinary spheres. As we have suggested elsewhere in this chapter, overcoming inequities in health care is a broad-based issue that requires interdisciplinary problem solving and community partnership. The certificate program seeks to address this need by cultivating a network of faculty at SFSU who are skilled in forming interdisciplinary teams and committed to service and to using these skills to address real-life problems affecting immigrant communities.

Future Directions: Challenges and Opportunities for Interdisciplinary Partnerships

In this section we identify some next steps for research and practice as we strive to strengthen the role of service learning to contribute to immigrant wellness and the education of health and language preprofessionals. These next steps are bolstered by our passion for and commitment to bridging university training programs and community-based organizations.

There are many challenges to building successful service-learning initiatives and sustaining community partnerships. Rubin (2001) observes that universities and community-based organizations, such as adult ESL programs and senior centers, have their own cultures and expectations for success. This leads us to ask, What areas of collaborations lead to meaningful differences in the training of nurses and adult ESL teachers, the career trajectories of university students, and in the health outcomes of immigrant elders? Ongoing dialogue about the nature and the goals of collaborations among faculty, students, and community partners is critical, but it is often too easy for faculty and students to retreat to their own "disciplinary silos" when the demands of academic life overshadow their efforts to integrate service learning into the curriculum. In this final section, we outline a few areas in research and practice that hold possibilities for capacity building and partnership.

Future Research Directions

Given the limited resources that often constrain partnerships between universities and the community, we should aim to be strategic and focus service-learning research on issues in health care that are the most critical in the immigrant elderly population. This point broadly refers to issues of the *practical relevance* (see Candlin & Candlin, 2003; also see Auerbach, 2002) of community service-learning initiatives in health care. We need to consider the application of community service-learning models to addressing those sources of disparity consistently identified in previous studies, such as the underenrollment of elderly immigrants in health insurance programs (Mold, Fryer, & Thomas, 2004) or their relatively low participation rates in cancer screening (Lin, Finlay, Tu, & Gany, 2005). This approach would likely lead to sustainability by attracting the attention of the medical community and funding. Related to this point, we need to bear in mind that various stakeholders may not agree which areas in health care are the most critical. We believe that research initiatives in service learning and health should be directly shaped by the input from immigrant elders themselves and culturally competent leaders in their communities. This approach serves to ensure that elderly immigrants and their communities are positioned at the center of service-learning research initiatives in health care.

Future Directions in Practice

There is a need for capacity building in colleges and universities so that students have the resources to pursue community service opportunities working with immigrant elders in collaboration with students from other disciplines. As illustrated by the ideas for collaboration in this chapter, several promising strategies exist for formalizing the process for students and faculty to engage in interdisciplinary exploration and community service work with immigrant populations. Also, as illustrated with the certificate initiative in Immigrant Family, Community, and Health Literacies, the community service being built around this certificate program will likely promote collaboration among faculty who are interested in looking for new ways to synthesize their interests in the immigrant experience. This in turn will expand the number of cocurricular opportunities students have to integrate community service with their academic training.

In addition to curricular innovation, colleges and universities can also create local scholarship funds that support students who are interested in combining their academic training with service to immigrant communities. In particular, colleges and universities can look for ways to support the academic and professional careers of students with bilingual and/or bicultural backgrounds who are interested in pursuing adult education or health professions careers.

Note

1. Focus groups were selected to reflect the diversity of older immigrants in the United States and a range of socioeconomic and educational backgrounds. The discussions with the immigrants were conducted in English, with interpretation in the languages of the participants. Special thanks to Hitomi Yoshida at Temple University and Nancy Hikoyeda at San José State University who organized and conducted focus groups and interviews. See Gordon, Yoshida, Hikoyeda, and David (2006) for more details about this study.

References

Auerbach, E. (Ed). (2002). *Community partnerships*. Arlington, VA: TESOL.

Candlin, C. N., & Candlin, S. (2003). Health care communication: A problematic site for applied linguistics research. *Annual Review of Applied Linguistics, 23,* 132–154.

Centers for Disease Control and Prevention & the Merck Company Foundation. (2007). *The State of Aging and Health in America 2007.* Retrieved November 2, 2009 from http://www.cdc.gov/Aging/pdf/saha_2007.pdf

Federal Interagency Forum on Aging-Related Statistics. (2008). *Older Americans 2008: Key indicators of well-being.* Washington, DC: U.S. Government Printing Office. Retrieved November 18, 2009, from http://www.agingstats.gov/agingstats dotnet/main_site/default.aspx

Gelmon, S. B., Holland, B. A., Seifer, S. D., Shinnamon, A., & Connors, K. (1998). Community-university partnerships for mutual learning. *Michigan Journal of Community Service Learning, 5,* 97, 97–107.

Gordon, D., Yoshida, H., Hikoyeda, N. & David, D. (2006). *Patient listening: Health communication needs of older immigrants.* [Electronic version]. Retrieved November 18, 2009, from http://www.projectshine.org/materials/healthliteracy

Gorospe, E. (2006). Elderly immigrants: Emerging challenge for the U.S. healthcare system. *Internet Journal of Healthcare Administration, 4*(1). Retrieved December 22, 2006, from http://www.ispub.com/ostia/index.php?xmlFilePath = journals/ ijhca/vol4n1/elderly.xml

Institute of Medicine. (2004). *Health literacy: A prescription to end confusion.* Washington, DC: National Academies Press.

Jacobson, E. (2003). Critical Sociolinguistics in the Adult ESOL Classroom [Electronic version]. *Radical Teacher, 68,* 13–17. Retrieved November 4, 2007, from http://findarticles.com/p/articles/mi_moJVP/is_68/ai_n6008646

Kutner, M., Greenberg, E., Jin, Y., & Paulsen, C. (2006). *The health literacy of America's adults: Results from the 2003 National Assessment of Adult Literacy.* [Electronic version]. Washington, DC: National Center for Education Statistics. Retrieved December 23, 2006, from http://nces.ed.gov/pubsearch/pubsinfo.asp? pubid = 2006483

Lin, J. S., Finlay, A., Tu, A., and Gany, F. M., (2005). Understanding immigrant Chinese Americans' participation in cancer screening and clinical trials. *Journal of Community Health, 30*(6), 451–466.

Mold, J. M., Fryer, G. E., & Thomas, C. H. (2004). Who are the uninsured elderly in the United States? *Journal of the American Geriatrics Society, 52,* 601–606.

Rubin, M. S. (2001). A smart start to service learning. In M. Canada & B. W. Speck (Eds.), *Developing and implementing service learning programs* (pp. 15–26). San Francisco: Jossey-Bass.

Rudd, R. E. (2002). A maturing partnership. [Electronic version]. *Focus on Basics, 5*(3), 1–8. Retrieved April 22, 2003, from http://www.ncsall.net/?id = 247

Rudd, R., Kirsch, I., & Yamamoto, K. (2004). *Literacy and health in America.* Princeton, NJ: Center for Global Assessment, Policy Information Center, Research and Development, Educational Testing Service.

Rudd, R., Soricone, L., Santos, M., Zobel, E., & Smith, J. (2005). *Health and adult literacy and learning, health literacy study circle + : Skills for navigation and access* [Electronic version]. Cambridge, MA: National Center for the Study of Adult Learning and Literacy and Harvard University School of Public Health. Retrieved from http://www.ncsall.net/?id = 1171

Schillinger, D., & Chen, A. (2004). Literacy and language: Disentangling measures of access, utilization and quality. *Journal of General Internal Medicine, 19,* 288–290.

Singleton, K. (2002). ESOL teachers: Helpers in health care. *Focus on Basics, 19*(C), 26–30.

U.S. Census Bureau. (2002). The older foreign-born population in the United States: 2000. *Current Population Reports: Special Studies.* Washington, DC: Author.

U.S. Department of Health and Human Services. (2000). *Healthy people 2010: Understanding and improving health.* [Electronic version]. Washington, DC: Author. Retrieved April 21, 2003, from http://www.healthypeople.gov/Document/table ofcontents.htm#under

U.S. Department of Health and Human Services. (2001). *National standards for culturally and linguistically appropriate services in health care.* Washington, DC: Office of Minority Health. Available from http://raceandhealth.hhs.gov/assets/pdf/ checked/finalreport.pdf

U.S. Department of Health and Human Services. (2005). *Healthy people 2010: The cornerstone for prevention.* [Electronic version]. Washington, DC: Author. Retrieved April 21, 2003, from http://www.healthypeople.gov/Publications/Corner stone.pdf

Williams, M. V., Parker, R. M., Baker, D. W., Parikh, N. S., Pitkin, K., Coates, et al. (1995). Inadequate functional health literacy among patients at two public hospitals. *Journal of the American Medical Association, 274*(21), 1677–1682.

Wrigley, H. S. (2001). *EL civics: Making the case for Just-in-Time Teaching.* [Electronic version]. Retrieved December 20, 2006, from http://www.brown.edu/De partments/Swearer_Center/Literacy_Resources/jitt.html

Appendix A

Recommended Online Resources

The Cross-Cultural Health Program

The Cross-Cultural Health Program addresses broad cultural issues that affect the health of individuals and families in ethnic minority communities and serves as a bridge between multicultural communities and health care institutions. This Web site provides information on cross-cultural health care and training programs for medical interpreters.

http://www.xculture.org/

Culture Clues

Culture Clues are tip sheets designed for clinicians to raise awareness about the health concepts and patient preferences of 11 cultural groups. The tip sheets include information for each culture about traditions in dealing with illness, how medical decisions are made, norms about physical contact, reducing communication barriers, and additional information sources. There are also information sheets on handling end-of-life care for Latino, Russian, and Vietnamese immigrants.

http://depts.washington.edu/pfes/CultureClues.htm

Diversity Rx

Diversity Rx promotes language and cultural competence to improve the quality of health care for minority, immigrant, and ethnically diverse communities. This Web site provides information on the organization's national conferences, health care news Listserv, and research on best practices in multicultural health care.

http://www.diversityrx.org

EthnoMed

The EthnoMed Web site presents information about the cultural beliefs and medical issues of newly arrived immigrant and refugee groups in the Seattle area, much of which can be applied to other geographic regions. The site contains culture profiles for health care providers and patient education materials translated into a variety of languages. The ethnolinguistic groups included are Amharic, Cambodian, Chinese, Eritrean, Hispanic, Oromo,

Somali, Tigrean, and Vietnamese. Other ethnic groups will be included as materials are prepared.

http://www.ethnomed.org/

Guide to Health Education Materials for Adults With Limited English Literacy Skills

Developed by World Education, this guide identifies a variety of resources that ESL teachers and health practitioners can use to help adult English-language learners access health information and appropriate health care.

http://www.worlded.org/us/health/docs/culture/

Harvard School of Public Health: Health Literacy Studies

This Web site offers materials concerning health literacy and health issues for adult learners, including curriculum ideas relating to doctor visits, disease prevention, and healthy aging. The site also provides innovative health literacy materials and links to related sites.

http://www.hsph.harvard.edu/healthliteracy/talk_drvisit.html

Health and Literacy Compendium

Developed by World Education in collaboration with the National Institute for Literacy, this Web site features an annotated bibliography of print and online health materials for use with limited-literacy adults. A wide range of topics are covered in this bibliography, such as links to publications discussing the connections between health outcomes and literacy, the assessment and development of effective health education materials, approaches for teaching "health with literacy in mind, and [teaching] literacy using health content," participatory approaches in education, and links to multilingual/multicultural health materials.

http://healthliteracy.worlded.org/docs/comp/

Health Literacy Resource Center

Developed by the California Health Literacy Initiative, this Web page is a central resource for health literacy information and training designed for literacy practitioners, health care professionals, adult literacy and ESL students, and the general public. The site offers multicultural and multilingual health resources; information on health literacy research, education, and policy; and a directory of people involved in health literacy initiatives.

http://literacyworks.org/healthliteracy/healthliteracyresourcecenter.html

Health Literacy Special Collection

Supported by the National Institute for Literacy, this Web site is a resource for teachers, students, and health educators, including those who teach people with limited literacy skills. It offers health curricula for ESL classes, resources in languages other than English, information about relationships between literacy and health status, and links to organizations dedicated to health and literacy education.

http://healthliteracy.worlded.org/

Understanding Health Literacy and Its Barriers

This site presents a bibliography of literature related to health literacy. Topics covered include strategies for improving health literacy, improving provider-client communication, cultural/cross-cultural competence for providers, assessing the readability level of health information material, and disease-specific information.

http://www.nlm.nih.gov/pubs/cbm/healthliteracybarriers.html

National Standards for Culturally and Linguistically Appropriate Services in Health Care

This Web site presents 14 national standards for Culturally and Linguistically Appropriate Services (CLAS) in health care developed by the U.S. Department of Health and Human Services, Office of Minority Health. The standards fall into three categories: culturally competent care, language access services, and organizational supports for cultural competence. The report also offers recommendations on implementation of the standards.

http://raceandhealth.hhs.gov/assets/pdf/checked/finalreport.pdf

Non-English-Language and Health Literacy Resources

This Web site, developed by the Consumer Health Reference Center at Treadwell Library, Massachusetts General Hospital, contains a list of resources for health education materials in languages other than English.

http://www2.massgeneral.org/library/chrc/noneng.html

Ask Me 3

This Web site is sponsored by the Partnership for Clear Health Communication, a coalition of national organizations working together to address the problem of low health literacy. The Web site provides downloadable information sheets for patients and providers about health literacy concerns, improving patient-provider communication, advocating for improved health literacy policy and increased funding, and research on health literacy issues.

http://www.askme3.org/PFCHC/

Project SHINE-MetLife Foundation Health Literacy Initiative

This project builds partnerships among universities and community-based organizations nationally to address the health literacy needs of elderly immigrants and refugees. Funded by MetLife Foundation, the initiative has developed health literacy curricula based on the needs identified by elderly immigrants. The units, which address a wide range of communication skills, health topics, and cultural issues, can be downloaded from the initiative's Web site.

http://www.projectshine.org/materials/healthliteracy/curriculum

The Stanford Geriatric Education Center

The mission of this federally funded consortium is to promote the cultural competence of health care professionals providing care to ethnic minority elders in the United States. The Web site provides information on curricula in ethnogeriatrics, online training modules for health care providers, and information about research and policy analysis.

http://sgec.stanford.edu/

System of Adult Basic Education Support

This Web site is designed to serve as a resource for adult educators who are interested in incorporating health topics into adult basic education and English as a Second Language classes. The site offers curriculum materials and training resources for teachers and program directors, as well as links to other sites and programs.

http://www.sabes.org/curriculum/health/index.htm

6

COMMUNITY-BASED HEALTH NEEDS ASSESSMENTS WITH CULTURALLY DISTINCT POPULATIONS

Joachim O. F. Reimann and Dolores I. Rodríguez-Reimann

Culturally and linguistically distinct U.S. populations face major disparities in health care. Financial reasons for this situation include lack of insurance (Mills & Bhandari, 2003), high service costs, and low patient income (Fiscella & Shin, 2005). Economics are not, however, the only barrier. Provider stereotyping, little cultural awareness, organizational inattention, language, and basic provider unavailability (e.g., in rural environments) also limit care. So-called minority groups thus tend to receive lower-quality services than the broader population, even when health insurance coverage is not a factor (Institute of Medicine [IOM], 2002). Disparities appear across oral and mental as well as general health services (U.S. Department of Health and Human Services [DHHS], 1999, 2000a, 2000b).

This reality has prompted multiple regulatory and policy initiatives. Some licensing boards have, for example, developed outlines highlighting cultural aspects of service provision (e.g., California Board of Psychology, 2004). On the federal level, the Office of Minority Health (2001) and the

This work was partially supported by Grant Number P60 MD00220, from the San Diego EXPORT Center, National Center of Minority Health and Health Disparities, National Institutes of Health. Its contents are solely the responsibility of the author and do not necessarily represent the official views of the National Institutes of Health.

Substance Abuse and Mental Health Services Administration (2000) have each developed national standards for culturally and linguistically appropriate care. Finally, DHHS's (2000b) *Healthy People 2010* lists as a primary goal, "eliminate health disparities."

Despite such efforts, progress toward culturally effective services has been modest (Wortley, 2005). One shortfall is that we know too little about the complex relationships between health care, economics, language, prevalent cultural norms, generational status, religious practices, and other factors in specific communities. This is especially true for groups that receive little positive attention, are not governmentally recognized as minority populations, live in remote or blighted locales, and/or face other unique challenges. The consequences can be significant individual and societal hardships. Limited prevention and inadequate (or no) treatment can cause longer-term personal distress, loss of productivity, and death. Delayed treatment is usually more intensive and therefore costly.

Culturally savvy health and social advocates often know of community needs, perceptions, access barriers, and other issues through their personal and professional experiences. Yet such anecdotal information tends to carry little weight with funding sources and policy makers. Lack of real evidence is thus a prime excuse for inaction.

Systematic community needs assessments are one way to gain such evidence. They can be catalysts for policy, resource, and service changes (Plescia, Koontz, & Laurent, 2001), and as such, they have been used in a variety of circumstances and locations (Beverly, Mcatee, Costello, Chernoff, & Casteel, 2005; Nolin, Wilburn, Wilburn, & Weaver, 2006; Wright, Williams, & Wilkinson, 1998). Aforementioned entrenched disparities highlight our need to increase the number of skilled people addressing care access. Educating students in best assessment practices is thus important. Given its hands-on nature, service learning through civic engagement is one potential tool in that process.

This chapter presents a brief overview of issues that faculty and students interested in conducting needs assessments may wish to consider. It describes (a) our experience with relevant interpersonal considerations and (b) technical and methodological issues. In addition it outlines some potential future directions. In this process the chapter largely draws on examples from two of our most recent assessments: Project Salaam, an evaluation of mental health needs among Greater San Diego's Middle Eastern and East African communities (Reimann, Ghulam, Rodríguez-Reimann, & Beylouni, 2005), and Project Saud Libre, which appraised mental health needs in Southern California's mostly rural Imperial Valley (Reimann, Rodríguez-Reimann, & Medina, 2006). Both projects entailed major participation by students as shown by coauthorships and acknowledgments on consequent articles and reports.

This chapter is by no means comprehensive but seeks to foster additional learning. While the focus is on health, it has applicability across other social issues. Basic topics (e.g., how teachers and students can access communities in respectful ways, how to obtain comprehensive and meaningful information, how to use such information to benefit society) tend to apply across disciplines.

Identifying Potential Scope and Communities of Focus

Not surprisingly, we have found assessments are most important when they address social groups that have received little systematic prior attention. This includes people living in blighted environments, refugee populations, and people from a host of national, regional, ethnic, socioeconomic, religious, tribal, kinship, and other backgrounds. Unfortunately, common societal, governmental, and research practices can hamper awareness of such communities. Racially Black immigrants from Africa, for example, are often classified as African American on demographic surveys. Yet they have little in common with the traditional history and experiences of African Americans (Summit Health Institute for Research and Education [SHIRE], 2005). Similarly, Arab Americans are often classified as White, limiting our knowledge of their situations (Samhan, 2000).

In other words, the richness of diverse experiences and attitudes within demographic groupings requires consideration. With Project Salaam we could not, for example, assume that people from Egyptian, Syrian, Lebanese, and Palestinian backgrounds espouse equivalent traditions, even though their countries are in fairly close geographic proximity (Reimann et al., 2005). Individuals within each group further vary in adherence to their own cultural norms. While such complexities might lead one to dismiss any cultural categories as irrelevant, Okazaki and Sue (1995) argue that if thoughtfully defined, group norms provide insights into major social issues. They are one important element in a continuum ranging from universal human experience to individual differences.

How have we then identified potential communities and areas of focus? Unlike many academic efforts, scientific publications are infrequently a prime resource. By definition, the idea is to find community needs that have received little or no research attention. Several alternate sources have been helpful to us in such instances. One was a review of published but nonacademic materials. This included community, faith-based, and non-English newspapers; culturally focused Web sites; reports from funding sources that support grassroots work; and so on. Some traditional academics resist considering materials that are not peer reviewed because fewer controls ensure such publications are well conceived and evidence based. In fact, grassroots sources may well have biased agendas and may make assertions without clear data. For us, however, they have also brought insights into legitimate community attitudes, concerns, and perceptions when we considered them from an open but discerning stance. In short, they generated ideas and hypotheses, if not necessarily firm conclusions.

Second, we have enlisted the assistance of staff, faculty, students, and on-campus groups with strong ties to local communities of interest who have provided valuable information and contacts. For example, they served as direct advisors and identified other individual, organizational, and community partners. Such partners have included faith-based organizations, kinship associations, social clubs, community nonprofits, and small businesses that cater to specific groups.

Additionally, interviewing professional stakeholders has been helpful. These included teachers, human rights attorneys, law enforcement officers, health care providers/workers, and others who have frequent contact with the group(s) of interest. They were often community members themselves. But, as Williams and Yanoshik (2001) point out, others who regularly interact with a group can also help identify prevalent needs. Finally, pilot focus groups have provided valuable directions. Effective outreach thus taps into the broadest spectrum of people who have frontline knowledge of neighborhood circumstances.

Stakeholders need not be a one-time information source. In both of our projects they were members of advisory councils that made ongoing recommendations about (a) the effort's scope and focus (e.g., mental, oral, or general health; illness-specific issues; immediate and long-term social circumstances), (b) culturally appropriate ways to approach participants, and (c) additional resources such as interpretation services. In summary, a potential assessment's direction and scope is determined by casting a wide net that taps into community-generated written materials, stakeholders, neighborhood leaders and organizations, and most important, the grassroots community members themselves.

Obviously, needs assessments often require considerable set up. Depending on academic timetables in service learning, completing an entire project is often impractical for one student cohort. But pilot assessments that set parameters for the broader effort, including who will carry it out, are also worthwhile. Later classes can then proceed with the full assessment, develop projects that distribute the results, and help implement recommendations.

While assessments involve many technical issues, we have found that their ultimate success largely depends on gaining the trust and assistance of community members. That requires meeting people on their own terms. In this context it is essential to understand what they believe, value, and practice. Cultural competence is the chapter's next topic.

Cultural Competence Basics

Many culturally and linguistically distinct groups have had poor experiences with researchers and health care providers. Negative encounters have ranged from basic insensitivity to major human rights abuses (Freimuth et al., 2001; IOM, 2002; Rolger, 1999). In addition, cultural taboos limit some people's willingness to participate in assessment efforts. Building trust and respect is essential. While maybe counterintuitive, that process begins with introspection rather than outreach. Well-meaning people can have unintentional biases toward those who are "different" (Tajfel & Turner, 1986), even when such biases are at odds with their egalitarian self-image (Dovido, Gaertner, Anastasio, & Sanitioso, 1992). Accepting this reality is the first and most crucial step toward cultural competence. In a study of physicians, for example, we found that knowledge about cultures per se and exposure to ethnic groups in clinical practice did not directly facilitate care. Rather, such care was most strongly predicted by acknowledging cultural factors and personal biases as important issues in service provision (Reimann, Talavera, Salmon, Nuñez, & Velasquez, 2004).

Accepting that we have biases is difficult. Our initial reaction may be: "That can't be; I'm not a bad person." But without acknowledging preconceptions, our efforts to understand various communities can become an exercise in viewing cultures "on parade." We may superficially examine a group's traditional food, music, dress, and customs from the sidelines and then judge them through our own background. In contrast, recognizing biases helps us suspend them and strive to understand a community's norms from its own point of view.

Consider the following example: A group of students and their professor were meeting with members of a grassroots organization for the first time. The students hoped the organization's members would help them find participants for the survey component of an assessment. The academic calendar left little time for what was to be accomplished, and they were eager to move ahead. As the meeting opened, community members talked at length about their families, philosophies, and other broad topics. They used some words and colloquial expressions the students did not understand. In addition, they apparently expected students and the professor to share similar personal information. Time passed, and the students' basic agenda remained unaddressed.

The students had two options. First, they could decide that working with this community group was useless because its members were disorganized, tangential, not task oriented, and unaware that time is valuable. On the other hand, they could suspend such initial judgments and recognize that the development of working relationships in some cultures focuses on shared personal understanding (Gudykunst & Ting-Toomey, 1988). The process of getting to know each other (including personal history, family background, etc.) was essential in that context. It established the comfort, trust, and loyalty productive efforts could be built on. Such an approach can feel incongruent with academic norms that tend to be more task than relationship oriented (Ibarra, 2001). Fortunately, the students chose to understand the community's dynamics and began to earn real trust and access.

Recognizing that cultural norms often serve an adaptive purpose can help guide how we view them. In short, norms perpetuate because on some level they work for the people who practice them (Kessing, 1974). This premise can help us identify cultural strengths that facilitate well-being. Some traditional practices have the desired health effects. Shapiro and Gong (2002), for example, reported that the Mexican practice of eating nopals (cooked prickly pear cactus) to fight diabetes is beneficial.

Notably, cultural competence does not require carte blanche acceptance of all behaviors people claim as tradition based. For example, some folk remedies are dangerous (Saper et al., 2004). Basic social justice is another important consideration. No cultural, religious, or other pretext excuses instigating violence and subjugating others. But mindfulness of our potential biases does help us more accurately separate the functional from the dysfunctional (in our own as well as in other cultures). Within that framework we can then critically review the pertinent literature, immerse ourselves in various communities, learn a new language, and do other things to increase our cultural effectiveness (Brach & Fraser, 2000; Campinha-Bacote, 1999). This process is a long-term commitment. Cultural proficiency is not automatically granted or denied by our ethnic group membership but is honed through lifelong learning (National Alliance for Hispanic Health, 2000; Reimann et al., 2004).

Assessment Structure, Content, Methods, and Procedures

Given their exploratory nature, we have found needs assessments most effective when they can yield unexpected information. Our work suggests that some common research methods have limited application in these circumstances when used in isolation. While quantitative surveys, for example, allow for statistical analyses, they require that we know the right questions to ask up front. Qualitative focus groups and interviews, on the other hand, involve a more open-ended process. Facilitators generally use structured protocols but can also follow up on important themes as they emerge. That is obviously important if we have little background about a population and/or subject (Maykut & Morehouse, 1994).

Unfortunately, resistance to some methods still exists. Rolger (1999) argues that procedural norms (the most commonly accepted research practices guiding specific disciplines) have hampered culturally effective studies. For example, the debate on whether qualitative or quantitative methods are better has raged for years and is fueled by academic traditions as much as substance (Proctor, 2005). In reality, each method has its strength. Qualitative results can be rich in their details. On the other hand, statistics used to analyze quantitative measures allow more assurance that what we observe is generalizable to broad populations and is not just because of chance. It is thus perhaps most helpful to view the two methods as potentially complementary. Focus groups and interviews, for example, can inform the content of follow-up surveys. Using mixed methods is consequently becoming more popular (Giddings & Grant, 2006). This matches our own experiences. Even when time constrains required us to use both techniques concurrently, identifying consistent themes across data types helped us gain valuable impressions of community needs (Reimann et al., 2005; Reimann et al., 2006).

Assessment Topic Areas

Once students and faculty have identified an appropriate design, the specific content of measures and protocols is shaped by the identified resources (discussed under "Identifying Potential Scope and Communities of Focus" on p. 84). What are frequent topic areas? Ferdman (1992) recommends a framework for exploring diverse populations. It entails attention to (a) the relationships of various societal groups to each other, (b) the cultural norms that tend to be shared by members of each group, (c) individual differences in how strongly (or if) group members embrace such norms, and (d) the environmental context affecting all the above. How these factors play out in real life varies with projects. But our most common assessment topics have been (a) who the participants are (e.g., demographics and background); (b) adverse experiences and stressors; (c) environmental toxins; (d) commonly reported problems, symptoms, or illnesses; (e) community perceptions about who is most at risk and why; (f) community coping efforts; (g) current health service usage patterns; (h) access barriers (e.g., rank ordering language, provider availability, economic, health insurance coverage; and (i) participant service requests, preferences, and recommendations.

Mental Health Needs Assessments

Given their highly sensitive nature, mental health topics require some additional discussion. In mental health-related efforts we have particularly considered a group's (a) cultural taboos and (b) other traditional perceptions on mental health. Since primary care is often the frontline and only treatment for emotional difficulties, assessing the care people receive from their family physician has been fruitful. What complaints do they bring in? What kind of advice and/or medications have they received?

While cultural taboos often exist, students should not be discouraged by presumptions that "nobody in our community will talk about that" or "they'll say its all physical." In Projects Salaam and Salud Libre, for example, we found that many people suffering major stressors just said "bad memory" when asked about consequences. Yet they readily acknowledged chronic nervousness, difficulties concentrating, sad mood, and feeling detached from others when asked about these symptoms as part of a checklist. Somatic complaints were less frequent (Reimann et al., 2005; Reimann et al., 2006). In other words, respondents were not "hiding" problems but simply did not recognize them as part of mental health. Concerns about "being crazy" were associated with psychotic symptoms (e.g., hearing voices) rather than stress responses. When elaborating how stressors affected them, respondents did, however, describe a variety of concerns, consequences, and coping efforts. This scenario again illustrates the positive interplay of qualitative and quantitative research methods. Surveys highlighted symptoms, and focus groups provided many details about their interpretation and impact on respondents' daily lives.

Beyond content, some major research considerations are language, literacy, confidentiality, and safety. These areas are discussed next.

Language and Literacy

Given that many cultural groups have non-English speaking backgrounds, language is often a prime issue. Language problems are consistently reported as a major barrier to health care (Jacobs, Agger-Gupta, Chen, Pitrowski, & Hardt, 2003). How do we ensure our surveys and protocols are culturally and linguistically valid? Are interpreters helpful, or do they just add a layer of potential miscommunication?

Translations are complex tasks because a literal word-for-word process is often insufficient. Colloquialisms, regional dialects, and other speech patterns are important factors in this scenario. For example, "I get the blues more often than most of my friends" literally translates in Spanish into "Consigo los azules más a menudo que la mayoría de mis amigos(as)." But the color blue is not a descriptor of mood in the Spanish language. So the translation makes no sense. An alternate translation is: "Comparado con mis amigos(as), me siento tirste más a menudo que ellos" (Compared to my friends, I feel sad more often than they do). That eliminates the "blue" reference and changes the sentence structure to something more natural sounding in Spanish. Given such issues, Rolger (1999) argues that translation effectiveness should use sufficient similarity rather than exact equivalence criteria. In short, each linguistic version of a protocol, survey, or instrument should convey the same core meaning even if that requires they be, strictly speaking, worded differently.

How have we addressed these issues? Two common techniques are *backtranslating* and *decentering* (Marín & Marín, 1991; Varricchio, 2004). Backtranslation involves several steps. First, a bilingual person from the population of interest translates the project's materials from his or her source language (e.g., English) to the target language (e.g., Farsi). Second, a similarly qualified but different person then translates the new versions back into their original language (e.g., English). The original and backtranslated English versions are then compared for equivalence. As one can imagine, they often have some differences. To reconcile these variations, the final English version should be revised to ensure it is conceptually identical with the measure's other languages. This is often called decentering.

Sometimes our own academic colloquialisms present problems. For example, in Project Salaam, our assessment of U.S. Middle Eastern communities, we were cautioned to avoid common research jargon such as "principal investigator" and "key informant." Such terms were likely to be confused with law enforcement. Given that many people in Middle Eastern communities in the United States believe they have been subjected to harassment by governmental entities since September 11, 2001, being perceived as investigators (or calling people informants) was not likely to gain us trust and access (Reimann et al., 2005).

Another consideration is literacy. Will participants be able to read your survey? Are materials best presented orally? This can involve more than educational considerations. Some tribal languages, for example, come from oral traditions whose spelling, characters, and other factors have not been fully codified. In those circumstances presenting surveys orally is the viable option, even if some may believe that written responses allow for more privacy.

Additionally, we have considered interpreter roles. It can be tempting to use people who are most available. The Office of Minority Health's (2001) National Standards on Culturally and Linguistically Appropriate Standards (CLAS) in health care, however, recommend that interpreters should be trained staff. An exception can be made if participants specifically request family members, presuming they are adults. The process of interpretation is another factor. In the traditional model, interpreters function as machinelike as possible. They try to keep their opinions and personalities out of the procedure. A more recent approach suggests interpreters can also serve as cultural brokers. They not only translate the words but can provide guidance that clarifies the cultural and historical context of what participants say (Singh, McKay, & Singh, 1999). We found this method particularly useful.

Using community health advisors (CHAs) is another way to gain culturally and linguistically effective community access. CHAs, sometimes called *promotoras*, are members of local social networks who have compassion for, and leadership in, their neighborhoods. They traditionally distribute health information and can thus help with practical needs assessment tasks. The use of CHAs is becoming more prevalent and has been specifically recommended by the IOM (2002). We cannot overstate the contributions CHAs made to Projects Salaam and Salud Libre. They were the essential keys to success in both efforts. One caveat in service learning, however, is that CHAs should not supplant hands-on experience by students. Instead, we have teamed CHAs with students, which allowed learning opportunities for everyone involved.

One final comment on this general topic: As described above, language considerations are often essential. Even fully bilingual community members are often most comfortable and forthcoming when they can describe personal issues in their traditional language (Javier, 2007). At the same time, language is not the be-all and end-all of culture. We cannot, for example, assume that monolingual English-speaking Latinos are ignorant of or uninfluenced by their group's traditions. We have thus checked our methods and procedures for cultural congruence, even when working with participants who spoke perfect English.

Confidentiality and Safety

While essential to all research, confidentiality often takes on special importance with culturally distinct populations. Suspiciousness of researchers' motivations in these groups is well documented (Reimann et al., 2005; SHIRE, 2005). Given past abuses, that suspiciousness is not entirely unfounded (Freimuth et al., 2001; Rolger, 1999). Some people may also fear repercussions from their own communities for "talking." A university's institutional review board (IRB) requires researchers to address confidentiality issues. But informed consent and other IRB procedures often require participant signatures that in and of themselves create a paper trail. We have found that many respondents wish to keep the information they contribute and the fact that they participate at all private. This is especially true for participants who have a history of being persecuted. In our experience IRB policies are most effective when they (a) allow potential volunteers to make viable consent choices but (b) do not require them to sign any documentation. It is important to advocate for such policies with IRBs that have not yet adopted them.

A related issue is participant safety, which requires preparing for many contingencies. For example, presume you are leading a focus group that discusses mental health, chronic disease, or any number of other stressful issues. The process is going well, and group participants feel safe and begin to divulge increasingly sensitive information. After the meeting, a participant tells you about some particularly difficult circumstances and that he or she is contemplating suicide. What do you do? The critical on-the-spot response may not be automatic for students or faculty members who are not also clinical practitioners. Setting up emergency protocols that quickly get people to needed resources is essential.

Participant Recruitment

As previously mentioned, individual stakeholders, advisory councils, and word of mouth have often helped us recruit participants. However, it must also be acknowledged that such community-generated samples have limitations. Referred to as *snowballing*, the method does not systematically access a representative cross-section of the study population (Okazaki & Sue, 1995). In short, it does not constitute random selection. Our partnership with a local mosque during Project Salaam, for example, attracted devout Muslims while reaching fewer (and even deterring some) secular and non-Muslim community members. A few presumed we had an Islamic agenda—even though we explicitly stated the contrary (Reimann et al., 2005). But for some assessments, nonrandom samples are most practical. Common random selection techniques (e.g., random-digit-dialed telephone surveys) only reach people who have phones, compete with a host of telemarketers, and do not lend themselves to identifying members of specific ethnic groups. In service learning these techniques may also keep students at phone banks rather than out in the community.

These circumstances make nonrandom sampling preferable for many efforts. We have sought to reduce accompanying problems by (a) gearing recruitment to all known components of a group, (b) thoroughly analyzing demographics of the final sample, (c) comparing these demographics to the broader community makeup, and (d) clearly specifying to whom findings could and could not be generalized.

Data Analysis and Interpretation

A full discussion of qualitative and quantitative data analyses is beyond this chapter's scope. But several points are worth noting. First, qualitative analyses have become increasingly standardized through computer programs and other methods (see Krueger & Casey, 2000). This greater consistency may enhance the acceptance of qualitative techniques in the long run. Service learning presents the advantages of practical hands-on exposure to advancing methods.

Second, reliability analyses can check the effectiveness of quantitative survey development/translation and fix some problems after data have been collected. Reliability's alpha statistics (e.g., Cronbach's alpha), for example, assess how well a set of questions measures a single underlying construct (e.g., anxiety, depression, health knowledge, attitudes toward care). Comparing the alphas of different linguistic versions of a survey shows how equivalently they performed across languages. In addition, reliability analyses (item-total correlations) identify which items helped measure a construct and which did not. Survey quality can thus be enhanced by removing a few "bad" items. In practical terms, these techniques have occasionally helped us shore up surveys after data collection was complete.

One caveat to reliability analyses with measures of health knowledge and awareness among traditionally underserved populations is noteworthy. For example, alphas are based on the assumption that knowing one fact about health makes it more likely a person will know other facts (be generally knowledgeable) in the same content arena. That makes sense if people have undergone structured education (e.g., a class). But it is less likely if bits of health knowledge in a community are picked up here and there in very informal ways ("so-and-so down the street said"). Consequently we have argued that less than ideal alpha levels do not necessarily mean a set of questions were poorly conceived in such circumstances (e.g., Yepes-Rios, Reimann, Talavera, Ruiz de Esparza, & Talavera, 2006).

Third and finally, a cautionary note about interpreting results: Significant average differences between demographic groups (e.g., males and females) have been all too often misinterpreted. Simply finding such differences does not mean we know why they exist. If we were to find that women are generally more health conscious than men, we would need to assess gender roles, not just gender per se, to clearly understand the phenomenon. Thus demographic differences can pilot more comprehensive follow-up studies. Yet sometimes researchers cite only demographic-based observations and then present consequent speculations as if they were direct results (Okazaki & Sue, 1995). There is nothing wrong with well-considered speculation. But direct conclusions and theorizing should be clearly distinguished.

Assessing the Assessment

In performing needs assessments we have frequently heard the following refrain: "So-and-so was through here a couple of years ago asking the same questions. But we don't know whatever happened. We never saw him or her again and nothing changed." Rolger (1999) calls this *hit and run* research. Such realities highlight our responsibility to the people we assess. One step in fulfilling that responsibility is to present results, conclusions, recommendations, and potential next steps to community members in follow-up meetings. In our experience, presenting draft findings has most often generated positive and lively feedback that enhanced our understanding of the populations we addressed even further. For students, direct reactions to their work added one more layer to their overall learning.

An additional method is to distribute information as widely as possible to key health care policy makers, workers, professionals, and other stakeholders. This includes writing reports in language understandable by the general public. Ideal distribution thus includes multiple civic and professional outlets (e.g., Reimann et al., 2005; Reimann, Ghulam, Rodríguez-Reimann, & Beylouni, 2007). Overall, we have found it most useful to start planning distribution contingencies before the assessment began, not when it was finished.

What then is an overall evaluation strategy? Not surprisingly, service learning is generally appraised on the two components of its name: How well did the project *serve* the community? What did students *learn* in the process? Needs assessments offer strong opportunities to succeed in both arenas. They can draw formal attention to important social and public health issues and give students opportunities to learn practical and collaborative research skills.

A number of evaluation resources exist, including Community-Campus Partnerships for Health, the National Service Learning Clearinghouse, and published literature (e.g., Blumenthal, Jones, & McNeal, 2001). Faculty can adapt basic templates to their individual projects. In general we have subdivided evaluation criteria into two classifications: intermediate and ultimate outcomes. Intermediate outcomes dealt with the conduct of the assessment itself (e.g., did sufficient numbers of people participate? Did they appear to trust the process? Did surveys show themselves to be valid and reliable? Was the consequent report adequately distributed? Did students learn tangible skills?). Ultimate outcomes addressed how well the long-term purpose of the assessment was fulfilled. If substantial needs were found, did the report influence policy decisions, resource availability, and service implementation?

On a practical level, intermediate outcomes are the most common criteria for student evaluations. They appraise how well an assessment's tasks and procedures were carried out. But it is also in faculty members' and their institutions' best interest to track ultimate outcomes, even if doing so is arduous and time consuming. Being able to show positive societal outcomes and alumni's use of the skills they gained in their later career strongly contributes to service learning's long-term credibility and acceptance (in academia and local communities), and thus its sustainability and growth.

Future Directions

Approaches described in this chapter are still in their infancy. In part, progress will be aided by reevaluating some academic traditions in research methods and information sources. Rather than making hierarchical judgments about which are good and which are bad, our challenge is to refine each, find their most effective applications, and identify how they best complement each other. If skillfully done, this process enhances rather than erodes academic quality.

Service learning is a potentially exciting opportunity for students. It brings them the practical chance to address social problems and gain technical and interpersonal skills, and it widens our base of people competent in such efforts. At the same time, student projects have some limitations. Students are by definition a transient population. Yet social change commonly requires long-term persistence. Refining institutional models that systematically enhance project continuity is important. The needs assessments themselves, disseminating their results, and implementing their recommendations are really potential components of a broader generational model. If each student cohort tangibly hands off its project segment to the incoming one (through orientations, introductions to the community, etc.), continuity is enhanced. Cohesive long-term models also potentially increase the variety of tasks and situations students are exposed to. Consequently, they and the broader community benefit.

References

Beverly, C. J., Mcatee, R., Costello, J., Chernoff, R., & Casteel, J. (2005). Needs assessment of rural communities: A focus on older adults. *Journal of Community Health, 30,* 197–121.

Blumenthal, D. S., Jones, A., & McNeal, M. (2001). Evaluating a community-based multiprofessional course in community health. *Education for Health, 14,* 251–255.

Brach C., & Fraser, I. (2000). Can cultural competency reduce racial and ethnic health disparities? A review and conceptual model. *Medical Care Research Review, 57*(Suppl. 1), 181–217.

California Board of Psychology. (2004). *Report of the California Board of Psychology: Accomplishments of the work group focused on human diversity.* Retrieved May 20, 2007, from http://www.psychboard.ca.gov/cont-edu/diversity-report.pdf

Campinha-Bacote, J., (1999). A model and instrument for addressing cultural competence in health care. *Journal of Nursing Education, 38,* 203–207.

Dovido, J. F., Gaertner, S. L., Anastasio, P. A., & Sanitioso, R. (1992). Cognitive and motivational bases of biases: Implications of aversive racism for attitudes toward Hispanics. In S. B. Knouse, P. Rosenfeld, & A. L. Culbertson (Eds.), *Hispanics in the workplace* (pp. 75–106). Newbury Park, CA: Sage.

Ferdman, B. M. (1992). The dynamics of ethnic diversity in organizations: Toward integrative models. In K. Kelley (Ed.), *Issues, theory, and research in industrial/ organizational psychology* (pp. 339–384). Amsterdam: Elsevier.

Fiscella, K., & Shin, P. (2005). The inverse care law: Implications for healthcare of vulnerable populations. *Journal of Ambulatory Care Management, 28,* 304–312.

Freimuth, V. S., Quinn, S. C., Thomas, S. B., Cole, G., Zook, E., & Duncan, T. (2001). African Americans' views on research and the Tuskegee Syphilis Study. *Social Science & Medicine, 52,* 797–808.

Giddings, L. S., & Grant, B. M. (2006). Mixed methods research for the novice researcher. *Contemporary Nurse, 23,* 3–11.

Gudykunst, W. B., & Ting-Toomey, S. (1988). *Culture and interpersonal communication.* Newbury Park, CA: Sage.

Ibarra, R. A. (2001). *Beyond affirmative action: Reframing the context of higher education*. Madison: University of Wisconsin Press

Institute of Medicine. (2002). Unequal treatment: Confronting racial and ethnic disparities in health care. Washington DC: National Academies Press.

Jacobs, E. A., Agger-Gupta, N., Chen, A. H., Pitrowski, A., & Hardt, E. J. (2003). *Language barriers in health care settings: An annotated bibliography of the research literature*. Woodland Hills, CA: California Endowment.

Javier, J. A. (2007). Language switching as communication. In J. A. Javier (Ed.), *The bilingual mind: Thinking, feeling, and speaking in two languages* (pp. 53–62). New York: Springer.

Kessing, R. (1974). Theories of culture. *Annual Review of Anthropology, 3*, 73–97.

Krueger, R. A., & Casey M. A. (2000). *Focus groups: A practical guide for applied research* (3rd ed.). Thousand Oaks, CA: Sage.

Marín, G., & Marín, B. V. (1991). *Research With Hispanic populations*. Newbury Park, CA: Sage.

Maykut, P., & Morehouse, R. (1994). *Beginning qualitative research: A philosophical and practical guide*. Washington, DC: Palmer Press.

Mills, R. J., & Bhandari, S. (2003). *Health insurance coverage in the United States: 2002*. (Current Population Reports, 2003.) Washington DC: U.S. Census Bureau.

National Alliance for Hispanic Health. (2000). *Quality health services for Hispanics: The cultural competency component*. (DHHS Publication No. 99–21.) Washington DC: U.S. Department of Health and Human Services.

Nolin, J., Wilburn, S. T., Wilburn, K. T., & Weaver, D. (2006). Health and social service needs of older adults: Implementing a community-based needs assessment. *Evaluation and Program Planning, 29*, 217–226.

Office of Minority Health. (2001). *National standards on culturally and linguistically appropriate services (CLAS)*. Washington, DC: Author.

Okazaki S., & Sue S. (1995). Methodological issues in assessment research with ethnic minorities. *Psychological Assessment, 3*, 367–375.

Plescia, M., Koontz, S., & Laurent, S. (2001). Community assessment in a vertically integrated health care system. *American Journal of Public Health, 91*, 811–814.

Proctor, R. W. (2005). Methodology is more than research design and technology. *Behavioral Research Methods, 37*, 197–201.

Reimann, J. O., Ghulam, M., Rodríguez-Reimann, D. I., & Beylouni, M. F. (2005). *Bringing communities together for wellness: An assessment of emotional health needs among San Diego's Middle Eastern, North African, and East African groups*. San Diego, CA: Islamic Center of San Diego.

Reimann J. O., Ghulam, M., Rodríguez-Reimann, D. I., & Beylouni, M. F. (2007). Project Salaam: Assessing mental health needs among San Diego's greater Middle Eastern and East African communities. *Ethnicity & Disease, 17*(Suppl. 3), 39–41.

Reimann, J. O., Rodríguez-Reimann, D. I., & Medina, M. (2006). *Proyecto Salud Libre: An assessment of the mental health needs in Imperial County's communities.* Brawley, CA: Clinicas De Salud Del Pueblo.

Reimann, J. O., Talavera, G. A., Salmon, M., Nuñez, J., & Velasquez, R. J. (2004). Cultural competence among physicians treating Mexican Americans who have diabetes: A structural model. *Social Science & Medicine, 59,* 2195–2205.

Rolger, L. H. (1999). Methodological sources of cultural insensitivity in mental health research. *American Psychologist, 54,* 424–433.

Samhan, H. H. (2000). Not quite White: Race classification and the Arab-American experience. In M. W. Suleiman (Ed.), *Arabs in America: Building a new future* (pp. 209–226). Philadelphia: Temple University Press.

Saper, R. B., Kales, S. N., Paquin, J., Burns, M. J., Eisenberg, D. M., Davis, R. B., et al. (2004). Heavy metal content of ayurvedic herbal medicine products. *JAMA, 292,* 2868–2873.

Shapiro, K., & Gong, W. C. (2002). Natural products used for diabetes. *Journal of the American Pharmacy Association, 42,* 217–226.

Singh, N. N., McKay, J. D., & Singh, A. N. (1999). The need for cultural brokers in mental health services. *Journal of Child & Family Studies, 8,* 1024–1062.

Substance Abuse and Mental Health Services Administration. (2000). *Cultural competence standards in managed mental health care services for underserved/underrepresented racial/ethnic groups.* (Publication No. SMA 00–3457.) Rockville, MD: Author.

Summit Health Institute for Research and Education. (2005). *Giving voices to the voiceless: Language barriers & health access issues of Black immigrants of African descent.* Woodland Hills, CA: California Endowment.

Tajfel, H., & Turner, J. C. (1986). The social identity theory of intergroup behavior. In S. Worchel & W. G. Austin (Eds.), *Psychology of intergroup relations* (pp. 7–24). Chicago: Nelson-Hall.

U.S. Department of Health and Human Services. (1999). *Mental health: Culture, race, and ethnicity.* Washington, DC: Author.

U.S. Department of Health and Human Services. (2000a). *Oral health in America: A report of the surgeon general.* Washington, DC: Author.

U.S. Department of Health and Human Services. (2000b). *Healthy people 2010* (2nd ed.): Vol. 1. *Understanding and improving health.* Vol. 2: *Objectives for improving health.* Washington, DC: U.S. Government Printing Office.

Varricchio, C. G. (2004). Measurement issues concerning linguistic translations. In F. Stromborg & S. J. Olsen (Eds.), *Instruments for health care research* (3rd ed., pp. 56–60). Sudbury, MA: Jones & Bartlett.

Williams, R., & Yanoshik, K. (2001). Can you do community assessment without talking to the community? *Journal of Community Health, 26,* 233–247.

Wortley, P. (2005). Who's getting shots and who's not: Racial/ethnic disparities in immunization coverage. *Ethnic Discourse, 15*(2 Suppl. 3), 4–6.

Wright, J., Williams, R., & Wilkinson, J. R. (1998). Development and importance of health needs assessment. *BMJ, 316,* 1310–1313.

Yepes-Rios, M., Reimann, J. O. F., Talavera, A. C., Ruiz de Esparza, A., Talavera, G. A. (2006). Colorectal cancer screening among Mexican Americans at a community clinic. *American Journal of Preventive Medicine, 30,* 204–210.

7

THE ROLE OF COMMUNITY-BASED PARTICIPATORY RESEARCH, CIVIC ENGAGEMENT, AND SERVICE LEARNING IN REDUCING HEALTH DISPARITIES

An Experience Using Community Health Theaters

Helda Pinzon-Perez

Health Disparities in the United States and Healthy People 2010

Health disparities in the United States have been amply documented by the National Healthcare Quality and Disparities Reports (NHQDR), which are periodically prepared by the Agency for Healthcare Research and Quality (AHRQ) as part of the mandate of Public Law 106–129, also known as the Healthcare Research and Quality Act of 1999 (AHRQ, 2004).

These reports provide detailed information on the status of health care disparities in the quality of and access to health care for communities in general and for congressionally designated priority populations. The 2007 NHQDR found that variations in the quality of health care services are diminishing, but disparities still exist (AHRQ, 2007). The Office of Minority Health and Health Disparities (OMHD, n.d.) has stated that variations are still present among ethnic and racial minority groups in the United States. According to the OMHD, the infant death rate among African Americans is more than double that of Whites, Hispanics in the United States have twice the risk of dying from diabetes than non-Hispanic Whites, American Indians and Alaska Natives have high death rates from unintentional injuries and suicide, and among Asian and Pacific Islanders, Vietnamese women have five times the risk of cervical cancer than do White women.

The key findings of the 2003 NHQDR indicated that inequality in the quality of health services still persists, disparities generate costs to society, and preventive care is still frequently not offered (AHRQ, 2004). Racial and Ethnic Approaches to Community Health (REACH) 2010 has listed six focus areas in which disparities in health access and outcomes have been documented: infant mortality, cancer screening and management, cardiovascular disease, diabetes, HIV/AIDS, and immunizations (OMHD, n.d.). In congruence with REACH 2010, the U.S. Department of Health and Human Services (DHHS, n.d.) has made a commitment, through Healthy People 2010, to eliminate health disparities by race and ethnicity, gender, education, income, geographic location, disability status, or sexual orientation. Healthy People 2010 delineates health goals and objectives for our nation and serves as a guideline for communities, health organizations, community-based entities, and people in general to design programs aimed at improving the health status of all people in the United States (DHHS, n.d.). The elimination of health disparities will require improved efforts in disease prevention, health promotion, public health, and health care delivery. It will also require enhanced knowledge of the determinants of health and disease in various U.S. populations.

Health Disparities and Health Literacy

Healthy People 2010 has placed a major emphasis on health disparities generated by health communication issues and health literacy limitations. Health literacy is defined in Healthy People 2010 as the capacity of individuals to obtain, understand, and use health information for decision making (Parker, Ratzan, & Lurie, 2003). Zorn, Allen, and Horowitz (2004) added that health literacy provides individuals with the tools to make health-related knowledge understandable and usable.

Zorn, Allen, and Horowitz (2004) indicated that the 2000 U.S. census revealed that 20 million people speak limited English, and 10 million speak no English at all. These authors provide data documenting that more than 90 million people in the United States have limited health literacy. Williams et al.'s (1995) study demonstrated that in a public hospital, 33% of English-speaking clients struggled to understand health materials, 25% could not read appointment information, and 42% did not understand prescription bottle labels.

People with the greatest health disparities are the ones who have lower health literacy levels and have less access to information, communication, and technology. (Research shows that populations with limited literacy are less informed about health issues and are less likely to engage in behavioral health changes (OMHD, n.d.).

Berkman et al. (2004) demonstrated that those with low reading skills have greater difficulty navigating the health care system and have a higher risk for poor health outcomes. These authors revealed that limited literacy is strongly related to low health knowledge, higher rates of chronic disease, and reduced use of preventive health services.

These findings reveal challenges for all levels of society including higher education. Community-based participatory research (CBPR), service-oriented pedagogy, and civic engagement are areas of higher education curricular design and scientific inquiry that can play a significant role in reducing disparities associated with health literacy.

The Role of CBPR in Reducing Health Disparities

CBPR is an interactive and collaborative process of scientific inquiry in which researchers and community members work together to identify research needs by designing research methodologies that are culturally appropriate for the participating stakeholders and by collecting and analyzing data with real-life applications and benefits for the participating population. According to AHRQ (2002), this research strategy engages community members, employs local wisdom in the understanding of health problems, motivates citizens to actively participate in the design of health-related interventions, and allows participants to invest in the process and outcomes of the research.

CBPR has proven to be an effective methodology to promote the health status and well-being of disadvantaged groups. Within these populations is an increased need to promote research that responds to various health challenges. Disadvantaged groups involve minorities, low-income populations, rural communities, and people with literacy challenges (AHRQ, 2002).

Effective community-researcher collaborations in CBPR are based on a paradigm that acknowledges community contributions, recruitment and training of disadvantaged populations to participate in research groups, improvement of health literacy, power co-ownership, and respect for diversity (Kone et al., 2000).

The benefits of CBPR in reducing health disparities have been amply documented. Kone et al.'s (2000) study revealed that CBPR increases the potential to develop culturally competent public health research agendas that effectively address community concerns. Israel (AHRQ, n.d.) mentioned that the benefits of CBPR in reducing health disparities are evident because it provides a real-life application to data, enhances the validity of the research, facilitates participant recruitment and retention, and provides an opportunity for the community to be actively involved.

Israel added that CBPR contributes to the reduction of health disparities by allowing disadvantaged populations to gather resources that communities can use, providing an opportunity for community and academic partners to share their expertise in public health issues, increasing trust, reducing cultural gaps between partners, and promoting the development of viable interventions and policy change (AHRQ, n.d.).

The role of CBPR in contributing to the Healthy People 2010 goal of eliminating health disparities can be illustrated in a community partnership that has gained national recognition. This partnership is between the community, the Health and Social Services Center in Detroit, community health centers, and university researchers formed to reduce the incidence of diabetes among economically challenged Latino residents. This CBPR explored the factors influencing the rates of diabetes in the participating population, the health resources available for this community, and the possible solutions to the problem. The project resulted in active community participation in collecting information and proposing interventions to reduce the risk and the effects of diabetes (AHRQ, n.d.).

The Role of Civic Engagement and Service Learning in Reducing Health Disparities

Reductions of health disparities in disadvantaged populations have long been sought-after goals in the movements of civic engagement and global justice in health. Health professionals and public health practitioners are now more open to incorporating the principles of service learning and active citizenry in health disparities and health literacy needs assessments, program design, implementation, and evaluation.

Civic engagement is frequently examined from two perspectives. At the personal level, it may be defined as the actions at the individual and collective levels aimed to identify and address issues of concern to the community (Carpini, 2006). At the organizational level, civic engagement is the institutional commitment to public purposes and responsibilities, which involves an engagement in a democratic way of life (University of Minnesota Morris, 2008). By 2004 institutional engagement gained national prominence when the presidents of 300 higher education campuses signed the Declaration on the Civic Responsibility of Higher Education, a pledge to strengthen civic engagement and service learning at their institution (Ehrlich, 2005). This declaration clearly placed higher education in the center of developing an active citizenry.

Consequently, the goal of developing students' skills related to active citizenry has been infused in the curriculum through service-learning efforts at many colleges and universities. In her research, Hanks (2003) demonstrated that civically engaged students in an undergraduate service-learning class could greatly contribute to the reduction of health disparities. In this class, students collaborated with community members in identifying what they needed and valued in health services, as well as their barriers to access care for their children. This experience was also very useful in helping middle-class college students understand people of different socioeconomic statuses and social classes (Hanks).

Cauley et al. (2001) indicated that service learning represents a means to increase awareness of health disparities among college students and to explore their roles in civic engagement.

Chin et al. (2004) have also demonstrated the benefits of civic engagement in reducing health disparities. The Health Disparities Collaborative was formed with the participation of 19 midwestern health centers to reduce the incidence of diabetes among disadvantaged groups. This experience demonstrated that civic engagement contributed greatly to the improvement of diabetes care in health centers as early as the 1st year of implementation of the program.

The Role of Health Theaters in Reducing Health Disparities

As we have seen, improved health literacy is a crucial element in reducing health disparities. Understanding health information is the first step toward accessing health services and adopting healthy lifestyles. The theme of the Eighth Annual Health Literacy Conference organized by the Institute for Healthcare Advancement (2009) was "Health Literacy: Bridging Research and Practice." This conference provided evidence on the value of research to explore alternative methodologies to increase health literacy in the United States (Alexander, 2009).

Health theaters, an educational methodology that involves the oral presentation of a script through performance, are being used as an effective methodology to increase health literacy in disadvantaged populations. Health theaters can be used to empower people to actively participate in their learning process.

In the United States, the program A Theater Approach to Educating Hispanic Girls About Healthy Bones is an example of innovative ways to improve health literacy and reduce health disparities in Latino populations. This collaboration between the National Alliance for Hispanic Health (2004) and the National Institutes of Health Osteoporosis and Related Bone Diseases resource center uses health theaters to educate Hispanic girls and their families on the importance of osteoporosis prevention and bone health promotion. This program demonstrated that a theater is effective because it adapts to the specific needs and realities of the Hispanic/Latino populations and can overcome difficulties generated by the diversity in literacy abilities of the participating groups (National Alliance for Hispanic Health, 2009).

The Youth Theater for HIV/AIDS Prevention Education is another example of the effectiveness of health theaters in health education. Funded by a grant from the Centers for Disease Control and Prevention, this project documented the value of theater in communicating HIV/AIDS prevention and education for Hispanic youth and their families (National Alliance for Hispanic Health, 2009).

Health theaters increase health literacy and reduce health disparities by allowing communities to understand and obtain meaningful and culturally appropriate health messages. In addition, health theaters empower community members by making them the creators and deliverers of important health information (National Alliance for Hispanic Health, 2009).

An Experience Using Community Theaters to Increase Health Literacy

Background

Theater productions are one of the best ways to reduce disparities associated with limited health literacy because they combine CBPR and service learning as well as promote civic engagement in higher education. This section describes the experience of developing community health theaters with male Latino agricultural workers in the Central California Valley during summer 2005.

Funded by a grant from the Office for Community Service and Civic Engagement at California State University, Fresno (CSUF), this program was developed with a CBPR approach in which the community members and the research team were active partners in the decision-making process. Students involved in this project were undergraduate, health science, or premedical majors, and were enrolled in a service-learning class.

This program was based on the fundamental understanding that community members can be seen as research experts because they have more knowledge of the reality of their communities than academicians or institutional representatives. Empowerment of farm-working males as community researchers was an essential component of this initiative in which each member of the team (farm-working males, community-based organization representatives, and CSUF faculty and students) cogenerated knowledge about the problem and jointly proposed alternative solutions.

This CBPR attempted to determine the effect of a community theater in knowledge, attitudes, and behaviors of Latino farm-working males living in the Central California Valley regarding their female partners' desire for a breast self-exam, an annual clinical exam, and a mammography. To date, few studies have attempted to recognize the role Latino males could play in their partners' decision to adopt early detection strategies for breast cancer.

Statement of Need

Breast cancer among Latinas living in the Central California Valley is a major public health problem; it is the major cause of cancer mortality among Hispanic women. The 5-year survival rates in Latino women are lower than those in other ethnocultural groups. Hispanics have been found to be at greater risk of mortality because of late-stage diagnosis and treatment (American Cancer Society, 2006). The incidence of breast cancer among Latino farm-working mothers in the Central California Valley is yet to be deter-mined because of the transient nature of this population.

Traditionally, women have been in charge of protecting the health of the family. In this traditional view, males have adopted a passive role in the prevention of disease and the promotion of health in the family environ-ment. Research has shown that males could play a major role in Latino wom-en's decision to adopt preventive actions (Delgado & Estrada, 1993). The positive influence Latino males can have on their partners to adopt breast cancer prevention behaviors needs to be further studied.

Traditional methods for motivating males to participate in health issues (e.g., lectures, class presentations) may lack sufficient involvement of the learner to produce a long-lasting effect. The use of community health the-aters as a methodology for breast cancer education with Latino males living in the Central California Valley needs to be studied in a context of CBPR.

Methodology

This project was a collaboration between faculty and students in the Depart-ment of Health Science at CSUF; a community-based organization, Migrant Head Start; and Latino male agricultural workers living in the Central Cali-fornia Valley. This project was reviewed and approved by the Committee for the Protection of Human Subjects at CSUF.

The first step involved recruitment of the community partners, which was conducted by Migrant Head Start personnel who have already built a relationship of trust and mutual respect in the community. From an ex-pected sample of 10, 8 participants decided to be involved in this program. Criteria for participation in this project included (a) being a male older than 18 years old and (b) being of Latino descent up to third generation.

The second step involved the development of two initial focus groups with Latino male farmworkers living in the Central Valley to determine their knowledge level, attitude, and behavior related to their female partners' compliance with health recommendations, such as monthly breast self-examinations, annual clinical exams, and mammographies, before the intro-duction of a community health theater program. To create an environment of comfort and security for participants, only males were allowed to attend these focus groups.

As part of the focus groups, the community members completed the Health Tree, an educational methodology that involves a visual portrayal of the causes, manifestations, and solutions of a health problem. This technique has been used with Latino populations in Latin American countries and the United States. Through this educational technique, participants are actively involved in recognizing the health needs in their communities, identifying the manifestations of community problems, and proposing a plan of action. According to Perez and Pinzon-Perez (1999), this pedagogical tool is very appropriate for low-literacy Spanish-speaking populations. The results of these focus groups and the Health Tree suggested a lack of knowledge among Latino farm-working males on the etiology, prevention, and early detection methods of female breast cancer. Participants stated their desire to learn more about this topic so they could become active partners in the protection of the health of their wife or sexual partner and suggested the creation of a theater script for breast cancer education.

The third step consisted of developing a community theater script on the role Latino males could play in the prevention and early detection of breast cancer. A theater group composed of three Latino male farmworkers and two CSUF students met a total of six times to discuss the needs of their community in terms of breast cancer education and to create a theater presentation that could respond to these needs. During the second meeting, a female participant was allowed by community members to be a part of the group. She was in charge of teaching about the fundamental issues involved in community theaters. Before admitting this female participant to the health theater, the participating males were asked for consent. They decided that this new member's participation would help them reduce their fear of acting in front of the public, and she could also be an active participant by playing the role of the mother in the script.

Constant reinforcement was provided to community coresearchers so they could participate in various capacities in the theater, such as organizing the community for the presentations, writing the script, and acting. Three community farm-working males participated in all stages of the process, including the presentations to the community.

The members of the health theater created a 20-minute script in Spanish to present breast cancer education to three communities they selected: Fresno, Parlier, and Selma. During the community presentation in Fresno, one of the attendees suggested to include in the script a line addressing the incidence of breast cancer among males. This suggestion was incorporated, and a new script was created to be presented in Parlier and Selma.

The participating Latino males, in collaboration with CSUF students and the faculty member involved in the project, created the dialogues in the script describing the reality of males and their cultural upbringing in their communities in relationship to motivating their wife/sexual partner to engage in breast cancer early detection (breast self-exam, clinical exam, mammography). The creation of these dialogues and script served as health education strategies to clarify misconceptions about breast cancer among the members of the health theater and the community at large, and to motivate Latino males to become active participants in the prevention of this community problem.

The group met at various locations, initially gathering at the Fresno Migrant Head Start office, but to increase participation the group decided to meet at the Parlier Migrant Head Start Office from 7:00 p.m. to 9:00 p.m., as many community members worked in the agricultural fields as late as 7:00 p.m. every day. During every meeting, participants were offered refreshments to create an atmosphere of trust and collegiality.

At one point, a suggestion was made by a Migrant Head Start representative to videotape the process and the community presentations. This suggestion was shared with the community participants who gave their approval. A modification of the research protocol was submitted to the Human Subjects Committee at CSUF's Department of Health Science, approval was granted, and subsequently a videotape was created describing this experience and the results of the study. A copy of the tape was given to the Migrant Head Start Program to be shared with the community participants.

The health theater made three presentations during the summer of 2005. The first presentation was to 17 migrant farmworkers living in Fresno and two members of the Migrant Head Start team. The second presentation was geared toward 20 community members from Parlier. The third presentation was made to 20 community members from Selma. Healthy refreshments were provided in all three presentations to provide an example of nutritionally appropriate snacks. After the theater presentations, the members of the community theater responded to questions from the audience related to breast cancer prevention and early detection.

The fourth step involved the development of another focus group (focus group number 3), which met after the community presentations. In this meeting participants completed the Health Tree again as a posttest method and answered the same six questions addressed in focus groups numbers 1 and 2 related to their knowledge level, attitude, and behavior toward female breast cancer prevention and early detection. The results of focus group number 3 revealed a significant improvement in participants' knowledge on breast cancer, a more positive attitude toward female breast cancer early detection strategies, and a greater willingness to talk about breast cancer with their spouse and children.

Outcomes

Community outcomes. This program succeeded in increasing participants' health literacy on breast cancer. Participating males increased their knowledge on breast cancer and became active promoters of health messages regarding breast cancer prevention in their families. The results indicated significant positive outcomes in terms of attitudes and behaviors of the participating Latino males.

Community members involved in the health theater talked to their wives about breast cancer and motivated them to do breast self-examinations and have clinical breast exams and mammographies (depending on age). These results are very encouraging and suggest the need for future programs with a similar methodology. There is a need to assess the impact on knowledge, attitude, and behavior among the community members who attended the theater presentations.

Student outcomes. Student involvement in this project was ample because they were constantly involved in every step of the process. Participating students developed community health skills such as group organizing, conflict resolution, health needs assessment, program implementation, program evaluation, and CBPR. In addition, students learned the value of active community participation in all phases of the service-learning educational encounters. As indicated by one of the students participating in the community theater, his experience in this service-learning class helped him understand the value of community theaters in reducing disparities related to health literacy, as well as helped him value the knowledge of community members and their willingness to actively participate in education.

This project was presented at the 2005 Annual Conference of the American Public Health Association as part of the student research proposals. In addition, the leading faculty member of this project and a student involved in it collaborated on an article on the lessons learned in service learning and participatory research, and published it in an online peer-reviewed teaching journal (Pinzon-Perez & Rodriguez, 2006). Students expressed great pride in their role as community collaborators and manifested their interest in taking additional service-learning courses.

Conclusion

Reducing health disparities and increasing health literacy is a task for everyone. Higher education institutions are called on to incorporate service-learning experiences to promote civic engagement as well as to increase CBPR on health disparities. Service learning, CBPR, and civic engagement can play a major role in the reduction and elimination of health disparities in the United States.

References

Agency for Healthcare Research and Quality. (2002). *Community-based participatory research-Conference summary*. Retrieved December 16, 2009, from http://www.ahrq.gov/About/cpcr/cbpr/

Agency for Healthcare Research and Quality. (2004). *National healthcare disparities report, 2003*. Summary. Retrieved December 15, 2009, from http://www.ahrq.gov/qual/nhdr03/nhdrsum03.htm

Agency for Healthcare Research and Quality. (2007). *Key themes and highlights from the National Healthcare Quality Report*. Retrieved December 15, 2009, from http://www.ahrq.gov/qual/nhqr07/Key.htm

Agency for Healthcare Research and Quality. (n.d.). *Community-based participatory research: Conference summary*. Retrieved December 16, 2009, from http://www.ahrq.gov/about/cpcr/cbpr/cbpr1.htm

Alexander, L. (2009, May). *Doing the right thing for the patient through health literacy education*. Poster presentation at the Eighth Annual Health Literacy Conference of the Institute for Healthcare Advancement, Irvine, CA. Retrieved December 16, 2009, from http://www.iha4health.org/html/posters%20online.pdf

American Cancer Society. (2006). *Exercise can prevent breast cancer in Hispanic women*. Retrieved June 3, 2006, from http://www.cancer.org/docroot/nws/content/nws_1_1x_exercise_can_prevent_breast_cancer_in_hispanic_women.asp

Berkman, N. D., DeWalt, D. A., Pignone, M. P., Sheridan, S. L., Lohr, K. N., Lux, L., et al. (2004). *Literacy and health outcomes*. Rockville, MD: Agency for Healthcare Research and Quality.

Carpini, D. (2006). *Civic engagement and service learning: Definition of civic engagement.* Retrieved June 3, 2006, from http://www.apa.org/ed/slce/civicengagement.html

Cauley, K., Canfield, C., Clasen, C., Dobbins, J., Hemphill, S., Jaballas, E., et al. (2001). Service learning: integrating student learning and community service. *Education for Health, 14*(2), 173–181.

Chin, M., Cook, S., Drum, M., Jin, L., Guillen, M., Humikowski, C., et al. (2004). Improving diabetes care in Midwest community health centers with the health disparities collaborative. *Diabetes Care, 27*(1), 2–8. Retrieved December 16, 2009, from http://care.diabetesjournals.org/content/27/1/2.abstract

Delgado, J., & Estrada, L. (1993). Improving data collection strategies. *Public Health Reports, 108*(5), 540–545. Retrieved December 16, 2009, from http://www.ncbi.nlm.nih.gov/pmc/articles/PMC1403428/

Ehrlich, T. (2005). *Civic engagement.* Retrieved November 11, 2005, from http://measuringup.highereducation.org/2000/articles/ThomasEhrlich.cfm

Hanks, C. (2003). *Health disparities research and service learning.* Retrieved December 16, 2009, from http://www.servicelearning.org/library/lib_cat/index.php?library_id=6496

Kone, A., Sullivan, M., Senturia, K. D., Chrisman, N. J., Ciske, S. J., & Krieger, J. W. (2000). Improving collaboration between researchers and communities. *Public Health Reports, 115* (2/3), 243–248.

National Alliance for Hispanic Health. (2009). *A theater approach to educating Hispanic girls about healthy bones.* Retrieved December 16, 2009, from http://www.hispanichealth.org/pdf/Healthy_Bones.pdf

Office of Disease Prevention and Health Promotion. (n.d.). *Healthy people 2010—Health communication.* Retrieved November 11, 2005, from http://www.healthypeople.gov/document/HTML/Volume1/11HealthCom.htm

Office of Minority Health and Heath Disparities. (n.d.). *About minority health.* Retrieved December 15, 2009, from http://www.cdc.gov/omhd/AMH/AMH.htm

Parker, R., Ratzan, S., & Lurie, N. (2003). Health literacy: A policy challenge for advancing high quality health care. *Health Affairs, 22*(4), 147–153. Retrieved December 15, 2009, from http://content.healthaffairs.org/cgi/reprint/22/4/147

Perez, M., & Pinzon-Perez, H. (1999). The health tree: An interactive needs assessment tool for Hispanic students. *Journal of Health Education, 30*(3), 186–187.

Pinzon-Perez, H., & Rodriguez, M. (2006). *Service learning in the classroom: Faculty and student viewpoints.* Retrieved December 16, 2009, from http://www.calstate.edu/ITL/exchanges/viewpoints/1247_Pinzon-Perez.html

University of Minnesota Morris. (2008). *Civic engagement at UMM.* Retrieved December 16, 2009, from http://www.morris.umn.edu/CurrentStudents/Civic.html

U.S. Department of Health and Human Services. (n.d.). *Goal 2: Eliminate health disparities.* Retrieved December 15, 2009, from http://www.healthypeople.gov/ data/midcourse/html/execsummary/Goal2.htm

Williams, M. V., Parker, R. M., Baker, D. W., Parikh, N. S., Pitkin, K., Coates, W. C., et al. (1995). Inadequate functional health literacy among patients at two public hospitals. *JAMA, 274*(21), 1677–1682.

Zorn, M., Allen, M. P., & Horowitz, A. M. (2004). *Understanding health literacy and its barriers: Current bibliographies in medicine 2004–1.* Retrieved August 2, 2007, from http://www.nlm.nih.gov/pubs/cbm/healthliteracybarriers.html

8

TEACHING PUBLIC HEALTH SECURITY THROUGH COMMUNITY-BASED AND CASE-BASED LEARNING

Louise Gresham, Sonja Ingmanson, and Susan Cheng

Everybody knows that pestilences have a way of recurring in the world, yet somehow we find it hard to believe in ones that crash down on our heads from a blue sky. There have been as many plagues as wars in history; yet always plagues and wars take people equally by surprise.

Albert Camus

The concept of public health security is a reality in public health and international communities. It gained prominence with the introduction of anthrax in the United States in October 2001 and expands against the background of the uncertainty of pandemic influenza. This chapter documents community-based and authentic case-based learning experiences that encourage students and faculty to explore the link between public health and national security as part of the master of science in public health degree with a specialization in global emergency preparedness and response at San Diego State University.

The Graduate School of Public Health's 700-level Emergency Preparedness and Response course offers learning opportunities that emphasize community engagement to promote critical thinking, problem solving, communication, organizational analysis, and values that are needed when leaders face pressures and unique circumstances in a health emergency (Grunder, 2004). Creating empathy and confidence in faculty and students is encouraged via the shared leadership roles of government, military, and humanitarian programs during disasters involving diverse target populations.

Our goal is to provide innovative and relevant learning experiences to educate a new generation of students to recognize the connection between wellness, public health, and national security. Given the unpredictability of influenza alone and its accompanying potential impact on the morbidity and mortality of populations around the world, and its real impact on the global economy and financial systems, these links can be fully explored. Inevitably students learn through their studies the link between the national security threat of infectious diseases and weapons of mass destruction to the well-being of individuals who seek security and stability in their daily lives. The learning experiences presented have immediate relevance to many disciplines, including communication, law, food security, laboratory sciences, public safety, engineering, nursing, and social work.

Learning Objectives

The emergency preparedness and response course is designed to result in the following learning objectives. At the end of the course students will have the ability to

- examine ethical issues related to the connection between public health and national security such as disease control, homeland security, and access to care;
- highlight principles of public health law in the context of health behaviors (quarantine, isolation, seeking health care), and confidentiality and privacy;
- apply epidemiological principles to understand surveillance, identification and analysis of disease patterns, outbreak control, and evaluation of the global public health impact of such efforts;
- apply principles of individual and community behaviors to the understanding of the occurrence, preparedness, response, mitigation of and recovery from public health emergencies;

- raise questions about the tensions between global public health and political, economic, cultural, and social development;
- develop skills that enhance responsible and shared leadership roles.

Methods

Throughout our program we integrate research and theory from Knowle's (1984) theory of andragogy (adult learning) with the assumption that adult learning is tied to problem solving, immediate value, and experiential learning. Unlike childhood education, adult learning is self-directed, and the individual often assumes responsibility for the decision-making process (Knowles, n.d.). Therefore, learning modalities need to approach adult education with a focus on experiential and problem-solving opportunities and the importance of and the rationale for the lesson, emphasizing process over content. Didactic classrooms may provide less impact than interactive simulations, case studies, or community-based learning. With this in mind, several projects incorporating vital elements of andragogy have been introduced into the course. The methods (a) inform research and case-based experiences, (b) provide student and faculty reflection, and (c) describe performance.

Students had the opportunity to participate in one of three learning projects: the Native American Alliance for Emergency Preparedness (NAAEP), the Red Cross, or the Smallpox Tabletop Exercise. In all three settings, graduate students review the literature and use critical thinking skills to understand the importance of government, military, and humanitarian programs during disasters and the dynamics of the health perspective of international relations and policy development. Each learning setting required multiple meetings with stakeholders, connected influence with decision making, and obtained input on community needs and values. Student activities included assessing needs through interviews; applying learning theory in mobilization; advocating and developing educational curricula; reflecting on personal beliefs, values, and attitudes about target populations; and reflecting on the needs of marginalized populations.

NAAEP

Students, along with Native American and public health experts, developed a clinic disaster preparedness survey to assess the readiness, such as knowledge and use of a central incident command system, of Native American health clinics in identifying and responding to man-made and natural disasters. The survey was administered in collaboration with federal and state Native American health agencies, and students were given the opportunity to conduct data collection. Survey items included the existence and components of an emergency operations plan (e.g., protocols/procedures, supplies, communications, staffing, and surge capacity), mandatory annual training of staff, components of biological/chemical terrorism preparedness (e.g., outbreak surveillance, sample retrieval and testing, isolation protocols in place, or prophylaxis/treatment supplies), and exercising the plan. Once the survey results were completed and collected, students created a data set, performed a descriptive analysis, and composed a final report to be discussed and disseminated to federal, state, and local Native American health organizations and agencies. A major finding of the survey was that clinics are far better prepared for a natural disaster than for a biological or chemical event. Federal and state officials use the survey to identify vulnerable clinics that need onsite technical assistance and to identify priority areas for additional funding, for example, supplying personal protective equipment such as N95 masks to the clinics.

In addition, students were able to join NAAEP staff in facilitating a 2-day workshop for clinic disaster preparedness plan development. Native American health clinic personnel from California were invited to attend to gain more knowledge, resources, and assistance in completing their clinic's emergency operations plan (EOP). Workshop topics included a history of public health disasters, risks and threats, risk assessment, the emergency Incident Command System, and testing the EOP. Students helped to facilitate discussion of technical, ethical, and social justice issues such as access to care/treatment while observing the problem-solving process for the Native American community.

A pre- and postevaluation assessed workshop productivity. Students used their knowledge in evaluation design to create a series of questions and statements based on the presented objectives. The workshop evaluation results were used to determine if the content of the workshop and the presenters effectively met the intended objectives. Any suggestions on adding or removing information from the presentations were used as references for updating future workshops. By participating in the workshop and evaluation, students were able to work with Native American health clinic personnel and NAAEP staff to aid in clinic disaster preparedness.

Red Cross

The student volunteers with the American Red Cross helped with its mission of providing care and comfort to those in need. Every year in San Diego and Imperial counties in California, disasters randomly strike hundreds of families. Homes and possessions are lost and lives are forever changed. Assistance during the wildfires and with Hurricane Katrina evacuees was part of student engagement. Volunteering for the Red Cross requires commitment and training, and students experience multiple interactions with victims when disaster strikes. Students evaluated the numbers of people assessed and the number of successful interventions and performed situational analyses.

Authentic Case-Based Tabletop Exercise

Students who are majoring in the public health program may be part of a 4-hour interactive biological agent tabletop exercise consisting of three modules, each portraying a response to a bioterrorism attack. The goals and objectives of the tabletop exercise require students to discuss the response and coordination issues that could arise during a bioagent emergency while in a nonintimidating atmosphere. The application of Knowles' (1984) theory is clearly demonstrated when students are given emergency management roles and asked to make decisions and respond to the storyline of an authentic scenario of smallpox, plague, or anthrax.

In Module I, Incubation, participants are confronted with the challenges of detecting and identifying a public health emergency. Module II, Initial Response, encompasses the period immediately following the detection of a suspected disease through the confirmation of the pathogen and the corresponding public health response from the appropriate agency. Module III, Continued Response and Recovery, focuses on issues raised by the public's reaction to what is happening with the emergency followed by discussion of midterm and long-term mitigation efforts.

Each module begins with a situation briefing. Participants then break out into designated groups to discuss probable actions and coordination efforts. Evaluation of the exercises consisted of questions posed at the end of each module to guide group discussion with staff from community emergency services and public health professionals. Interaction and the expression of opinions among groups is encouraged to promote communication, to better integrate response activities, and to reach consensus. As an evaluation, observers noted the ability of the students to articulate concepts and reflections on operational and policy-level aspects in a public health emergency. Emphasis is on developing the best possible response through problem identification, coordination, discussion of ethics and social justice, and the integration of capabilities, innovation, and resolution.

Evaluative Framework of Authentic Engagement

The research- and case-based experiences described above are considered an evaluative framework of authentic engagement. The key components of the framework are the sustained, interactive involvement of stakeholders from multiple segments affecting the Native American community, acknowledgement of community views and contributions, and decision making based on community values and aspirations (Knowledgeworks Foundation, 2005).

Evaluation was based on surveys and observation of workshop and tabletop environments and demonstrated student successes in all goal categories for purposeful civic learning (Howard, 2001). Table 8.1 presents a sample of student reflection categorized for select goal categories.

Future Directions

Devastation caused by bioterrorism acts or widespread disasters such as a potential pandemic influenza outbreak and the December 26, 2004, tsunami has shown how complicated and challenging it is for health professionals to help people during these health emergencies. There is a consensus among many health leaders to build a stronger public health workforce that can not only respond to large disasters requiring multidisciplinary and massive response on an immediate and long-term basis but can also detect potential threats before they become big problems.

Several experts in the field note that although the number of students who volunteer for social or public health programs remains constant, the link between these activities and a greater sense of civic engagement remains elusive for many students (Ehrlich, 2005; Rhoads, 2003; Saltmarsh, 2005). Working with the California State University Disaster Management Faculty Consortium, our goal is to build the number of community links and authentic case-based learning scenarios that compel faculty and students to

TABLE 8.1
Civic Learning Goals

Goal Categories for Purposeful Civic Learning	Student Reflections
Political	• "The experiences have given me resources to want to become more active in the community in organizations with [public health] programs or education." • Differences in peoples' reactions to illness could lead to panic, discrimination, even racial quarantine."
Leadership	• "How decisions are made and how leadership is shared depending upon the type and stage of an emergency was new to me." • "Working with public health professionals from around the world and watching them develop rapid-assessment strategies was amazing. It was here that I became aware that we each have a civic responsibility to each other and it worked."
Inter- and Intrapersonal	• "The combined disaster of Hurricane Katrina and the levees breaking was of historic proportions. The opportunity to work with the evacuees day to day and month to month was deeply moving." • "I have never had concerns about working with people of different class structures but understanding assess their needs[AU: WORD(S) MISSING?] was deeply moving." • "The woman told me how she felt that our work at the Red Cross saved her life and now she has a place to live and a job. From her point of view she felt more empowered."
Social Responsibility	• "I had never contemplated the complexities of implementing public health policies (like potential quarantines) in a sovereign nation such as Native American reservations; although collaborations are necessary, compassion and respect [are] just as vital." • I didn't realize until I joined the project (NAAEP) that few decisions or actions are implemented without many agencies and specialties represented, and that my opinion as a student and a future public health professional would be given equal weight and respect on the project." • The ability to contribute to the real process of public health action (like the development of emergency plans for Indian health clinics) is empowering and deeply rewarding."

contemplate the public health–national security connection and their immense responsibility and ethical obligations. Other institutions have similarly galvanized to improve quality of life via service-learning activities (Schneider, 1998). In this way we may instill the knowledge, skills, and values to unite the powerful and the powerless during circumstances of panic, suffering, and the spread of disease, while concurrently gaining traction to protect the civil liberties of global populations (Eckenwiler & Cooper, 2004).

Public health security is a concept that targets socially responsible leaders capable of addressing disasters that occur in unscripted circumstances and who will directly build capacity in an otherwise shrinking public health workforce (Marcus, Dorn, & Henderson, 2006). Our intention at San Diego State University is to remain as current on and relevant as possible to community needs while advancing the science, policy, and practices related to global emergency preparedness and response. The texture of the national discussion about civic engagement will mature as new generations of graduates are trained to recognize links between wellness, public health, and national security, and, importantly, to recognize opportunities to overcome obstacles to an investment in global health.

References

Eckenwiler, L., & Cooper, E. O. (2004). Paying the ultimate price: Emergency health professionals grapple with obligations during crises. *Quest, 7*(2), 22–25. Retrieved from http://www.odu.edu/ao/instadv/quest/payingprice.html

Ehrlich, T. (2005). Service-learning in undergraduate education: Where is it going? *Carnegie Perspectives.* Retrieved from http://www.carnegiefoundation.org/perspectives/service-learning-undergraduate-education-where-it-going

Grunder, P. (2004, February–March). *Homeland security and civic engagement: A report of the Second Annual Summit,* San Francisco. Retrieved from http://www.league.org/league/projects/homeland_security/files/Homeland%20Security%20White%20Paper.pdf

Howard, J. (2001). *Service-learning course design workbook.* Ann Arbor: Edward Ginsberg Center for Community Service, University of Michigan.

Knowledgeworks Foundation. (2005). *10 principles of authentic community education.* Retrieved from http://www.kwfdn.org/resource_library/_resources/10principles.pdf

Knowles, M. (n.d.). *Androgogy.* Retrieved from http://tip.psychology.org/knowles.html

Knowles, M. S. (1984). *The adult learner: A neglected species* (3rd ed.). Houston, TX: Gulf.

Marcus, L., Dorn, B., & Henderson, J. (2006). Meta-leadership and national emergency preparedness: A model to build government connectivity. *Biosecurity and Bioterrorism: Biodefense Strategy, Practice and Science*, 4(2), 128–134. Retrieved from http://www.hks.harvard.edu/sites/npli/PDFs/MetaleadershipBiosecurity.pdf

Rhoads, R. (2003). How civic engagement is reframing liberal education. *peerReview*, 5(3), 25–28. Retrieved from http://www.aacu.org/peerreview/pr-sp03/pr-sp03 research.pdf

Saltmarsh, J. (2005). Civic promise of service learning. *Liberal Education*, 91(2), 50–55. Retrieved from http://www.aacu.org/liberaleducation/le-sp05/le-sp05perspec tive2.cfm

Schneider, M. K. (1998). Models of good practice for service-learning programs: What can we learn from 1,000 faculty, 25,000 students, and 27 institutions involved in service? *AAHE Bulletin*, 50(10), 9–12. Retrieved from http://www.aahea .org/bulletins/articles/schneider.pdf

SECTION THREE

COMMUNITY PARTNERSHIPS

9

FROM PROJECTS TO PARTNERSHIP

Using Ethnography to Engage Students

Charles N. Darrah and Katie Plante Smith

Adelina sat on the park bench, juggling an interview instrument and tape recorder while she tried to make Alice comfortable. Adelina had just met Alice at Friday's neighborhood food distribution program and was trying to finish the interview before the woman returned home with her bag of food, a grandchild in tow. "How do you personally define healthy?" Adelina asked. "What are the characteristics of a healthy person?" Alice thought and exclaimed, "God! Do I really know somebody that's healthy?" Adelina was shocked, for while she expected that specific answers to the question would vary, the ability to formulate an answer seemed obvious. Now she sat a few blocks from the university that identifies itself as "powering Silicon Valley," facing a woman who could not identify a healthy friend or acquaintance.

Encounters such as Adelina's can be disconcerting, but they can also provide a foundation to build skills as a researcher, a deeper knowledge about a community, and opportunities to reflect on how to integrate academic experiences into one's career and life. Adelina was enrolled in an ethnographic research methods course designed to help students develop skills as researchers while generating data that can inform real-world decision making. The goal of this chapter is to describe the organization of the course and its outcomes from the perspective of the instructor and the student assistant who was enrolled in the class. The presentation is intended to be frank and prag-matic so the reader can judge the merits of the approach as well as its limita-tions. However, this story goes beyond a single course, for it traces how adopting a project-based model of instruction can ultimately develop into a partnership between the instructor and an organization.

An Ethnographic Approach to Civic Engagement

Community engagement has a lengthy history in the Department of Anthro-pology at San José State University, grounded largely in the realities of the region and the constraints on student learning. Located in Silicon Valley, a global center for entrepreneurship and technological innovation, the univer-sity is a magnet for people from around the world and forms a natural labora-tory on the rearrangement of family, community, technology, and the course of life. An important implication is that anthropologists, who are typically enamored of exotic places, can find themselves compelled to study the local and familiar. Furthermore, university classrooms are filled with students whose lives and communities reflect the realities of migration. They seek to use anthropology not simply to understand other societies but to understand the one they're in and their place in it. The department has traditionally addressed student and community needs through a model of apprenticeship in which students work closely with faculty on research projects designed to address regional needs.

Ethnographic Methods (ANTH 149), the department's cultural anthro-pology research methods course, has been taught regularly by Darrah since 1991. The course addresses the familiar topics of similar courses, such as problem formulation, design, sampling, data collection methods, analysis, and presentation of findings. The heart of the class is teaching students to develop skills in participant observation and note taking, and to develop semistructured (open-ended) interview instruments to use to conduct inter-views, structured observation, and qualitative (textual) analysis (see Appen-dix A for the course reading list). The pedagogical strategy involves learning about a method from lecture and readings, practicing and discussing it in class, and then applying it in the real world. Students are subsequently asked to reflect in writing about each experience and then share their writings with each other.

Rather than completing disconnected assignments or individual projects, the class is organized into a single research team that undertakes a project for a partner. Partners have included the Santa Clara County Office of Education, Junior Achievement, Working Partnerships/Massachusetts Institute of Technology, the Tech Museum of Innovation, Joint Venture/Smart Valley, and the Institute for the Future. A representative of the partner organization visits the class and explains the organization's problem or question and the actions it hopes to take. The students query the partner and then brainstorm research questions in groups of four to five students. Gradually, they agree on a major research question and several subordinate ones and then develop questions for the instrument the team will use in interviewing. Darrah takes the results of the brainstorming, compiles an often lengthy list of possible questions, and then distributes it to the students at the next meeting. The groups critique and refine the questions, and the instructor offers advice on how to eliminate questions that inadvertently stifle an interview (e.g., questions requiring yes or no answers). He then compiles the actual instrument to be used based on the questions the students generated and his own experiences as a fieldworker. The goal is to create an instrument that will have the highest probability of successfully eliciting the perspectives of the interviewees, thereby resulting in a positive experience for the students.

Although students may be more or less interested in the course project, they understand that being trained in the appropriate use of research methods is the goal of the course; one's personal interest in the topic is ultimately irrelevant, and the benefits of the group project are immense. First, it creates a focus and sense of mission that is often lacking in classes. Second, depending on the partner and the topic, it permits students to link training in methods with addressing practical problems and human needs. Third, it creates a collection of data that is comparable and more extensive than what any single student could generate. This allows students to place what they have learned from one interviewee in a much larger context; certainty is challenged and humility is nurtured.

As one student put it,

> After my assignments were turned in and graded I often felt dissatisfied knowing that no further attention would be paid to my hard work. The importance of our assignments in ANTH 149 went way beyond a grade; the conclusions we made based upon our research had the potential to affect hundreds of people and our community. Even though, as a student,

this project created more pressure than any of my other class work, it also caused me to become much more deeply dedicated, concerned, and interested.

Project Number 1: Five Wounds/Brookwood Terrace Neighborhood

This project emerged when the Health Trust became the Department of Anthropology's community partner in Project SHINE (Students Helping in the Naturalization of Elders), a national service-learning program. The department and the Health Trust agreed to create a research-based approach to civic engagement focusing on issues of health. Other university departments were independently working with the Health Trust to create ways to use the talents of university students to improve regional responsiveness to health issues and to provide educational experiences that increased the likelihood that students would choose careers involving public service. The Five Wounds/Brookwood Terrace neighborhood, adjacent to the university, has historically been one of the city of San José's poorest. The population includes a substantial and established Portuguese community, as well as many recent immigrants from Latin America and Southeast Asia. A major local employer had shut down, and a nearby hospital was in the process of doing so.

Following classroom visits by a repesentative from the Health Trust and San José's Strong Neighborhoods Initiative, the class began developing the questions for the interviews. Each student was to conduct two interviews using different instruments. The first interview was designed to capture data about the interviewee's everyday life to be analyzed as context for health and medical decisions. The second interview addressed specific health-related behaviors. Meanwhile, the students began their participant-observation exercise to better understand life in the neighborhood. Some took self-organized tours, while others focused on particular shops or other locations. From the start, students learned surprising lessons. Some women said they felt a raw sexism when they entered social settings occupied exclusively by males; other women in class explained the tacit rules for such encounters. An African American male announced that he felt uncomfortable in a predominantly Mexican American neighborhood that was very different from where he had grown up. Several students later confided that it had never occurred to them that members of ethnic minorities might feel uncomfortable in non-White neighborhoods. A student who had grown up in the neighborhood and then left doubted that he could undertake the emotional journey back via participant observation. When he did, he found himself informally interviewing someone who had dated one of his relatives.

According to one of the students,

> A classmate and I decided to tour the neighborhood for our participant observation assignment on a Saturday morning. As we walked, we were discussing things we saw as well as taking notes. I felt as if we were definitely sticking out, and people did give us odd looks. It was obvious that I was outside of my comfort zone because I felt awkward and embarrassed. I was concerned that people would not want me there snooping around. This made it difficult for me to open up and talk with the people we came across as we walked.

San José's Strong Neighborhoods Initiative staff identified potential interviewees. Many on the list turned out to be uninterested, and the contact information for others was outdated. Students independently found interviewees by walking and bicycling through the neighborhood, and others worked through a grassroots food distribution program. The process was time consuming and ambiguous, but it provided access to people whose voices would otherwise never be included.

While the participant observation and scheduling of interviews was proceeding, the class continued developing the interview instruments. They practiced interviewing in class, learning how to simultaneously follow the instrument, maintain eye contact with the interviewee, and make sure their recorder was working. Above all, they struggled to really listen to what the person sitting across from them was telling them so they could probe to provide more details and follow up important points that were raised.

As one student described it:

> Many of the interview questions were personal and interviewees felt comfortable enough to open up to the students. For me, this created an instant connection between myself and the interviewee. This connection seemed to happen with the majority of the students. As we shared stories and experiences in class, we also shared our concerns for the well-being of these individuals. Interviewees became more than a component of a research project; they became humans we could relate to.

Attendance in class remained high, and each session was an opportunity for the research team to touch base. Each class began with time for students to present any difficulties or successes. Sometimes these presentations were very mechanical and brief. Other times they were quite elaborate, troublesome, or complex, and could take half the period. Often the questions were new for the instructor.

For example, this student said,

> The daily discussions were the key to keeping my confidence high. On a few occasions, I did doubt my ability to be successful with this project. But, after hearing that other students were having difficulties, and these difficulties could be resolved, I always felt much better about my own progress. Hearing other students talk about some of the successes they had had was also very motivational to me.

As an interview was completed, the interviewer transcribed it and inserted pseudonyms. Transcribing was tedious, if not painful, but it has been a powerful component of the course. It teaches students that they do not really hear people accurately; they write down what they think the person was saying, as illustrated by the following:

> Transcribing was extremely tedious and, by far, the most difficult and time-consuming part of the project. It was also, however, the most eye opening. When I transcribed my interviews, I was able to catch many particularly important statements that I overlooked during the initial interview. It gave me an opportunity to better absorb what was said, and really pick out issues that seemed most important to her [the interviewee].

The Health Trust provided multiple copies of each interview, and the students each read 10 interviews in class and analyzed them following guidelines provided by the instructor. The goal of analysis was to discover the recurring themes that cut across interviews and the domains in which people organized their thinking. The important findings are summarized as follows:

- Many interviewees mentioned the concept of a healthy lifestyle that involved diet and exercise but was threatened by stress. Health education that addresses their particular risk factors and cultural heritage might be valuable, yet the importance of adopting a healthy lifestyle was already widely accepted.

- Few residents acknowledged they had achieved a healthy lifestyle. Factors that prevented people from practicing what they acknowledge to be important were diverse. Chronic diseases may take decades to develop, and concern about them clearly took a back seat to the immediate, pressing problems of earning a living and, in some cases, basic survival. Health simply paled compared to the immediacy of finding work in an unstable economy and of developing skills for the future. An implication was that interventions should probably focus resources on removing obstacles to what residents already believe they should do as well as improving their awareness of desirable behaviors.
- It is, however, unwarranted to conclude that health issues are irrelevant to the residents. Many lives were constrained by coping with a medical condition, either an individual's own or someone else's. In fact, many interviews included a description of a medical issue the interviewee's life revolved around. Our research team noted it was often difficult to determine if (a) people were relatively poor and facing an uncertain financial future because of poor health or (b) because of their poor health they had become economically poorer. Regardless, coping with poor health may contribute in significant ways to preventing many residents from overcoming their uncertain economic futures.
- Economic security, family solidarity, and cultural identity were intertwined in the lives of many residents. Faith in education to provide a more secure future was widespread and its importance cut across jobs, family, and cultural identity. Indeed, education was the broadly acceptable means for achieving personal and community improvement. The relative emphasis on job skills, economic uncertainty, family, and cultural identity suggested that any program to support healthy lifestyles could be targeted as a means to help achieve the goals that residents already articulate as important. The importance of education suggests the value of a single, comprehensive information center designed to address resident needs, including health education and job training.

Students met in groups and discussed the specific lessons they wanted to communicate to the Health Trust. These were written on the blackboard and then consolidated as the subjects of seven posters the class would prepare and display at a meeting in the community. One group per poster was formed, and students spent the remainder of the session designing the poster and delegating duties. At the final class session students arrived with graphics and snippets of text to affix to the freestanding poster boards that had been provided. A few days later, the posters were displayed at the community showcase and reception.

A student had this to say:

> To me, the showcase event was a terrific idea. I felt so connected to the project that I wanted everyone to know about what we found and how necessary it was to act on these findings. Also, students rarely have the opportunity to take pride in their work and present it in a forum such as this.

During the final examination period, students discussed the skills they had developed, with the instructor acting as blackboard scribe. This step is crucial, for students may have skills and yet not think of themselves as skilled. Initially the call for skills was greeted by awkward silence, but gradually the ideas started pouring out and soon the board was covered. As the session progressed, students became aware that they had done things that required skills they had never deemed worthy of mentioning. The power of the assignment is twofold: The capacity of the group to identify skills far exceeds that of any individual, and the skills are publicly and collectively validated. Skills mentioned included large, complex ones such as interviewing, which students then broke down into smaller components (e.g., developing research and instrument questions, asking questions, self-presentation, managing logistics, and probing). Participant observation and structured observation were similarly noted and then decomposed into constituents. Discussion became quite sophisticated, as students talked about the importance of seeing what is there and describing it and seeing what could be but is not there. Gradually, students began to mention teamwork, managing time under pressure, maintaining humor and flexibility under ambiguous conditions, and moving beyond their comfort zone. Several students commented that they had never thought they could handle such challenges and were thrilled they had done so.

By most accounts, the project was a success. Although each stakeholder would undoubtedly emphasize different facets of it, the project likely succeeded academically for the following reasons.

First, the team dynamics were conducive to achieving the project goals. The project was complex, and new challenges emerged almost daily. Not everything went smoothly, but the Health Trust partner and instructor respected each other and talked frequently to prevent problems from escalating. More importantly, interests were aligned. The Health Trust was working with the university in a way that is consistent with its mission to improve health outcomes. The basic goal of supporting the university because it is a local producer of talent who will stay in the area and address community needs was a familiar one. It allowed Darrah to teach methods in a context where students felt they were acting constructively in the world. The project thus rested on a mutually beneficial professional relationship in which interests were aligned. No one was asked to do anything against his or her individual interests or those of the organization. They were able to see the relationship between research and action. But these outcomes, of course, only make sense within the sets of the individual values of the partners who drove the project and saw its present and future merits.

Second, because Darrah has long taught the class, he is comfortable with the ambiguity and disorder that can surround such projects. The course is structured so that lectures and readings are loaded early in the term, which leaves more slack time at the end to buffer the inevitable crises. The class is not a tightly scripted one, but it relies on trusting that students will learn from being placed in new situations, as long as they are well prepared, know their concerns will be addressed, and they will not be asked to pay a price in grade if someone else fails to deliver on a promise.

> From a student stand point, the most significant factor in the success of this project was the fact that the professor was honest and we all had complete trust in him. Constant readjustments and time constraints were manageable because it was clear that he had our best interest in mind. We felt comfortable enough to open up, ask questions, and ask for help, which made our work significantly less complicated.

Third, Darrah is a full professor who can devote considerable time to the course without worrying about its impact on tenure or promotion. It is not clear that junior faculty would feel similarly protected or that they could invest time in the course instead of preparing publications.

Fourth, the project is consistent with core anthropological assumptions and values. It is trying to capture insider perspectives, which are generally not typically included in discussions. It looks from the bottom up and challenges received views. Students read an anthropologist's book describing her field-work, so they understand the uncertainty and anxiety that always surrounds fieldwork. They were able to contextualize their own feelings in the grander enterprise of anthropology since the very hassles that frustrated them were evidence that they too, were becoming anthropologists. Especially significant here was the possibility of action and the gradually increasing awareness that this research was indeed real and might be linked to tangible outcomes in the community. The effect was galvanizing as students progressed from sim-ply taking another class through conducting research for the Health Trust to working in and for the community.

> Because this project was so different, students tended to care more about this assignment than those from any other class. This made it more likely for frustration to arise when things went wrong. We were more dedicated to this project and wanted defined outcomes because of the new attach-ments we made to the people and community.

Of course not everything worked, and like all courses this one is a work in progress. A constant concern is the logistical one of finding the interview-ees and scheduling the interviews. In fact, this is the main requirement of partners: Either the nature of the sample is irrelevant so students can easily find interviewees, or the partner must provide access to interviewees. In this case, the logistics of finding interviewees in the neighborhood were formida-ble, and it was the capacity of the Health Trust to deliver them that was appealing. Still, the project was within one day of being cancelled by Darrah when the Strong Neighborhoods Initiative staff delivered the list of names. A list promised by a source in the Health Trust failed to materialize.

The 16-week semester creates tension between accomplishing the curric-ular goals of the course and accommodating the realities of real-world re-search. It changes the timing of the curriculum because students must be moved quickly into the field if the unforeseen crises are to be resolved early so students can move through transcription and analysis. A result is that top-ics such as sampling and research design are covered midsemester while stu-dents are completing the transcriptions. Analysis is invariably compressed, as is ethnographic writing and learning to present data.

> For students, having extra leeway with time helped. This was especially true because we had to work around the interviewee's schedules, as well as

wait for them to return our calls or e-mails. In a few instances, students waited and waited only to find themselves with very little time to do the assignments and no prospective interviewees.

Although intentions were good, the neighborhood became swamped with students from several classes, all trying to help. The result was that some people were contacted repeatedly. A related issue was the possibility of action. We were conducting the research for the Health Trust, but its ability to take action in the neighborhood was ambiguous. While the Health Trust was facilitating the university endeavor, it was unclear if its goal was to develop a program to help this neighborhood or develop a model that could be used regionally. In effect, the Health Trust could only change the discourse about the neighborhood and increase the probability of certain actions. The result was raised expectations and limited capacity to deliver anything except more research.

> Because of this, some students could have been led to feel as if all of their efforts and research were not going to be used, as if the information we gathered from our work was insignificant. This is especially true because we all desperately wanted to see some good come out of our work. We are now permanently connected to these people and we do not want to let them down.

A further complication is that the Health Trust benefited not just from the student-collected data but from the possibility of analysis and interpretation by Darrah who effectively became a professional consultant, yet report writing could not be completed until after the semester if it competed with other commitments.

Project Number 2: The Health Trust Volunteers

Following the mixed success of the Five Wounds/Brookwood Terrace project and discussion of the lessons learned, the Health Trust and Darrah decided to undertake a second project, one linked even more directly to implementation. The organization had taken satisfaction surveys of its volunteers, and while the results were useful they were limited in a way very familiar to ethnographers. They provided answers to a set of predetermined questions, but they did not necessarily capture the questions and concerns that were most

salient to the volunteers. The result was that while the answers were comparable and amenable to statistical analysis, they neither suggested specific recommendations for how to best organize volunteers in the Health Trust
programs nor how volunteering could best be implemented in the organization's strategic planning.

Potential interviewees were identified by the Health Trust's program
staff and by Elizabeth Sills, director of Community Partnerships. The goal
of sampling was to identify people who would be reflective about their experiences as volunteers and who would be willing to share them with the inter-
viewers. In effect, interviews were conducted with a sample of "successful"
volunteers who were generally satisfied and who had a track record of participation in one or more Health Trust programs. The focus on successful volunteers allows the Health Trust to think about the strategic implications of
the experiences of a population that supports its programs. Second, such volunteers constitute a resource the Health Trust may wish to maintain and
develop. Specifically, if volunteer labor is indeed valuable, then attrition becomes an important issue. Successful volunteers have already passed a thresh-
old of commitment, and retaining (and retraining) them may be a necessary
complement to attracting new volunteers.

The interview protocol was constructed to address topics such as how
volunteering fit into the interviewee's life, the skills and knowledge the interviewee used in volunteering, how the experience of volunteering affected him
or her, and how the interviewee envisioned the Health Trust in optimistic
and pessimistic scenarios. The class again was organized as a single research
team, except that 23 volunteers from five different programs were each interviewed twice using different instruments. The major findings can be grouped
into four clusters.

- The logistics of volunteering were significant to volunteers. Simplicity
  of tasks was valued, as were clear directions, since both allowed volunteers to contribute immediately. Flexibility in who could participate
  in programs was valued as was flexibility in how someone can volunteer. Volunteers were generally very busy, and flexibility allowed them
  to help under conditions they controlled.
- Volunteering was a moral act, and so the Health Trust too was swept
  into a moral calculus. From the perspective of most volunteers, perceived program inefficiencies were personally annoying and virtually

immoral, for they were interpreted as poor use of scarce resources that should be directed at unmet client needs.

- The staff members of a program were important insofar as they got things done but also as models for the good and compassionate community member. Recognition or acknowledgment was expected as part of basic civility, but ways of doing so that appeared to be costly were criticized. Again, such recognition represented resources that from the perspective of most volunteers could and should be directed at meeting client needs.

- Individuals thought of themselves as volunteering for the clients through the Health Trust but not as volunteers of the organization. Volunteering was a way to transcend or go beyond everyday life through connecting with other like-minded people, especially with clients. Individuals volunteered for clients through the vehicle of the Health Trust. A result was the creation of a community that people joined and whose members expressed values that might otherwise be lacking in their experiences. The Health Trust was less distinctly identifiable than its programs, and it might not have been sufficiently well known in the region. Volunteers often said they did not understand what it was or what it did, and they identified themselves as volunteers of specific programs and not the Health Trust.

- Finally, volunteering was seen and experienced as a means to achieve personal growth, which in turn was facilitated through education. Accordingly, the volunteer experience was an educational one, and it could be a focus of further education.

The Health Trust is currently incorporating the report into its strategic planning process and exploring its implications for program planning, training and communication, and interacting with other organizations. The project was a clear success, and students had the opportunity to see their efforts translated directly into action. Still, the project was arguably less compelling because the students were working on behalf of the Health Trust and not directly for community members in need.

From Project to Partnership

The two projects described in this chapter mark a gradual shift from a project-based to a partnership-based model of curriculum. The shift is subtle, but its consequences are nonetheless very real. Projects are bounded in time and scope of work. Regarding time, the project activities are bounded by the familiar constraints of the semester or quarter and the needs of the owner of the project. Less obviously, the relationship between instructor and owner terminates when the project is completed and its results are delivered. Additional projects may be conceptualized, but each must be negotiated. From the perspective of a course instructor, projects are comparable, and the one that best meets pedagogical goals may be selected. This allows projects to be adjusted as frequently as a course is offered, and it allows instructors to avoid falling into the rut of discovering the same thing repeatedly. It also helps minimize the impact on organizational owners since alternative organizations can be approached, and besides, projects have become routinized so they can be easily supported by an organization with minimal impact on its time. There are, however, significant drawbacks. As projects become formulaic they may lose the edginess that appeals to students. Having completed the same or a similar project before, new findings may not be especially valuable and it may be difficult to connect them to organizational policies or practices. Of course, insofar as projects are not formulaic, they must be conceptualized and negotiated anew whenever the course is offered.

A partnership-based approach solves some of these dilemmas while creating others. It is not necessarily easier, but it clearly is different. A partnership entails an ongoing relationship that reduces the need to sell or explain the very idea of a project to potential owners. It becomes based on shared assumptions and expectations about the needs of the partner, further reducing the transaction costs of creating new projects. A robust partnership also allows the community partner to have access to skills and knowledge it might otherwise lack, thereby augmenting its own capabilities. Furthermore, it can increase the probability that a specific project can be directly linked to organizational goals and acted upon.

Despite its advantages, the partnership-based approach also creates work of a different sort for both partners. Organizational or community partners need to better understand the rhythms and incentives university instructors operate under as well as their own needs for data that could be met through a project. Doing so can transform the way they think about the mission of their own organization, its policies, and even daily practices. Likewise, for a partnership to endure and thrive, instructors cannot simply view their partners as providers of learning experiences for students, much less engage in projects in which the benefits flow one way. Instructors must come to understand that the constraints on organizations are real and specific, and that hosting projects is not without costs, such as in staff time. Partnerships as those described here thus require the work of the partner to be taken seriously, and for each partner to be deeply involved in the fate of the other. Such sensitivity takes time and effort, but it also models the very behavior and skills that will serve our students well.

A partnership-based approach in effect still includes projects, but those projects become embedded in longer-term relationships that are themselves multistranded. One strand is built of formal or informal agreements between the organization and the instructor, and it exists apart from personal relationships. The other strands are woven from the ties between the faculty member and specific individuals in the partner organization. These ties are personal and professional, and they require attention and maintenance. Although, in general, partnerships work best when each partners' self-interests are addressed, sometimes partners are asked to do something that meets the other's needs with little immediate gain in return. Partnerships are based on such reciprocity and the faith that things will even out in the long term. If they do not, then the partnership is likely doomed.

Finally, a partnership approach also has implications for how instructors view and interact with students. While the model can be one of a research team, the instructor clearly must be in charge of it: The students and organizational partner reasonably expect it. However, being in charge is different from simply being the professor as expert. Expertise is assumed, as is experience and a willingness to understand the very real stress of at least some students, regardless of how worthy the project. The solution suggested here involves creating mutual expectations as accountable professionals who exhibit the very behaviors that students will need in their careers. The partnership-based approach is one way to model professionalism a little sooner than students may have anticipated.

Appendix A

Course Reading List

Agar, M. (1996). *The professional stranger* (2nd ed.). New York: Academic Press.

Bernard, H. R. (2002). *Research methods in anthropology: Qualitative and quantitative approaches* (3rd ed.). Walnut Creek, CA: AltaMira Press.

Darrah, C. N., English-Lueck, J. A., & Freeman, J. M. (2003). Shock-absorbing and sense-making: American families and a public anthropology. *Anthropology News, 44*(2), 12.

Fetterman, D. M. (1997). *Ethnography: Step-by-step*. Thousand Oaks, CA: Sage.

Hammersley, M., & Atkinson, P. (1983). *Ethnography: Principles in practice*. New York: Tavistock.

LeCompte, M., & Schensul, J. J. (1999). *Designing and conducting ethnographic research*. Walnut Creek, CA: AltaMira Press.

Perry, R. J. (2003). *Five key concepts in anthropological thinking*. Upper Saddle River, NJ: Prentice Hall/Pearson.

Schensul, S. L., Schensul, J. J., & LeCompte, M. (1999). *Essential ethnographic methods: Observations, interviews, and questionnaires*. Walnut Creek, CA: AltaMira Press.

Spradley, J. P. (1979). *The ethnographic interview*. San Francisco: Holt, Rinehart and Winston.

Spradley, J. P. (1980). *Participant observation*. San Francisco: Holt, Rinehart and Winston.

10

THE ACCIDENTAL
SERVICE LEARNER

The Role of Graduate Education in
Community Service Learning

Jonathan Sills

Cardiovascular disease (CVD) includes medical conditions that affect the heart as well as the blood vessels (Bankhead et al., 2003; Cooper et al., 2000; Raza, Babb, & Movahed, 2004). The most common cardiovascular medical disorder is coronary heart disease, which irrespective of race, ethnicity, and gender is the leading cause of death in the United States (Kochanek, Murphy, Anderson, & Scott, 2004). Provided that health promotion and prevention strategies are implemented on an individual level, risk factors associated with CVD are modifiable (Bankhead et al.; Raza et al.). In an effort to increase screening opportunities and positive health behaviors among individuals who experience significant barriers to medical services, public screening events have been underwritten by various community health agencies (Bankhead et al.).

In the summer of 2003 a community-university collaborative was formed with stakeholders from the Health Trust, a nonprofit hospital conversion foundation; San José State University (SJSU); and the AmeriCorps Bridging Borders project to work toward the goal of reducing health disparities in Santa Clara County, California. The centerpiece of the effort was the Open-Air Health Fair (OAHF). As a doctoral student in clinical psychology at Pacific Graduate School of Psychology at Palo Alto University, I became interested in how interdisciplinary teams function to address the emerging health needs of diverse patient populations, and I joined the collaborative effort. My experience clearly demonstrated the value that a service-learning experience can bring to graduate studies.

Serving the Community

The OAHF was held at the San José Flea Market, which attracts roughly 80,000 visitors a week and serves as a major retail center for Latino and Asian immigrants residing in Santa Clara County. On the day of the event, 500 residents of Santa Clara County were provided with comprehensive CVD risk factor screening, education, and referral. Participants entered a covered pavilion the size of a football field where they were greeted by student health ambassadors who spoke Spanish, Vietnamese, Chinese, Tagalog, and English. While participants were waiting to see a health care professional, the students used a consent form and survey instrument (see Appendix A and Appendix B) as a framework to discuss and record participants' health beliefs, behaviors, and hopes (Poss, 2001; Sheeran, Conner, & Norman, 2001; Strecher, Champion, & Rosenstock, 1997; Sutton, 2002, Weinstein, 1993).

Upon completion of initial survey instruments, participants were escorted to one of six identical areas where clinical services were provided. Nursing students met participants in each area and administered clinical services. Participants were given the opportunity to have their blood pressure checked, their body mass index (BMI) quantified, and their blood drawn so that information related to cholesterol levels could be calculated. Participant demographic information, behavioral risk factors, and clinical results were analyzed, and a personal CVD-related risk factor profile was generated. Health science students provided participants with basic behavioral health education. *Promotores*, community health workers, provided participants with additional health information and aided in referral to community clinics when subsequent health services were required.

The demographics of the clients being served provided students and faculty a unique opportunity to work with segments of the population most at risk. The vast majority of participants served were immigrants with an average of 11 years of residency in the United States. Roughly 50% indicated that they use local emergency room services as their usual place for medical care, and 25% indicated that they do not have any particular place they go for medical care; 35% of participants reported having left school by eighth grade, and 8% reported they had no formal education (Sills, 2008).

When comparing participant demographic characteristics to the broader California population—as captured by the California Health Interview Survey—observed differences suggest that OAHF participants were less educated, were recent immigrants, and included a greater number of individuals who use emergency room services for their primary source of medical care (Sills, 2008; UCLA Center for Health Policy Research, 2003).

Analysis of clinical CVD risk factors showed that over 57% of participants had total cholesterol scores at dangerously high levels. BMI scores indicated that roughly 49% of participants were overweight, and 30% of participants were obese at the time of screening. Systolic blood pressure scores showed that 40% were prehypertensive, and 10% showed signs of hypertension. Diastolic blood pressure scores showed that 33% of participants were prehypertensive, and 10% showed signs of hypertension (Sills, 2008).

Stakeholder Perspectives

As the convener and primary financial supporter of the event, the Health Trust has successfully demonstrated that a community-university collaborative can effectively deliver comprehensive CVD risk factor screening in a nontraditional environment to traditionally underserved residents. Complementing the Heath Trust's goals, SJSU faculty took part in the OAHF to provide a service-learning opportunity for over 250 students. SJSU nursing, health science, and management information systems (MIS) faculty modified their traditional classroom content to include curriculum and field assignments that culminated in a service experience. The variety of disciplines represented each had specific orientations, backgrounds, and teaching objectives.

SJSU nursing faculty supported service learning by having their students take part in the provision of supervised medical procedures, which included blood pressure checks, quantification of participants' BMI, and blood draws that allowed for rapid analysis of cholesterol levels. Students were challenged to apply their emerging clinical skills in a dynamic environment while facing participants' language barriers and limited health literacy. This environment required flexibility in the delivery of clinical services and sharpened the student's ability to communicate clinical health information to participants, family members, translators, and other health professionals (Sills, 2008).

SJSU health science faculty facilitated learning by having students take part in the delivery of wellness messages at the health fair. To help participants reduce their risk of developing CVD, student teams were encouraged to create and deliver interactive educational activities. An important component of the assignment was to shape accessible health messages for a diverse immigrant population. The health science faculty organized the students into working teams that were reflective of the culturally diverse population expected to attend the OAHF.

SJSU MIS faculty encouraged students to develop a computer application that could support data collection in a manner that was mobile, reliable, secure, and user friendly. Since participants would be accessing different services at the health fair, a critical component of the computer application was that it protect participant privacy while maintaining the necessary accuracy to record data from multiple sources in a centralized system. Using a tablet PC, MIS students were effective in meeting these requirements and demonstrated that a portable electronic medical record management system could be implemented in a dynamic community environment (Sills, 2008).

As a research student, my primary role in the project involved evaluation. To gather the relevant data required to complete an evaluation, I worked with stakeholders in OAHF planning meetings and developed interview instruments used by students to survey participants multiple times during the health fair (see Appendix A and Appendix B). Because participants included representatives from a wide variety of ethnic groups, survey instruments needed to be provided in a number of languages including Spanish, Vietnamese, Chinese, Tagalog, and English. Moreover, based on the number of participants who were expected to take part in the OAHF, the variety of clinical services being offered, and the environment where the services were to be delivered, gathering participant data was expected to pose significant logistical challenges, including language and cultural barriers that could only be met with the support of students familiar with the languages and cultures (Sills, 2008). The students' support was integral to the successful gathering of participant consent, baseline information, and follow-up data collection (see Appendix A and Appendix B).

Student members of the AmeriCorps Bridging Borders program working alongside the Health Trust's promotores team provided continuity of care as well as help in facilitating successful data gathering. Promotores are known as guides to health care systems in traditionally underserved communities (Dower, Knox, Lindler, & O'Neil, 2006a; Dower, Knox, Lindler, & O'Neil, 2006b; Ro, Treadwell, & Northridge, 2004). They work in a variety of settings, such as clinics, hospitals, community-based organizations, faith-based organizations, and public health departments (Dower et al., 2006a, 2006b; Ro et al.). Consistent with the tradition of promotores, this group acted as cultural health ambassadors, advocates, and mediators between participants and clinical health service providers throughout the screening process. AmeriCorps members and promotores conducted intake interviews to record participant's demographic information and behavioral risk factors (Centers for Disease Control and Prevention, 2004). They provided culturally accessible health information, informal counseling, and referrals to local community health clinics.

A Shared Learning Environment

The OAHF provided a unique venue for students, faculty, and community partners to understand the changing demographics of the community, identify health disparities among community residents, and develop new approaches to the delivery of health services. The OAHF expanded the traditional role of the student, and in doing so increased the community's access to culturally competent health care services.

The context for learning extended beyond the students, supporting health care providers in gaining a better understanding of the needs of traditionally underserved residents. Traditional roles of expert and recipient were dismissed as all stakeholders—students, promotores, community members, and health care providers—contributed to a shared learning environment. The pursuit of integrated services among multiple stakeholders contributed to enhanced communication among a group of providers working more effectively as individuals and as a part of a team to provide health care to an underserved community.

The Health Trust's director of community health promotion reflected on the experience:

> The Open Air Health Fair provides a place for students and *Promotores* to
> gain a better understanding of their identity as health professionals while

volunteering in the community. As they become more experienced in delivering health information the need for additional education and reflection becomes a critical part of the process.

The reflection has become as important to our *Promotores* as it is for the students that are participating in a service learning experience. In that sense, the role of the students has been transformative in the way that we approach our *Promotores* work and the development of community leaders and peer educators.

The *Promotores* became better in their role as a result of gaining confidence by working in a setting outside their neighborhood that they initially found challenging and intimidating. Everyone involved seems to be changed as a result of participating in this experience. The Health care providers have shared with us the learning that they have experienced as a result of working alongside the *Promotores* and the students (Sills, 2008).

The reciprocal nature of learning in this unique collaboration elevated the level of engagement of all stakeholders. The impact of service learning extended beyond the targeted student population and helped shape the perspective of individual health care providers as well as strengthen emerging community health systems.

Lessons Learned

I have integrated the value of this experience by actively engaging in dialogue with fellow stakeholders, students, and my faculty advisor. During these discussions, I often reflect on my role in the OAHF collaborative and the development and evaluation of a CVD risk factor prevention program targeting an underserved immigrant population. Among my initial goals in participating in the project were to gather data for my dissertation and evaluate the feasibility of providing screening services in a community setting. I anticipated my role in the collaborative would provide me with the opportunity to directly apply what I had learned in the classroom. I was eager to conduct data collection and present findings related to participants' CVD risk factors, health beliefs, and behaviors. In addition, by taking part in the OAHF collaborative, I had the opportunity to broaden my understanding of how health care providers work across disciplines.

My first impression of the various stakeholders led me to believe that while we would be working together, our objectives were different. During initial discussions with the team of stakeholders, it became clear that a variety of factors contributed to the reason stakeholders wanted to participate in the OAHF. For the community partners, the event is an opportunity to advance their organizational mission. For the faculty, it is an opportunity to provide their students with a service-learning experience that solidifies the lessons learned in the classroom. What I was not aware of until completing the project was that my own learning would be informed by the experience of working alongside other professionals, community members, students, and by providing service to the community.

Through my participation at the OAHF I was able to expand my understanding on how the delivery of health care services can be modified to better meet the needs of a community. As a result of my service-learning experience, I have gained greater insight on how barriers to access, language, and patient preferences contribute to disparities in the delivery of health care services (Singh & Deedwania, 2006). Service-learning experiences strengthen the understanding that health care providers, by meeting participants in their own community, must at times think beyond disciplines and their traditional clinical roles to adequately serve clients' needs (Simpson, Dixon, & Bolli, 2004). Cultural awareness, knowledge, respect, recognition, and appreciation of differences allow greater interdisciplinary functioning of the team. My experiences related to the OAHF allowed me to better integrate classroom lessons with my clinical practice while enhancing my confidence in my ability to work effectively in service to the community.

Conclusion

Years later the community has rallied to keep the OAHF in place, as it has come to be a stable and regular source of care for many in the community. The alternatives are more expensive and require months of waiting prior to receiving an appointment. The data that was collected for my dissertation has helped to inform the discussion regarding health disparities as well as bring additional attention to the nature of health services that are currently available to Santa Clara County residents (Hospital Counsel of Northern and Central California, 2007).

The OAHF continues to be a dynamic learning environment, allowing diverse stakeholders to explore the problems of and the potential solutions for the emerging health needs of community residents. The OAHF has provided a vehicle for hundreds of students to contribute to the delivery of care for underserved populations, and I am confident many have continued their pursuit beyond their classroom experience as I have.

References

Bankhead, C. R., Brett, J., Bukach, C., Webster, P., Stewart-Brown, S., Munafo, M., et al. (2003). The impact of screening on future health-promoting behaviors and health beliefs: A systematic review. *Health Technology Assessment, 7*(42), 1–92.

California Health Interview Survey. (2001). *Adult Public Use File.* Los Angeles, CA: UCLA Center for Health Policy Research.

Centers for Disease Control and Prevention. (2004). *Behavioral risk factor surveillance system survey questionnaire.* Atlanta: Author.

Cooper, R., Cutler, J., Desvigne-Nickens, P., Fortmann, S. P., Friedman, L., Havlik, R., et al. (2000). Trends and disparities in coronary heart disease, stroke, and other cardiovascular diseases in the United States: Findings of the national conference on cardiovascular disease prevention. *Circulation, 102*(25), 3137–3147.

Dower, C., Knox, M., Lindler, V., & O'Neil, E. (2006a). *Advancing community health worker practice and utilization: Focusing on financing.* San Francisco: National Fund for Medical Education.

Dower, C., Knox, M., Lindler, V., & O'Neil, E. (2006b). *Funding community health worker programs and service in Minnesota: Looking to the future.* San Francisco: National Fund for Medical Education.

Hospital Counsel of Northern and Central California. (2007). *2007 Santa Clara County Community Health Assessment.* Retrieved November 29, 2009, from http://www.hospitalcouncil.net/cgi-bin/default.asp?AID=197

Kochanek, K. D., Murphy, S. L., Anderson, R. N., & Scott, C. (2004). Deaths: Final data for 2002. *National Vital Statistics Reports, 53*(5), 1–115.

Poss, J. E. (2001). Developing a new model for cross-cultural research: Synthesizing the Health Belief Model and the Theory of Reasoned Action. *Advances in Nursing Science, 23*(4), 1–15.

Raza, J. A., Babb, J. D., & Movahed, A. (2004). Optimal management of hyperlipidemia in primary prevention of cardiovascular disease. *International Journal of Cardiology, 97*(3), 355–366.

Ro, M., Treadwell, H., Northridge, M. (2004). *Community health workers and community voices: Promoting good health.* Atlanta: National Center for Primary Care at Morehouse School of Medicine.

Sheeran, P., Conner, M., & Norman, P. (2001). Can the theory of planned behavior explain patterns of health behavior change? *Health Psychology, 20*(1), 12–19.

Sills, Jonathan R. (2008). Predictors of exercise and dietary change among immigrant Latinos following cardiovascular risk factor screening. *Dissertation Abstracts International: Section B: The Physical Sciences and Engineering, 69*(1-B), 699.

Simpson, D. R., Dixon, B. G., & Bolli, P. (2004). Effectiveness of multidisciplinary patient counselling in reducing cardiovascular disease risk factors through non-pharmacological intervention: Results from the Healthy Heart Program. *Canadian Journal of Cardiology, 20*(2), 177–186.

Singh, V., & Deedwania, P. (2006). Dyslipidemia in special populations: Asian Indians, African Americans, and Hispanics. *Current Atherosclerosis Reports, 8*(1), 32–40.

Strecher, V. J., Champion, V. L., & Rosenstock, I. M. (1997). The health belief model and health behavior. In D. S. Gochman (Ed.), *Handbook of health behavior research 1: Personal and social determinants* (pp. 71–91). New York: Plenum.

Sutton, S. (2002). Using social cognition models to develop health behaviour interventions: Problems and assumptions. In D. Rutter & L. Quine (Eds.), *Changing health behaviour: Intervention and research with social cognition models* (pp. 193–208). Buckingham, UK: Open University Press.

Weinstein, N. D. (1993). Testing four competing theories of health-protective behavior. *Health Psychology, 12*(4), 324–333.

APPENDIX A

Self-Report Measure for Baseline and Postscreening
Information–English

October 2005 Flea Market Survey:
Tracking Health Beliefs

1) Have you ever been told that you have high cholesterol?
YES .... _____
NO .... _____
REFUSED .... _____
DON'T KNOW .... _____

2) How old are you? _____

3) Are you male or female?
MALE .... _____
FEMALE .... _____

4) Would you describe yourself as . . .
[CODE ALL THAT APPLY.]
WHITE .... _____
BLACK OR AFRICAN AMERICAN .... _____
VIETNAMESE .... _____
MEXICAN .... _____
AMERICAN INDIAN OR ALASKA NATIVE .... _____
OTHER PACIFIC ISLANDER .... _____
EAST INDIAN .... _____
OTHER (SPECIFY): _____
REFUSED .... _____

5) About how many years have you lived in the United States?
[FOR LESS THAN A YEAR, ENTER 1 YEAR]
_____ (NUMBER OF YEARS)
_____ YEAR (FIRST CAME TO LIVE IN U.S.)
REFUSED .... _____

6) What is the highest grade of education you have completed and received credit for?
NO FORMAL EDUCATION .... _____
GRADE SCHOOL .... _____
HIGH SCHOOL OR EQUIVALENT .... _____
2-YEAR JUNIOR OR COMMUNITY COLLEGE .... _____
4-YEAR COLLEGE OR UNIVERSITY .... _____
GRADUATE OR PROFESSIONAL SCHOOL .... _____
VOCATIONAL, BUSINESS, OR TRADE SCHOOL ..... _____

7) What is your zip code? _____ (ZIP CODE)
REFUSED .... _____

8) Would you say that in general your health is excellent, very good, good, fair or poor?
EXCELLENT .... _____
VERY GOOD .... _____
GOOD .... _____
FAIR .... _____
POOR .... _____
REFUSED .... _____

Please circle a number on the scale from 1 to 10.

9) How serious a threat to your health is having high cholesterol?

1	2	3	4	5	6	7	8	9	10
Not Serious		Somewhat Serious		Serious		Very Serious			Extremely Serious

10) How likely is it that you have elevated cholesterol?

1	2	3	4	5	6	7	8	9	10
Not Likely		Somewhat Likely		Likely		Very Likely			Extremely Likely

11) If a health care professional were to tell you that you should eat a diet lower in fat, how confident are you that you would do this?

1	2	3	4	5	6	7	8	9	10
Not Confident		Somewhat Confident		Confident		Very Confident			Extremely Confident

12) If a health care professional were to tell you that you should start or maintain an exercise program, how confident are you that you would do this?

1	2	3	4	5	6	7	8	9	10
Not Confident		Somewhat Confident		Confident		Very Confident			Extremely Confident

13) How confident are you that eating a diet low in fat and engaging in exercise would improve your health and make you feel better?

1	2	3	4	5	6	7	8	9	10
Not Confident		Somewhat Confident		Confident		Very Confident			Extremely Confident

14) How important do you think it is to maintain a diet low in fat?

1	2	3	4	5	6	7	8	9	10
Definitely Not Important		Probably Not Important		No Opinion			Probably Important		Definitely Important

15) How important do you think it is to exercise regularly?

1	2	3	4	5	6	7	8	9	10
Definitely Not Important		Probably Not Important		No Opinion			Probably Important		Definitely Important

16) How important is it to your family that you maintain a diet low in fat?

1	2	3	4	5	6	7	8	9	10
Definitely Not Important		Probably Not Important		No Opinion			Probably Important		Definitely Important

17) How important is it to your family that you exercise regularly?

1	2	3	4	5	6	7	8	9	10
Definitely Not Important		Probably Not Important		No Opinion			Probably Important		Definitely Important

18) I intend to start or maintain a diet lower in fat?

1	2	3	4	5	6	7	8	9	10
Definitely No		Probably No		No Opinion		Probably Yes		Definitely Yes	

19) I intend to start or maintain a regular exercise program?

1	2	3	4	5	6	7	8	9	10
Definitely No		Probably No		No Opinion		Probably Yes		Definitely Yes	

PLEASE STOP ANSWERING QUESTIONS NOW
AND GO TO SCREENING AREA

FOLLOW-UP

Now that you've gotten your test results, I'd like to ask you a few more questions.

20) Would you say that in general your health is excellent, very good, good, fair or poor?

EXCELLENT .... _____
VERY GOOD .... _____
GOOD .... _____
FAIR .... _____
POOR .... _____
REFUSED .... _____
DON'T KNOW .... _____

Please circle a number on the scale from 1 to 10.

21) How serious a threat to your health is having high cholesterol?

1	2	3	4	5	6	7	8	9	10
Not Serious		Somewhat Serious		Serious		Very Serious		Extremely Serious	

22) How likely is it that you have elevated cholesterol?

1	2	3	4	5	6	7	8	9	10
Not Likely		Somewhat Likely		Likely		Very Likely		Extremely Likely	

23) If a health care professional were to tell you that you should eat a diet lower in fat, how confident are you that you would do this?

1	2	3	4	5	6	7	8	9	10
Not Confident		Somewhat Confident		Confident		Very Confident		Extremely Confident	

24) If a health care professional were to tell you that you should start or maintain an exercise program, how confident are you that you would do this?

1	2	3	4	5	6	7	8	9	10
Not Confident		Somewhat Confident		Confident	Very Confident		Extremely Confident		

25) How confident are you that eating a diet low in fat and engaging in exercise would improve your health and make you feel better?

1	2	3	4	5	6	7	8	9	10
Not Confident		Somewhat Confident		Confident	Very Confident		Extremely Confident		

26) How important do you think it is to maintain a diet low in fat?

1	2	3	4	5	6	7	8	9	10
Definitely Not Important		Probably Not Important		No Opinion		Probably Important		Definitely Important	

27) How important do you think it is to exercise regularly?

1	2	3	4	5	6	7	8	9	10
Definitely Not Important		Probably Not Important		No Opinion			Probably Important		Definitely Important

28) I intend to start or maintain a diet lower in fat?

1	2	3	4	5	6	7	8	9	10
Definitely No		Probably No		No Opinion		Probably Yes		Definitely Yes	

29) I intend to start or maintain a regular exercise program?

1	2	3	4	5	6	7	8	9	10
Definitely No		Probably No		No Opinion		Probably Yes		Definitely Yes	

30) I intend to follow-up with a health care professional to discuss my screening results.

1	2	3	4	5	6	7	8	9	10
Definitely No		Probably No		No Opinion		Probably Yes		Definitely Yes	

31) I intend to get more information about how I can live a "heart healthy lifestyle?"

1	2	3	4	5	6	7	8	9	10
Definitely No		Probably No		No Opinion		Probably Yes		Definitely Yes	

32) Finally, can I have your phone number so that we can follow-up with you in the future?
YES my phone number is _____ .
NO .... _____

That is all the questions I have. I really appreciate your time and cooperation. You have helped yourself and community with a very important health survey. Thank you.

For Health Ambassadors:

Please indicate the primary language this survey was administered in? (check one only)
_____ English
_____ Spanish
_____ Vietnamese
_____ Cantonese
_____ Mandarin
_____ Tagalog
Other _____

APPENDIX B

Telephone Follow-Up Measure

October 2005 Health Fair Participant 1 Month Follow-Up Survey

Name: _____ ID#_____ Date_____

General Health Perception:

1) Would you say that in general your health is excellent, very good, good, fair or poor?

EXCELLENT . . . . _____
VERY GOOD . . . . _____
GOOD . . . . _____
FAIR . . . . _____
POOR . . . . _____
REFUSED . . . . _____
DON'T KNOW . . . . _____

Beliefs and Behavior: Please circle a number on the scale from 1 to 10.

2) Since the health fair, how much have you been able to *reduce* the fat in your diet?"

1	2	3	4	5	6	7	8	9	10
Not At All		Minimal		Moderate		Large		Very Large	
Haven't Tried		Reduction		Reduction		Reduction		Reduction	

3) Since the health fair how much have you *increased* your exercise?

1	2	3	4	5	6	7	8	9	10
Not At All		Minimal		Moderate		Large		Very Large	
		Increase		Increase		Increase		Increase	

4) How serious a threat to your health is having high cholesterol?

1	2	3	4	5	6	7	8	9	10
Not Serious		Somewhat		Serious		Very Serious		Extremely	
		Serious						Serious	

5) How likely is it that you have elevated cholesterol?

1	2	3	4	5	6	7	8	9	10
Not Likely		Somewhat		Likely		Very Likely		Extremely	
		Likely						Likely	

6) Since the health fair how much have you *increased* your fat intake?

1	2	3	4	5	6	7	8	9	10
Not At All		Minimal		Moderate		Large		Very Large	
		Increase		Increase		Increase		Increase	

7) Since the health fair, how much have you *reduced* your exercise?

1	2	3	4	5	6	7	8	9	10
Not At All		Minimal Reduction		Moderate Reduction		Large Reduction		Very Large Reduction	

Information/Physician Follow-up: Please answer Yes or No

8) What place do you USUALLY go to when you are sick or need advice about your health?

DOCTOR'S OFFICE/KAISER/OTHER HMO .... ⎯⎯

CLINIC/HEALTH CENTER/HOSPITAL CLINIC .... ⎯⎯

EMERGENCY ROOM .... ⎯⎯

SOME OTHER PLACE (SPECIFY):⎯⎯⎯⎯⎯⎯⎯⎯⎯⎯⎯

NO ONE PLACE .... ⎯⎯

REFUSED .... ⎯⎯

DON'T KNOW .... ⎯⎯

9) Since the health fair did you *attend* a medical appointment to discuss your results?

    YES⎯⎯   NO⎯⎯

10) Since the health fair, have you gotten more information about risk factors for heart disease?

    YES⎯⎯   NO⎯⎯

11) Since the health fair, have you avoided any information about risk factors for heart disease?

    YES⎯⎯   NO⎯⎯

12) What were your total cholesterol results given during the health fair?

    Desirable⎯⎯   Borderline High⎯⎯   High Cholesterol⎯⎯

13) What country were you born in?

    Mexico⎯⎯   USA⎯⎯   Other (specify)⎯⎯⎯⎯

14) What could we do to improve the health fair?

⎯⎯⎯⎯⎯⎯⎯⎯⎯⎯⎯⎯⎯⎯⎯⎯⎯⎯⎯⎯⎯⎯⎯⎯⎯⎯⎯

⎯⎯⎯⎯⎯⎯⎯⎯⎯⎯⎯⎯⎯⎯⎯⎯⎯⎯⎯⎯⎯⎯⎯⎯⎯⎯⎯

⎯⎯⎯⎯⎯⎯⎯⎯⎯⎯⎯⎯⎯⎯⎯⎯⎯⎯⎯⎯⎯⎯⎯⎯⎯⎯⎯

Thank you for taking the time to answer these questions. Good Bye.

Telephone Administrator:

What was the primary language this survey was administered in? (Check one only)

⎯⎯ English

⎯⎯ Spanish

Other ⎯⎯⎯⎯⎯⎯⎯⎯⎯⎯⎯⎯⎯⎯⎯⎯⎯⎯⎯

11

THE ECONOMY OF
ABUNDANCE

Developing Service Learning on a Grand Scale in a
Rapidly Changing Environment

Kathleen M. Roe, Andrea Nance, Alvin Galang, Anna Bingham,
German Blanco, Ryan Duhe, and Kenneth Lee

T
he service-learning literature clearly identifies a well-defined and
manageable project as a key predictor of student and course success
(Connors & Seifer, 2005; Eyler & Giles, 1999; Hollander, Saltmarsh, & Zlotkowski, 2001; Metz & Hesser, 1996). Typically, successful
projects are based on a doable unit of community service, a class of 15–30
service learners, enough time for students to prepare with confidence, plenty
of lead time for communication and coordination with the community partners, and structured, reinforcing opportunities for reflection from the beginning through the end of the term. These good practices make good sense
when the community is the setting for learning. How then did our service-
learning project become the health education component for a huge community health fair just 7 weeks into the semester in an introductory course with
nearly 100 students? And how did the Health Science (HS) 104 Health Fair

The authors would like to thank the Health Trust for its vision and support of the Open-Air Health Fair
and the involvement of the SJSU Department of Health Science. We specifically acknowledge Gary
Allen, Todd Hansen, Sheree Dela Pena, Cynthia York, Elizabeth Sills, Rachel Poplack, and Debra David
for their role in the early days of this collaboration. We also thank the 2006 TAs, Amy Carlson, Mikiko
Inoue, Joy Mulhern, Julieta Pomares, and all the fall 2006 students.

become one of the signature experiences of the health science department at San José State University?

This chapter describes the experience of student-initiated integration of service learning into a community health promotion course. We begin with the instructor's quest for a new way of teaching community-based analysis, a group of civic-minded students, and their idea to take our learning out of the classroom. We describe our introduction to the Open-Air Health Fair, the evolution of our relationship with the Health Trust, a local nonprofit hospital conversion foundation that operates health promotion programs and provides grants to health-related organizations and initiatives in the geographic area surrounding the City of San José, and our first, second, and third health fair efforts. We share our own good practices and the things we learned along the way, drawing upon our department's principles, core values, and university context. We conclude with our commitment to service learning and the combination of champions, resources, skills, and sensibilities we have found support the unique economy of abundance that makes this educational adventure work for the community, our partner, the students, and the faculty.

HS 104: Community Health Promotion

HS 104 is one of the introductory courses in the health science major and minor at San José State University. The three-unit course is offered every fall semester and is open to sophomores and juniors who have completed the lower-division general education course HS 1, Understanding Your Health. HS 104 meets twice a week for 1 hour and 15 minutes. It is designed to introduce students to the social ecological approach to community health, using the spectrum of prevention (Cohen, Chavez, & Chehimi, 2007) as the conceptual and organizing framework. The course explores the many factors that influence community health and successful strategies to promote health, prevent disease, and enhance community capacity and resilience. Additional course objectives include

1. To learn to understand and describe communities in context, using multiple sources and presentation styles
2. To explore key community health concepts, including risk, resilience, and evidence-based analysis

Traditionally, HS 104 requires weekly readings from a variety of sources; practical, hands-on, short homework assignments; exams; at least one paper; and active class participation.

A recurring challenge with HS 104 has been effectively helping students make the paradigmatic shift from approaching health with a personal and disease focus to a population-based, social ecological perspective. Undergraduates bring a grand curiosity to studying health. The one-semester personal health prerequisite seems to only whet their appetite for all the things they could explore about the human body and disease. Health science is a "discovery major"; students in HS 104 often come from science, prenursing, or business backgrounds. Their enthusiasm for learning about health is often matched only by their resistance to shifting their frame of reference from the endless possibilities at the individual level to the complex context of health from a social systems perspective. Over the years, numerous short assignments and practical projects have been developed to support this analytical shift. By the end of the semester, most students could (albeit often reluctantly) think at the community level, but few embraced that unit of analysis with the enthusiasm that was generated by studying personal health—until HS 104 met the Open-Air Health Fair, the Health Trust, the Flea Market, and service learning.

The First Open-Air Health Fair at the San José Flea Market

The first Open-Air Health Fair at the San José Flea Market was held in October 2003, before HS 104 became involved. The San José Flea Market, established in 1960, is the oldest continuously operating flea market in California and the largest open-air market in the United States. According to its Web site (see http://www.sjfm.com/), over 4 million people visit the flea market each year, with 80,000 visitors each week and 50,000–60,000 visitors each weekend. The 120-acre flea market contains 1,000 open-air stalls for over 6,000 sellers, 100 food carts, 25 restaurants, and California's largest farmer's market. A covered pavilion in the center is the setting for events and festivals throughout the year. The flea market is a primary shopping and social venue for Latino, Vietnamese, Chinese, Filipino, and Afghani families in the region. It is clearly a place of abundance.

The first health fair was a collaboration between flea market management and the Health Trust. A children's event sponsored by the Health Trust in the pavilion the previous summer demonstrated the flea market's potential for outreach to the local multicultural population. The flea market's management and the Health Trust's staff were eager to try something that would combine health services and education at this exciting and eclectic venue.

The essence of the Open-Air Health Fair was established at that first event. As designed by the Health Trust, the fair offers three primary and interrelated services: (a) health risk factor screenings, (b) referral and on-site insurance enrollment, and (c) health education. Early health fairs also offered flu shots, on-site blood and bone marrow drives, and breast cancer screening through a mobile mammography van.

The scope of the Open-Air Health Fair is evident in the numbers served: In October 2003 over 2,000 screenings and flu shots were administered by Health Trust staff, per diem nurses, and qualified nursing students over the 2-day weekend event. Over 30 volunteers from local schools and health organizations offered resource information and lighthearted health promotion activities.

A second health fair in April 2004 served similar numbers but involved over 240 volunteers. The impact of screening in this unique community setting was clear. Of the 502 people who received cholesterol screening, 19% were found to have high cholesterol levels and 34% were borderline; 11.6% of the 502 receiving glucose screening had levels outside the recommended range. One in five (20%) of the 487 screened had elevated blood pressure. Half (49%) of the 246 tested for body mass index were overweight, 21% obese. Half of the 200 people in a convenience sample of 200 waiting for screening reported they do not see a doctor regularly. These data were sobering and compelling. Even as Health Trust staff participants immersed themselves in the massive organizational undertaking needed to turn an empty pavilion into a safe and welcoming screening, referral, and educational venue—literally overnight—they were beginning to imagine even greater possibilities. One of those dreamers—an AmeriCorps volunteer based at the Health Trust—was also a student in HS 104.

From Clothing Drive to the Health Fair—HS 104 Gets Into the Game

HS 104's path to the Open-Air Health Fair began with an animated class discussion near the end of fall 2003 about ways to apply the class material on community health to a real community setting. Led by a student who had just participated in the April health fair, the students suggested a class project should replace an upcoming exam. Although the 55 students in the class ultimately agreed to an ambitious winter clothing drive for homeless families, this student suggested that future HS 104 classes "should really get involved in the health fair—It's *perfect* for this class!" The seed was planted.

The students' engagement in the winter clothing drive, including research on homeless families, services, and prevention strategies, brought a welcome energy to the course. The spontaneous nature of the project selection and implementation was fun, although with 55 students and only 4 weeks left in the semester, it sometimes felt barely manageable. The class delivered three truckloads of donations to a homeless services program near the campus and received a commendation from its director for the quantity and quality of the donations.

From a teaching perspective, however, the activity was not quite right. It was unilateral by design, with students collecting resources but leaving them at the agency and driving away. While rich with opportunities to learn and practice team and organizational skills, the activity did not really challenge or stretch students' capacities to understand, analyze, or act on community health problems from an ecological or systems perspective. And with little risk for California college students in collecting and giving away winter clothing, there was limited potential for transformative learning. And yet, the students and instructor were now excited about community-based learning. A deeper, more engaging, and more reciprocal learning activity was needed—and so HS 104 turned to the Health Trust and the Open-Air Health Fair.

A New Partnership—The Health Trust and the SJSU Health Science Department

Following up on the student's recommendation, the HS 104 instructor began talking with the Health Trust's director of community partnerships about the possibility of including HS 104 in the upcoming fall 2004 Open-Air Health Fair. This was the beginning of a creative and productive relationship between the SJSU health science department and the Health Trust. The partners agreed that a service-learning project based at the health fair would not only enhance students' learning about the issues and methods of community health but would also provide service that would benefit the community through deployment of engaged and excited health education volunteers. The multicultural student population of SJSU, a majority minority campus for many years, all but guaranteed diverse language and cultural skills in any HS 104 cohort—an added benefit for serving the culturally diverse population that regularly visits the San José Flea Market. The Health Trust leadership welcomed the opportunity to contribute to the development of the public health workforce by providing the setting and resources for this intensive introduction to community health. The activity, like the setting, was another place of abundance.

The new academic and community partners worked closely that summer to develop an assignment for the 65 students registered for the 2004 fall semester (10 more than the year before) that would be meaningful to the students and useful for the health fair and its attendees. The planning team was fortunate to add an SJSU student who was pursuing a master of public health degree to serve as an AmeriCorps volunteer at the Health Trust and who, incidentally, had taken HS 104 as an undergraduate several years before. He became HS 104's first teaching assistant (TA). The Health Trust assigned him to the course to assist in planning and coordinating the service-learning activities. Another AmeriCorps volunteer worked behind the scenes on materials and displays.

The new partnership between the Health Trust, HS 104, and AmeriCorps volunteers proved critical to managing what was quickly becoming a bigger enterprise than initially imagined. In 6 weeks, the combined group managed to develop interesting and engaging educational booths promoting healthy messages and introducing simple ways to enhance diet and physical activity. The booths were based on Salud Para Su Corazon (Heart Health), a cardiovascular community education curriculum supported by the National Heart, Lung, and Blood Institute (NHLBI, 1999). Specific curriculum modules, such as Make Heart Healthy Eating a Family Affair, were selected for the booths by the Health Trust staff and the AmeriCorps TA then assigned to student teams. Booth frames, materials, and props were arranged by the Health Trust. Students had to pass a quiz on the knowledge base of their booth's educational messages before being cleared for the health fair. This division of labor allowed the instructor to guarantee the knowledge and competencies of the 65 students without also having to worry about booth design and activities—a critical factor in a project of growing ambition and community responsibility.

The mid-October health fair date pushed the class to be ready very quickly. As the date got closer, increasing amounts of class time had to be devoted to sessions on contingency planning, the flexibility needed in community-based work, and the basics of educational outreach. The TAs dedicated HS 104 instant message hours—Mondays through Thursdays, 8:00 p.m.–10:00 p.m.—were well used by students as the teams scrambled to be ready.

The First Year: We Did It!

Over the two days of the 2004 health fair, the instructor, the AmeriCorps member, and 65 HS 104 participants provided health education at nine inter-active booths to more than 1,000 adults, teens, and children over a period of 14 hours. Despite unseasonably cold and rainy weather, the flea market's health fair pavilion was a lively, entertaining, and educational place. The students' reactions at the fair, their enthusiasm in the days afterward, and the "ahas!" revealed in their reflection papers and discussion during the class de-briefing clearly demonstrated the wisdom of the early insight that the project would be perfect for this class.

In discussion and reflection papers, the participating students consis-tently described the experience as useful, challenging, and meaningful, saying that it gave them "real world application of the theoretical and statistical information presented in class." The instructor found that the paradigmatic shift from individual to community unit of analysis clicked after the health fair, with students eager to learn more about community-level risks and pro-tective factors and to be better able to imagine community-based interven-tions. Best of all, the service learning reinforced values of hope and civic engagement among the undergraduates: "During my childhood, I spent many weekends at the Berryessa Flea Market. It was especially rewarding to be a part of something that addressed an important need in my immediate community."

The Health Trust reported that student involvement significantly ex-panded the health education possibilities at the health fair, brought a unique energy to the event, and the students' language skills helped extend outreach and education to health fair visitors who spoke Spanish, Vietnamese, Can-tonese, or Tagalog, but little or no English. The AmeriCorps volunteer had the satisfaction of successfully coaching 65 students and nine health education booths in just 6 weeks. The instructor was delighted to see the students become a cohesive and enthusiastic group while meeting critical learning objectives.

The scale of the health fair increased with the 10 additional students but so did its impact. If we could manage the scale, we all agreed it was well worth doing again. Looking to 2005, the instructor pledged to center the Health Fair as the primary learning activity of the first half of the semester; the Health Trust pledged course support through additional AmeriCorps volunteers.

AmeriCorps Bridging Borders: Another Key Partner

Four AmeriCorps members serving at the Health Trust were assigned to work with HS 104 as peer TAs for the 2005 fall semester. Their contributions, along with the supervision and guidance provided by the Health Trust, were instrumental in transforming the health fair from a fun and promising group activity to a structured undergraduate learning experience. The TAs provided in-class support during the 15 minutes devoted to team time at each of the 14 class sessions prior to the health fair. The TAs also worked closely with the Health Trust staff to make certain that class efforts to develop the educational booths, including the health screenings and publicity, were well coordinated with the Health Trust and mutually reinforced the goals of the event.

The TAs were challenged by managing a community project that continued to draw more participants and was clearly becoming more ambitious and complex each year. To facilitate student learning and better serve the culturally diverse flea market patrons, the instructor decided to move away from the NHLBI curriculum and let the class teams develop their own educational priorities, messages, activities, and materials. For numerous reasons, HS 104's enrollment increased by an unprecedented 50%, from 65 in fall 2004 to 96 in 2005. We were nervous. The enrollment growth was clearly an asset in a university context in which resources are allocated to departments based on full-time equivalent student census. However, we knew that a 96:1 student-faculty ratio seriously challenged the economy of scale deemed appropriate for service learning. However, we were also mindful of our commitment to the community and the Health Trust. It seemed the only way forward was to learn from the past, move ahead with the second Health Fair, and then decide if we had outgrown our capacity to deliver a meaningful service to the community, our students, and our partners.

Incorporating Lessons From Fall 2004 Into the New Plan for Fall 2005

One of the most significant differences between fall 2004 and fall 2005 was the opportunity to be more deliberate about planning for educational effectiveness in the second year. Key contributing factors included the addition of the four AmeriCorps members to the teaching team, the ability to plan over the summer, and the specific and very helpful feedback preserved in the 2004 students' reflective papers and course evaluations. Planning was also enhanced by the growing buzz in the department about the fun and importance of the health fair. In just one semester, HS 104 was transformed from a traditional classroom-based course to a community-based course involving a weekend service-learning project. The change in faculty thinking and the student approach to learning happened remarkably fast. This successful transition allowed the planning team to focus on the educational experience without having to convince students of the benefits of service learning.

The first matter to address was class size. The 50% enrollment growth presented opportunities and challenges. Since more students were involved, the potential for expanding the topics, activities, and language capabilities of the health education booths was exciting (abundance!). At the same time, the challenge of coordinating 96 students with just 7 weeks between the 1st day of class and the 1st day of the health fair in a course not focused on health education methods and materials was daunting. Clear communication, careful planning, deliberate group management, and outside of class support by and for the volunteer TAs were critical. Two of the TAs were class members in fall 2004; two were currently enrolled in the course. These unique and different insider perspectives provided invaluable critique and innovation that kept the student experience in the mix as the instructor focused on managing the course to meet its broader objectives, and the Health Trust staff focused on planning and managing an increasingly complex community event.

After 2 weeks of class sessions on the foundations of community health and health promotion, the 96 students formed 9 groups and began working in and outside class on their assigned booths. Students were instructed to design activities that focused less on teaching and more on engaging participants in informal discussions of simple health promotion messages that would reinforce what had been talked about during the screenings. Each TA supervised two to three teams, keeping in constant communication with the Health Trust on the progress of the booths, learning objectives, messages, and related activities.

As they worked in their teams, students were expected to use and develop their skills in small-group communication, teamwork, and leadership. They were also expected to draw from class sessions on culturally appropriate outreach methods, the behavior change process, and the stages of change in relation to cardiovascular disease. Moving away from a standardized curriculum allowed freedom for the students to be creative in their booth and activity designs. However, each team was required to receive approval from its TA and the instructor on the key background information, theoretical framework, and change strategy that informed the booth's educational messages and activities. Several indicators were used to determine group and individual grades in the 2nd year, including the quality and effectiveness of the booth, the group process as observed during team meetings and documented in weekly written team updates, evidence of individual effort, and the quality of the final individual reflection papers.

The TAs were consultants to the teams, but it was the responsibility of each group to manage the time, effort, skills, and contributions of all members so that (a) everyone participated, (b) the booths were completed on time, and (c) the activities and materials met the standards required for an educational community service. Teams were also expected to staff their booths from 10:00 a.m. to 5:00 p.m. on Saturday and Sunday.

The Health Trust agreed to fund and/or supply all reasonable props for each booth (e.g., poster board, pens) and to translate and/or reproduce the teams' educational materials (e.g., handouts, resource lists). A benefit of this arrangement was that students learned to manage their big ideas within the limited resources of a nonprofit agency as they worked with their TAs to negotiate exactly what the Health Trust could provide. The dimensions and locations of the booths were provided for students during the 2nd week of planning so that the teams were working with realistic expectations of the setup of the fair. The instructor, the AmeriCorps members, and the Health

Trust staff had to trust the teams to design and execute engaging and dynamic booths as it was not logistically possible for the teams to actually put them together until the 1st day of the health fair.

Seeking the Balance of Content and Process in a Service-Learning Course

HS 104 meets twice a week for 75 minutes. Prior to the health fair, held at the end of the 7th week of the semester, each class session incorporated a formal presentation of key community health promotion concepts during the 1st hour and time for the teams to apply those concepts in a specific planning activity during the last 15 minutes of class. The fast learning curve was reinforced through related individual and/or group homework assignments. An enhanced conceptual framework this time included definitions of community health promotion, the epidemiologic profile of the county, health disparities, introduction to cardiovascular disease; the health belief model, stages of change, community norm change, and the principles of culturally competent outreach. The instructor struggled daily to decide which content and in-class learning activities could be cut to make room for the concepts and time necessary as the teams prepared for their days of community service.

Coordinating So Many (and Increasing) Moving Parts

One of the most important developments in the 2nd year of HS 104's experience was the system for communication between the students, the instructor, and the Health Trust. While the students worked feverishly on their educational booths, the Health Trust staff was working with a growing cadre of partners to make this a community event, sponsored but not dictated by the Health Trust. As with any community-organizing project, this introduced elements of innovation, uncertainty, and constant adjustment as each partner's commitment and specifications were established and then integrated into the overall project. To keep the students' efforts on track and in support of the evolving event, several practical communication strategies were put in place: (a) the TAs met weekly with Health Trust staff for check-in, updates, and coordination; (b) one TA served as a direct liaison between the course instructor and the Health Trust; (c) a class Listserv was established to provide regular updates and information to all teams between classes, (d) the TAs worked together to make sure the booths were coordinated and the teams were making appropriate progress. The instructor continually revised in-class activities and homework assignments to meet course objectives and to support the emerging and immediate needs of the project.

The 2nd Year: Benefits and Challenges of Such a Large Class in Action

The fall 2005 Open-Air Health Fair was held October 8 and 9. The event was larger, more varied, and more complex than previous fairs because of the Health Trust's growing sense of what was possible, the participation of more community partners, and growing public anticipation of this now well-publicized event.

Without the standardized curriculum from the year before, some booths worked better than others. Active Kids was extremely popular, because of the Bounce House that was rented to provide an opportunity for very young children to experience the differences in heart rate before and after physical activity. The students quickly learned, however, that it was almost impossible to do anything beyond supervising bouncing children at their booth—the gimmick eclipsed the educational moment. Other booths provided intimate educational opportunities, from walking with pedometers to low-fat cooking. Some booths were just more popular than others, leaving students at the less-popular booths underused and disappointed.

An unanticipated challenge in the 2nd year came from the diverse class's language skills. Although the 96 students spoke a total of 15 different languages and dialects, only 20 spoke Spanish and only 6 spoke Vietnamese. In contrast, most of the adults leaving the screening area and in need of health education spoke Spanish and very little or no English. The students quickly realized that their planned activities were too knowledge oriented and explanation based. Without the corresponding language abilities, they found it difficult to explain the meaning of blood pressure or the use of a pedometer, despite great interest from booth visitors and the students' own excitement. This limitation was particularly significant because the 2nd day of the health fair was also the closing day of Binational Health Week, and the San José Flea Market was a well-publicized venue for closing-day festivities. As a result, most of the adults attending the Sunday health fair spoke Spanish as their primary—and often only—language.

Despite the language barriers, by the end of the weekend thousands of people had come to the health fair, and over 500 participated in comprehensive cardiovascular disease risk factor screening, referral, and education. Over half (57%) of those screened had dangerously high total cholesterol scores; 30% were obese and 49% overweight as indicated by their body mass index; blood pressure scores indicated that 40% were prehypertensive and 10% showed signs of hypertension. It is estimated that over 2,000 adults and children were exposed to the messages, activities, and resources of the nine health education booths. A follow-up study with a sample of 200 screening participants found that among those who had initiated a behavior change recommended at the health fair the most common variable was an educational interaction with the students (Sills, 2006).

Reflection on Action

Student reflection papers and class discussions in the days following the health fair identified three primary challenges to overall effectiveness and individual satisfaction: (a) the pressure to develop booths from scratch in such a short time, (b) the unanticipated language barriers, and (c) the uneven participant interest in each booth. However, the students agreed that the experience stimulated unique and valuable awareness, reflection, and questions about community health, health promotion, and their own professional preparation priorities.

Students and TAs agreed that TA supervision and assistance had been critical and the liaison role between the Health Trust and the instructor prevented any number of potential planning problems. The students agreed (95%) they had learned important group skills and were now more interested in health disparities (77%) and culturally appropriate health services and materials (72%) than they had been before participating in the health fair. They spoke of their initial nervousness but ultimate ease with adjusting their booth plans to accommodate what they learned once the health fair was under way. Many students spoke of the value of the experience in helping them understand the community's need for basic health education that they had not previously realized. One of the most powerful lessons learned was the limitations of even well-trained college students and professionals if they can not speak the languages of the community, and the related need for a diverse and multicultural workforce. Nearly all of the students (98%) said they learned a great deal by participating in the health fair and nearly everyone (95%) recommended that the assignment be continued the next year.

Is It Getting Too Big? Rethinking the Commitment and the Constancy of Change

In an ironic but perhaps predictable twist, just as the students' enthusiasm for the health fair reached an all-time high, the instructor and the Health Trust staff were beginning to rethink involvement for the year ahead.

From the Health Trust's perspective, the event was extremely time and resource intensive. The organization's mission was evolving as a result of an intensive and exciting strategic planning process—would the health fair still fit the new mission? The Health Trust's growing role as community convener and collaborator was going to involve the staff in several very high profile and complex events in October 2006—could it possibly do the health fair as well? Perhaps most important, a change in the university's AmeriCorps grant and some staffing changes at the Health Trust meant a much smaller group available to help the HS 104 class prepare for their roles, and that the staff with the most health fair experience would have many other priorities in the weeks leading up to the event. Some questioned if it was time to turn the health fair over to other community collaborators. As late as April 2006, the Health Trust was leaning toward declining the lead role and significantly scaling back its involvement.

At the university the HS 104 instructor was similarly starting to wish for an economy of scale that would make service learning a little easier to manage. The energy, focus, and organization required to create a meaningful community-based experience for so many students in such a short time, while also meeting the content requirements and broader learning outcomes of the course, was daunting. Once or twice had been fun, but as a long-term community commitment? Could the instructor do this again without compromising the quality of the two other very different courses she teaches in the fall semesters? What if she couldn't maintain the energy required to pull this off? What if the course needed to be reassigned to another instructor—who would be willing to take on such a complex and public project? Without AmeriCorps members, how could she possibly coordinate 100 students? Wasn't there a smaller, less-intensive community project somewhere that would work just as well? As preenrollment data indicated the class would be even bigger in fall 2006, she wondered whether service learning was worth it. Maybe the course had outgrown the method—a good idea now on an untenable scale.

In the end, it was commitment to the community and community-based education that brought all parties back to the health fair. The Health Trust was moved by the urgency in its community partners' appeals for the health fair to continue under the Health Trust leadership. A countywide planning committee had already selected the Open-Air Health Fair as the setting for the closing ceremonies of the 2006 Binational Health Week celebration, which would bring thousands more people to the already popular flea market. At the end of the day, the Health Trust's newly endorsed vision—helping to make Silicon Valley the healthiest region in the country—made it almost impossible to turn away.

The core values and principles of the SJSU health science department (http://www.sjsu.edu/healthscience/about/mission) brought the class back for another year: core values of health, community, diversity, and balance; the principles of relevance and participation, partnership, and civic engagement. Most important, the department principle that that which is not given away is lost reminded the instructor that the talents, skills, imagination, and abundant goodwill of 100 plus undergraduates were gifts to be used in service of our community, not squandered in an easier traditional course design. With the partners back at the table, the 2006 Open-Air Health Fair was a go. And, with 2 years' experience behind us, the third health fair was the best ever.

The Economy of Abundance: Champions, Resources, Skills, and Sensibilities

In its 3rd year, the Open-Air Health Fair finally attained all the ingredients of a well-developed community service-learning experience. The enterprise had passionate champions in the classroom, the community, and our organizational partner. The 2006 experience was focused on a task that was needed, beneficial, and appropriate to the student learners and the community they served. The class and the community were supported by adequate resources, and although it always seems the timeline is too fast, the scope of the task was doable with the time and resources available. The student activity was linked to specific learning objectives and an overarching conceptual framework, which allowed the instructor to emphasize the knowledge and sensibilities of community-based practice. Although the class was big, students worked in teams of a manageable size with appropriate supervision. The assignments facilitated multicultural, interdisciplinary, integrative, and intergenerational learning as students worked in teams and with TAs, the instructor, the Health Trust staff, and, eventually, community members. Perhaps most important, the fall 2006 health fair experience and all that led up to it was reciprocal, providing a true and real-time exchange between the student learners and the community members they served. Our project is big, but it provides an economy of abundance that is dynamic, responsive, and meaningful to us all.

References

Cohen, L., Chavez, V., & Chehimi, S. (2007). *Prevention is primary: Strategies for community well-being.* San Francisco: Jossey-Bass.

Connors, K., & Seifer, S. (2005). *Reflection in higher education service-learning.* Retrieved from http://www.ccph.info

Eyler, J., & Giles, D. (1999). *Where's the learning in service-learning?* San Francisco: Jossey-Bass.

Hollander, E., Saltmarsh, J., & Zlotkowski, E. (2001). Indicators of engagement. In Kenny, M.E., Simon, L.A.K., Kiley-Brabeck, K., Lerner, R.M., *Learning to serve: Promoting civil society through service learning* (pp. 31–49). Boston: Kluwer.

Metz, S., & Hesser, G. (1996). Principles of good practice in service-learning. In B. Jacoby & Associates (Eds.), *Service-learning in higher education* (pp. 26–52). San Francisco: Jossey-Bass.

National Heart, Lung, and Blood Institute. (1999). *Salud para su corazon: Your heart, your life.* (NIH Publication No. 99–3674). Rockville, MD: U.S. Department of Health and Human Services.

Sills, J. (2006). *Predictors of exercise and dietary change among immigrant Latinos following cardiovascular risk factor screening.* Unpublished doctoral dissertation. Pacific Graduate School of Psychology, Palo Alto, CA.

12

USING SERVICE LEARNING TO
TEACH COMMUNITY
NUTRITION

Marjorie Freedman

H
ealthy People 2000: National Health Promotion and Disease Prevention Objectives (U.S. Department of Health and Human Services [DHHS], 1990) identified goals and objectives that if reached by the year 2000 would advance the health of Americans. *Healthy People 2010: Understanding and Improving Health* (DHHS, 2000) was issued 10 years later, and it too provided an agenda for overall health improvement. It focused on two overarching goals: increasing the quality and years of healthy life and eliminating health disparities, and identifying 10 leading health indicators including physical activity, overweight and obesity, environmental quality, and access to health care.

Dietary factors contribute to four of the leading causes of death in the United States: coronary heart disease, some types of cancer, stroke, and diabetes (National Center for Health Statistics, 2004), and diet plays a significant role in the development of other acute and chronic conditions such as hypertension, osteoporosis, iron deficiency anemia, and dental caries (DHHS, 1988). Overweight and obesity, which have consistently and relentlessly increased in prevalence over the past 20 years in children and adults (Centers for Disease Control, 2009), are linked to increased mortality and morbidity as well as billions of dollars in associated health care costs (DHHS, 2001). Thus, nutrition-related activities are essential to health promotion and advancing a number of Healthy People 2010 objectives (see Table 12.1).

TABLE 12.1

A Sampling of Healthy People 2010 Objectives for Nutrition and Overweight

Objective	Baseline %	Current Estimate % (1999–2002)	Target % (2010)
Increase the proportion of adults who are at a healthy weight	42	33	60
Reduce the proportion of adults who are obese	23	30	15
Reduce the proportion of children who are overweight or obese	11	16	5
Increase the proportion of persons age 2 years and older who consume at least two daily servings of fruit	28	28	75
Increase the proportion of persons age 2 years and older who consume no more than 30% of calories from fat	33	33	75
Increase the proportion of persons age 2 years and older who meet dietary recommendations for calcium	46	Limited data	75

Note. From *Healthy People 2010. Nutrition and Overweight,* by U.S. Department of Health and Human Services. Retrieved November 15, 2009, from http://www.healthypeople.gov/Document/HTML/Volume2/19Nutrition.htm and http://www.healthypeople.gov/Data/midcourse/pdf/fa19.pdf

Unfortunately, tracking progress toward meeting the Healthy People 2010 objectives indicates the only nutrition objective that significantly moved toward its target was related to increasing food security. Available data suggest little or no progress for Healthy People 2010 objectives aimed at promoting healthful diets; all objectives relating to the weight status of adults and children have showed a trend of moving away from 2010 targets (DHHS, 2007).

Community nutritionists are charged with developing programs and policies that improve people's overall health and well-being (Boyle & Holben, 2010). They work to increase people's nutrition awareness and knowledge and ultimately change behaviors with respect to diet and food habits. If we are to make any progress in meeting the goals of Healthy People 2010, community nutritionists need to take a much more active role in the community, not only by educating consumers but advocating for environmental change.

To bring Healthy People 2010 objectives to life, I decided to incorporate service learning into my community nutrition class and asked the students several questions: Why are teens spending more time in front of computer and video screens rather than spending time outdoors? How can this trend be reversed to meet the objective of increasing the proportion of teens who exercise for at least 20 minutes a day/3 times a week from 64% to 85% by the year 2010? Why does the low-income Hispanic mother serve her child Tampico juice drink rather than Tropicana 100% juice? How can this habit be changed to meet the objective of increasing the proportion of people aged 2 years and older who consume at least two daily servings of fruit? And how does a working but uninsured father of four know if he is at risk for, or already has, hypertension, type 2 diabetes, or high blood cholesterol levels, and what can he do about it? How can we reach this father to meet the objective of increasing the proportion of people appropriately counseled about health behaviors and reduce the proportion of families that experience difficulties or delays in obtaining health care or do not receive needed care for one or more family members?

Working in the community provides students with opportunities to engage in important and necessary work, become involved with cross-cultural experiences, and increase their civic and citizenship skills. It might also motivate them to become advocates for environmental change—to lobby for increased access to more fresh fruits and vegetables, healthier vending options in community centers and libraries, and healthier foods in schools and after-school programs. Quite honestly, I wanted students to step out of their comfort zone and understand that their future roles as community nutritionists would best be realized by their becoming socially responsible learners—applying their professional knowledge and skills to the betterment of society. Through service learning I wanted to convey to students that by immersing themselves in their community they could better understand root causes of social problems, and this understanding coupled with classroom instruction would allow them to ultimately make a difference in their community.

Class Organization, Academic Design, and Logistics

As a new tenure-track faculty member in the Department of Nutrition and Food Science, I had little to no experience with service learning before designing and teaching my community nutrition class, which is offered every spring to graduating seniors and graduate students at San José State University. Previous instructors assigned students an agency visit, but my gut feeling was that visiting an agency would be dull compared to the richer experience of actually participating in a community organization. To this end, I designed a syllabus that included 20–25 hours of service learning as a class requirement (see Appendix A).

However, to my surprise, the initial reaction of many students was negative. Did they really have to spend 20–25 hours doing service learning in addition to class assignments and exams, their already full course load, work schedule, and family commitments? And were they only going to receive 3 credit hours for this class? Despite grumbling, I persisted and decided to let the chips fall as they may. After all, 20–25 hours over the course of 10 weeks (not counting startup time, spring break, and finals) amounts to only 2 hours per week. Surely, I reasoned, students could spend 2 hours a week volunteering in the community.

With a class of over 40 students, my goal was to provide a wide variety of community experiences for students to choose from. Being new at teaching service learning, I thought, *the more agencies, the more choices, the better!* Though I successfully placed 48 students in 32 different community agencies/projects (see Table 12.2), it required an enormous amount of time before and during the semester.

To be able to offer a wide variety of opportunities to my students, I made personal contact with community agencies prior to the start of the semester. I began with agencies already working with our Center for Community Learning & Leadership (CCLL); for example, Sunday Friends, After School All Stars, Boys and Girls Club), and then created new agency partnerships. Contact was initially made by phone and/or e-mail. It was always followed with a face-to-face meeting, where programs, potential needs, and the scope of student service learning were discussed. At the start of the semester, I distributed a list of all service-learning opportunities to students (including location, dates, times, and project description). Based on their schedule, language skills, and interests, I matched them with community organizations and agencies. Through e-mail, I introduced students to their agency contact, and left the rest (personal contact and follow-up) to them. Throughout the semester, I was available for advice, troubleshooting, and to provide needed resources and guidance.

TABLE 12.2
Community Nutrition Service Learning Partners and Service Learning Projects (spring 2006)

Service-Learning Partner	*Service-Learning Project Description/Requirements*
After School All-Stars	**Cold Foods Cooking Program:** Develop and present nutrition education lessons to at-risk middle school students attending after school program.
American Cancer Society	**Spring Into Health Program:** Work with ACS on health program geared toward 4th and 5th graders and their caregivers. Student will participate in training calls, format letters to schools, mail packets, help at schools as needed to implement program. Good clerical skills.
Boys and Girls Club	**Health and Life Skills Programs:** Develop and present programming for school-age children on (a) nutrition and oral hygiene, (b) food and body/muscle development, and (c) decision making and health.
Children's Health and Disability Program, County Health Department	**Feeding Dynamics:** Create low-literacy brochure on feeding dynamics; pilot test on parents at a community event.
City of San José	**Healthy San José:** Collect and document information regarding vending machine offerings throughout city of SJ (airport, city buildings, libraries, Parks and Rec.). Research policies existing in other cities with respect to healthy vending, advocate for local change.
City of San José, Public Library; Books for Little Hands Program	**Kids in the Kitchen:** Prepare and deliver nutrition education materials, including simple recipe preparation, to multicultural adults who care for preschoolers.
City of San José, Public Library	**Snack Smart:** Write a grant proposal focusing on teaching 4th–7th grade children about healthy snacks that includes food preparation and demonstrations, creation of a cookbook, and interactive games.
Congregation Shir Hadash/Most Holy Trinity	**Community Health Fair:** Students will (a) solicit donations of materials to hand out, (b) develop culturally appropriate interactive educational materials and activities for children and families, and (c) participate in the health fair. Tagalog, Vietnamese, and Spanish speakers needed.
Community Diabetes Project	**Community Diabetes Project:** Provide culturally appropriate nutrition education and hands-on workshops that support existing programs for diabetics. Spanish speaking a plus.

TABLE 12.2 (Continued)

Service-Learning Partner	Service-Learning Project Description/Requirements
Community Health Partnership	**Stanford Pediatric Weight Control Program:** Be trained to teach 6-month pediatric weight control program, offered in English and Spanish. Long-term commitment necessary.
Community Mapping Projects	**Community Access:** Map access to all sources of food on campus and within 1-mile radius around campus. Digital camera and computer skills necessary.
Diabetes Society of Santa Clara Valley	**Nutrition Classes:** Help teach weekly classes to clients with diabetes; student must have completed medical nutritional therapy and be familiar with nutritional needs of diabetic patients. **Diabetes Education and Counseling:** Work with children attending diabetes camp.
Doctor's Hospital of Manteca	**National Nutrition Month:** Prepare interactive activities for staff at hospital during National Nutrition Month.
Emergency Housing Consortium: Life Builders	**Making Healthy Food Choices on a Limited Budget:** Pilot test a program regarding educating residents of homeless shelter about healthful, economic food choices and cooking tips on a limited budget; introduce to WIC, food stamps, other public assistance programs.
Gault Elementary, Santa Cruz	**Breakfast/Snack Smart:** Involve children in preparation of healthy snacks and provide nutrition education to 3rd grade students in a public elementary school.
Generations-Wellness Centers	**Spring Chickens:** Develop and present multicultural nutrition education materials for seniors participating in diet and exercise programs.
Health Trust and Children's Discovery Museum	**Community Health Fairs:** Students will (a) solicit donations of materials to distribute, (b) develop culturally appropriate interactive activities and educational materials for children and families, (c) participate in activities at community health fairs.
InnVision	**Drop-In Nutrition Education:** Prepare and present relevant health-related information to low-income, uninsured women with children.
John XXIII	**Senior Nutrition:** Prepare and present culturally relevant nutrition and health-related information to Asian seniors. Cantonese/Mandarin speakers needed.

Mid-Peninsula Housing Organization	**Community Garden/Nutrition Project:** Develop an integrated, intergenerational health education programs focusing on nutrition and community gardens. Work with children at garden site implementing program.
Pediatric Lifestyle Clinic	**Lifestyle Counseling:** Work with pediatrician and dietitian to provide culturally competent nutrition information about diet and physical activity to families attending clinic.
Rainbow Recovery Foundation	**Nutrition Matters for Women in Transition:** Work with house managers and residents of transitional housing for women recovering from drug addictions. Educate and help with menu panning, food preparation, shopping, and basic life skills. Develop nutrition resource manual for house managers and residents.
San José Conservation Corps	**Student Nutrition Action Team:** Develop and present interactive and fun nutrition education materials to at-risk high school students.
San José State Child Development Center	**Parent Assessment and Education:** Provide basic nutrition screenings and information to parents whose children attend the child development center.
San José Unified School District: Steps to a Healthier US	**Parent Education Day/Evening:** Plan and present interactive learning activities to staff, students, and families. **Teen Health Council:** Work with teens/their advisors to create interactive booths for health fairs at local high and middle schools.
School Health Clinics	**GoGirlsGo:** Develop and present nutrition education materials to high school girls.
Second Harvest Food Bank	**Brown Bag/Family Harvest Programs:** Provide nutrition information to Brown Bag sites for low-income seniors (various ethnicities) and Family Harvest sites for child nutrition education.
Sunday Friends	**Nutrition Games:** Develop and implement family-based nutrition games (e.g., nutrition jeopardy, bingo) for low-literacy clients. Spanish speaking a plus
Volunteers for Outdoor California (VOC)	**Nutrition Manual:** Develop a food service manual for use by Project Support Coordinators in meal planning and preparation for VOC land stewardship project.

TABLE 12.2 (Continued)

Service-Learning Partner	*Service-Learning Project Description/Requirements*
YMCA	**Curriculum Development and Implementation**: Work with YMCA and Santa Clara County After School Collaborative on culturally competent curriculum, recipes, and cookbooks. Organize family events and work with branches on Healthy Kids Day.
YWCA	**Preschool and After-School Nutrition Programs**: Develop rotating menus; provide nutrition guidance to center directors who work with children aged 6 wks to 12 yrs.

Was it worth it? At the end of the semester, one busy full-time student who had a job, a new husband, and whose service learning was working with transitional high school students wrote:

> The most important lesson I learned throughout this project was how much I truly want to be a nutritionist and specifically, how much I want to work in the community. I am glad something good came out of this experience and that in the end, I can look back on this project and this class in a positive light. I realized that working in the community can be discouraging and is hard work but can also be incredibly rewarding. Furthermore, I recognized how much the community needs us and how much work there is to be done. The fact that we can make such a difference in the livelihood of the people in the community, the country, and even the world is why I am determined to continue my studies in this field and work hard when I am out of school and in the community. What I discovered most through working at Andrew Hill High School is how important it is that we provide the tools to individuals in every community to be able to live a long and healthy life. Every individual in this country has the right to live a healthy life and I plan to work with individuals, community leaders, and legislation to ensure that the appropriate tools are provided to make this happen.

I was vindicated.

Community Partners and Individuals Served

In Santa Clara County, community organizations serve an extremely diverse population. Thus, by volunteering with these organizations, students experienced working with children, the elderly, and everyone in between. Many agencies serve children and teenagers who benefited from interactions with college-age students. Students worked with people who spoke English, Spanish, Portuguese, Farsi, Vietnamese, Russian, Tagalog, Mandarin, Cantonese, and Korean. Every attempt was made to match the language skills of students with the community partners/clients they served, although this was not always possible. Some community partners served low-income individuals, people who were homeless or in transitional housing, or people recovering from substance abuse. Knowledge of nutrition was minimal in most cases.

Students mainly acted as a nutrition resource for members of the community, increasing awareness about the role of nutrition in health and providing basic culturally relevant nutrition information to target populations. Students were role models for high school students and looked at as experts by less-educated and less-nutritionally informed members of the community. Most organizations did not have someone trained in nutrition on staff, nor could they afford to hire a registered dietitian or nutrition consultant. Thus, students provided valuable services to community organizations that would probably not have had the opportunity to provide nutrition education to their clients.

One organization that students volunteered with was Second Harvest Food Bank of Santa Clara and San Mateo counties. They participated in Operation Brown Bag, a self-help program that gives low-income seniors a bag of groceries each week, and Family Harvest, which provides monthly groceries to low-income families with minor dependent children. Since many recipients of these programs do not speak English, students were challenged to provide nutrition information using posters and other visuals that could be easily understood despite language barriers. Translated educational materials were a necessity. This experience brought to life what one student working with Operation Brown Bag had read in a textbook. She wrote:

> Through this experience, I was able to work with the elderly population of our area and I was shocked. I had no idea the diversity of our elderly population. I have worked in community nutrition before with a younger population, mostly Spanish speaking, and I expected all Spanish speakers in this population too. I assumed this especially living in this area of California. In Mountain View and Palo Alto the Brown Bag clients are almost exclusively Russian. I am currently taking a class in Cultural Foods and our text helped explain this. It stated: "Policy in the former Soviet Union required aging parents to leave if their children wished to emigrate. One result is that Russian immigrants are one of the oldest populations in the United States: 20

percent are older than 65 years" (Kittler and Sucher, 2000). In Campbell, there is a large Iranian elderly group. Maria Goretto, a site off Senter Road, is entirely Vietnamese. Areas of East San Jose that I expected to be Hispanic were mainly Chinese or Korean. Areas near Milpitas were Chinese and Filipino. I was surprised wherever I went. I learned after about the third visit, however to have my car full of materials in every language. I never knew the types of ethnicity at a site until I arrived.

Student Evaluation and the Student Perspective on the Learning Experience

Students were required to keep a journal of their experiences, fill out the Student Evaluation of Community Placement Form (see Appendix B) provided by the CCLL, and write a reflective paper at the conclusion of their project, adapted from materials provided by CCLL (see Appendix C). Grading was based on student writings and reflections rather than community accomplishments.

What did students learn? Although difficult to fully assess and measure, their writings about community experiences were enlightening and showed their experiences did, in fact, enhance their academic learning as well as broaden their understanding of diversity and social responsibility. For example, one student who worked in an elementary school wrote:

> This experience was very rewarding to me. I truly felt like I made a difference in the way children performed and felt at school. I think I also made an impact on the students about taking care of themselves by eating well and exercising. I came into this project with big expectations about teaching students about basic nutrition, however when feeding them became more important, my expectations changed along with my focus. I soon became very satisfied with providing and preparing snacks with them. They have been extremely appreciative and were always very pleased to see me. Their teacher has commented that her classroom environment has become a better learning environment due to my efforts.

Another, who worked at a high school, wrote:

> My entire experience was eye-opening. I had never worked with high school students before which is a challenge all in itself but I also had never worked with a primarily Hispanic population and with students that were

from a lower socioeconomic class. It was hard to hear students tell me that their parents would not let them buy this or that because it was too expensive. This program made me realize that being a nutritionist is not just about telling people how to eat and how to live a healthy lifestyle. As a registered dietitian informing people on how to make "healthy" choices is going to be the easiest part of my job. The biggest challenge is going to be making sure they have the tools to be able to live a long and healthy life. This includes working hard to make sure the environment and community supports this objective and I am well aware that this is not going to be an easy task to achieve.

And, another, who worked with women in recovery, wrote:

It's always a bad idea to enter into a situation knowingly carrying expectations. The main expectation I had of which I was unaware was that I figured everyone would shut up and listen to me when I spoke and not interrupt everyone else when they spoke. The most common emotion I had was overwhelm, followed by frustration, hopelessness (bound ever so tightly to helplessness), utter shock, and guilt for not being able to do enough.

In conclusion, this was a quick-and-dirty, thrown-into-the-fire way of learning how to assess a group's needs and design a potential program totally from scratch. I have to admit that I'd probably never make a career of it because there's little money in it and I have these student loans to pay. These skills are definitely transferable, however, because these women and their children represent a segment of the real world that I am bound to encounter in my professional life again and again.

When asked if the service component was meaningful to the course material, one student responded, "Yes. After all how can you do community nutrition without being in the community? It is like taking a cooking class and never cooking anything." Another wrote, "Yes, I felt that my service activities helped me better understand some of the issues that were lectured about in class. An example would be childhood obesity, for I was able to witness how kids were eating and how active they usually are. Furthermore, I was able to understand how city and government funding or lack of funding directly affects the community of those who utilize the Boys and Girls Club."

Measuring change in personal skills and attitudes is also difficult but I believe best reflected by the student's own self-assessment in journal entries and reflective writing as illustrated here:

> The most valuable thing that came out of my service-learning experience was probably my own personal growth. I never realized that helping kids could be so rewarding. I would always look back on what my experiences were as a teenager, and I use this to better interact with the kids so that they have better opportunities for excelling in school and with their overall health. I can only hope that all the information that I put forth to the kids will affect them positively, whether the change be from reconsidering junk food, or realizing that they should be more active and playing sports instead of video games. Ultimately, I would like to work with kids in the future so that they have positive role models to look up to.

Feedback From Community Partners

Most community partners were enthusiastic about working with San José State University nutrition students and provided feedback via phone or e-mail. One e-mail expresses appreciation for my student working with alternative high school students:

> My co-leader and I were extremely pleased with DM's presentations. She tailored the information to suit the students' interests and habits and did a great job at eliciting participation from the students. We really appreciate her efforts and time. Our crew recently won a pizza party, and all the students said "we need to have lots of vegetables on our pizza." I was ecstatic about their request. Every bit counts. Thanks again.

Another, who works for an organization that provides preschool and after-school care to children aged 6 weeks to 12 years, wrote:

> Today I met with KW so she could give me her completed work. She produced many pages of activities for the children to work on. Really great stuff and it will be used quite a bit. In addition, she gave me directions to three games that she came up with: healthy hopscotch, food guide pyramid, and food label scavenger hunt. The directions are clear, and I think they're good for various ages of children. The kids will learn quite a bit (as I'm sure staff will!) from participating in these games. Overall, I have to

say that I'm very impressed with KW's work. She was given a task that seems simple to us, because we know the environment. But to dive into this and really understand what we're working with, to see the struggle, and then to give us some clear directions, was very challenging, and I know it took effort and time on her part. She worked well on her own and gave us some materials we can easily work with. Our staff will thank her for the coordination, which makes putting all of this into place much easier. Thanks so much for sharing your students!

One successful project engaged students in political learning and showed how citizen groups could effect change in their communities. Specifically, students provided important background information and research to support a healthy vending initiative in public libraries and buildings in the city of San José. When the initiative was being heard by the city council, students attended the meeting dressed as fruits and vegetables, holding signs in support of the initiative. After the initiative was unanimously passed, a letter from the city council staff expressed gratitude for student involvement.

> Just wanted to email on behalf of Councilmember Yeager—and express our gratitude for your support today and throughout this entire process. We wouldn't be celebrating today without all of your assistance. There is nothing like the words of people who work day in and day out with the community to bring us out of the office and into reality. We look forward to working with you all in the future—great job everyone! There is still much work to be done—so we'll be in touch. Can't believe I forgot . . . please express our gratitude to your dedicated students as well . . . their presence was wonderful!

University Recognition

Each year the CCLL and the provost honor students, faculty members, and community organizations make outstanding efforts to integrate community service and academic learning. I was honored when my student Sally Chaves received the award for outstanding student. The following is a description of her efforts.

> Sally Chaves, RN, a graduate student in community nutrition class has remarkable commitment and dedication to her service-learning project. She works weekly at the Pediatric Lifestyle Clinic (a satellite clinic of Valley

Medical Center located in East San Jose), under the supervision of Dan Delgado, MD. The Clinic treats mostly Hispanic children—all overweight, and most at significant risk for type 2 diabetes. Sally has exceeded the number of hours of service learning required for the class. Her desire to go beyond what is expected makes her efforts so remarkable and worthy of commendation. After only a few weeks of work at the clinic, Sally was given the responsibility of a team member and now she takes care of her own patients. She developed Spanish language skills to be able to communicate with children and their parents. She also assists on translating the clinical material from English into Spanish for those practitioners who do not speak Spanish. Sally is integrating her existing medical background with her recently acquired knowledge regarding nutrition to make a difference in the lives of these children and their families. These experiences with children and their families have deeply affected her, and have strengthened her resolve to do something meaningful for the underserved population after she graduates from SJSU [San José State University]. She exemplifies what service learning is all about—the integration of service to the community, the development of social responsibility and the maturity to reflect on how this experience contributes to learning and the betterment of the community at large.

Putting It All Together and Recommendations to Others

Students enrolled in the community nutrition class benefited from participating in service learning, as it not only allowed students to gain firsthand knowledge of and experience with social problems and issues that directly affected the health and well-being of members of their community but also to reflect on their experiences. Reading about a health objective (e.g., increasing the number of people age 2 years and older who consume no more than 30% of calories from fat) and influencing policy change so that vending machines in public libraries and community centers frequented by children are not allowed to stock snack foods high in fat are two very different experiences. Knowing they can be part of the process and reflecting on their own participation in the community, allows students to realize that what they have learned in class is not simply of academic importance but has social relevance as well.

Students who participated in service learning were able to make a difference in their community—from educating low-income families about consuming more fruits and vegetables and decreasing their intake of sugar-sweetened beverages to providing important health screening information to uninsured adults. They were better able to understand some of the barriers that individuals face when trying to reach Healthy People 2010 objectives and to work toward environmental change to remove some of these barriers. Although no direct assessments either of the community organizations or the people they serve were made, this is an area of growth that will be explored in future service-learning projects.

Service-learning classes require instructors to be organized, well connected, and available to students outside the typical school hours for consultation and observation. An understanding of community resources, community problems, and, in some cases, local politics is helpful. What works well is giving students clear expectations before their service learning begins and checking in with them during the course of the semester to address ongoing problems or issues. It is necessary to make sure community partners know what to expect from students with respect to time, ability, and expertise. Open channels of communication between all parties involved is key to successful service learning.

My experience with service learning has been positive, despite the additional and sometimes overwhelming amount of work necessary especially at the start of the semester. I have been pleased to see students who are quiet or shy in class connect with children in the community. I am thrilled when a student who struggles with English successfully communicates with an elder who speaks the same language as the student and is able to provide important information that might otherwise be unavailable. I am surprised when students rally around an issue they believe in, just because it's the right thing to do and not because they receive extra credit for doing so. Finally, I learned that unless we take the classroom into the community, and train our students to translate academic knowledge into social and civic action, we have little hope of making any headway into solving the serious health issues facing Americans today and in the future. Our students are the future, and we must not only provide them with academic knowledge but also help them to hone their personal skills and develop their inner beliefs and self-esteem so they will be successful when they graduate from our institutions of higher learning.

References

Boyle, M. A. & Holben, D. H. (2006). *Community nutrition in action: An entrepreneurial approach*. Belmont, CA: Thomson/Wadsworth.

Centers for Disease Control and Prevention. *Overweight and obesity*. Retrieved November 15, 2009, from http://www.cdc.gov/obesity/index.html

National Center for Health Statistics. (2004). Deaths: Final data for 2002. *National Vital Statistics Reports, 53*(5). Retrieved November 15, 2009, from http://www.cdc .gov/nchs/data/nvsr/nvsr53/nvsr53_05acc.pdf

U.S. Department of Health and Human Services. (1988). *The surgeon general's report on nutrition and health* (DHHS Pub. No. 88–50210). Washington, DC: U.S. Government Printing Office. Available from http://profiles.nlm.nih.gov/NN/B/ C/R/T/

U.S. Department of Health and Human Services. (1990). *Healthy people 2000: National health promotion and disease prevention objectives*. Washington, DC: U.S. Government Printing Office. Available from http://odphp.osophs.dhhs.gov/pubs/ HP2000/

U.S. Department of Health and Human Services. (2000). *Healthy people 2010: Understanding and improving health*. Washington, DC: U.S. Government Printing Office. Available from http://www.healthypeople.gov/

U.S. Department of Health and Human Services. (2005). *Healthy people 2010: The cornerstone for prevention*. [Electronic version]. Washington, DC: Author. Retrieved April 21, 2003, from http://www.healthypeople.gov/Publications/Corner stone.pdf

U.S. Department of Health and Human Services. (2001). *The surgeon general's call to action to prevent and decrease overweight and obesity*. Rockville, MD: U.S. Government Printing Office. Available from http://www.surgeongeneral.gov/topics/ obesity/calltoaction/CalltoAction.pdf

Appendix A

Syllabus, San José State University

Community Nutrition (NuFS 114A)

Course Information

- Class meets M–W 12:00–1:15 in CCB 102; Course Code 35091 (3 units)

Faculty Information

- Marjorie Freedman, MS, PhD, Assistant Professor
- Office: CCB 202; Office Hours: M–W 11:00–12:00 or by appt.
- **Phone:** (408) 924–3105; **E-mail:** mfreedman@casa.sjsu.edu
- Faculty Web page: http://www.sjsu.edu/faculty_and_staff/ faculty_detail.jsp?id = 1070

Course Description: Nutrition problems; public policy, advocacy and legislation; government programs; needs assessments; management of community services.

This course will provide basic knowledge and skills relevant to the practice of community nutrition. We will cover the concept of community, the role of nutrition in health promotion, and perspectives for resolving community nutrition problems. Needs assessment issues and national and state community nutrition programs, determinants of health outcomes, measurement of nutrition and health status, food, and nutrition policy, legislative issues and management of community programs will be covered. Finally, the concepts and knowledge required for the delivery of community nutrition services will be applied to program planning, intervention, and program evaluation.

Course Objectives: By the end of the semester, students will be able to

1. Explain characteristics, functions, and processes of a community and identify the role of nutrition in health promotion.
2. Describe objectives of, and services provided by, community nutrition programs discussed in class.

3. Distinguish between local, state, and federal food and nutrition programs.
4. List the basic goals of a community assessment.
5. Describe how a community assessment can be conducted including specification of the types of data that are relevant.
6. Describe the different methods for assessing nutritional status and health in the community, and give examples of the appropriate use of each method.
7. Be familiar with sources of data for conducting a community assessment, including those on the Internet.
8. Apply knowledge from other disciplines such as epidemiology, anthropology, and health education to a community nutrition assessment.
9. Describe the legislative and regulatory process, and discuss ways to influence policy.
10. Demonstrate an understanding of the processes involved in designing, implementing, and evaluating a community nutrition program.

Prerequisites:
NuFS 106A. Senior standing and instructor consent.

Required Course Materials:
Boyle, M. A. & Holben, D. H. (2006). *Community nutrition in action* (4th ed.). Belmont, CA: Thomson/Wadsworth.

Evaluation:

	Points	% of Grade
Midterm	100	26.7
Case Study (choose 1 of 4)	50	13.3
Legislative Assignment	25	6.7
Community Project	100	26.7
Final (noncumulative)	100	26.7
Total Points	**375**	**100.0**

Grading:

A	94 – 100%	C+	78 – 79
A –	90 – 93	C	70 – 77
B+	88 – 89	C –	68 – 69
B	84 – 87	D	60 – 67
B –	80 – 83	F	< 60

Extra Credit (EC) Options:

- EC options are available throughout the semester and will be posted on WebCT. I will choose students for EC based on response to postings as well as unique talents. Students can receive a maximum of 20 EC points. A write-up using the EC form, and submitted to WebCT within 1 week the EC event is necessary to receive EC points. No exceptions!
- If you sign up for EC (involving showing up somewhere) and you do not show up, you forfeit the opportunity to participate in future EC events.

Academic Integrity Statement:

"Your own commitment to learning, as evidenced by your enrollment at SJSU, and the University's Academic Integrity Policy requires you to be honest in all your academic course work. Faculty is required to report all infractions to the Office of Student Conduct & Ethical Development." The policy on academic integrity and student conduct are found at http://sa.sjsu.edu/judicial_affairs/index.html

Students are expected to follow university policy regarding plagiarism & cheating. If you are unfamiliar with the issue of plagiarism, I strongly advise you to complete the library tutorial on plagiarism at http://tutorials.sjlibrary.org (sign in as a guest). Results of this tutorial will NOT be collected. Any work, including term papers, that are plagiarized will receive a zero, the student will be reported to Office of Student Conduct and may receive an F in the class. I strictly enforce this policy every semester!!

Campus policy in compliance with the Americans with Disabilities Act:
"If you need course adaptations or accommodations because of a disability, or if you need special arrangements in case the building must be evacuated, please make an appointment with me as soon as possible, or see me during office hours. Presidential Directive 97-03 requires that students with disabilities register with DRC to establish a record of their disability."

Tentative Course Schedule

Please note that this is a tentative schedule and during the semester the instructor may adjust the schedule if necessary to maximize the students' learning of a particular topic.

Date	Topic	Reading	Assignments/Other
W 1/24	Introduction: Green Sheet and Assignments		
	Nutritionists in Action: Working in the Community		
M 1/29	Opportunities in Community Nutrition	Ch 1	Finalize community projects 2/2
W 1/31			
M 2/5	Assessing Community Resources	Ch 2	Last day to drop classes
W 2/7			
M 2/12	Assessing Nutritional Status	Ch 3	Last day to add classes
W 2/14	Principles of Epidemiology	Ch 4	Case Study (1) p. 111
M 2/19			
W 2/21	National Nutrition Agendas	Ch 6	Case Study (2) p. 194
M 2/26			Case Study (1) Due
W 2/28	Policy Making	Ch 7	
M 3/5	Obesity & Public Health Policy	Ch 8	Case Study (2) Due
W 3/7			
			Case Study (3) p. 269
M 3/12	Public Policy		Guest Speaker
W 3/14	Health Care Systems	Ch 9	
M 3/19	Catch up, Review		Case Study (3) due
W 3/21	Midterm Chapters 1–4, 6–9		
	SPRING BREAK		
	Community Nutritionists in Action: Delivering Programs		
M 4/2	Food Insecurity	Ch 5	
W 4/4	Domestic Hunger Programs		Guest Speaker
M 4/9	Mothers and Infants	Ch 10	
W 4/11	WIC Program		
M 4/16	Children and Adolescents	Ch 11	Case Study (4) p. 379
W 4/18	Working with Families in the Community		Guest Speaker
M 4/23	Children and Adolescents; School Nutrition		Legislative Assignment due
W 4/25	Growing Older	Ch 12	Case Study (4) due
M 4/30	Designing Interventions	Ch 15	
W 5/2	Cultural Competency	Ch 16	
M 5/7;	Marketing Nutrition	Ch 18	
W 5/9			
M 5/14	Catch-up, Review		Final Write-up Due
T 5/22	FINAL EXAM 9:45–12:00		

Assignments:

Assignment 1. Case Study (50 pts) Due per schedule above, no late papers accepted. Choose ONE of the FOUR case studies below. Read the case study and answer questions (for your own knowledge—do not turn in) under "Foundation: Acquisition of Knowledge and Skills." Then, using the information you have gathered, write and turn in the answers to all questions under headings labeled Steps 1–4.

a. Case Study 1: Epidemiology of Obesity, p. 111
b. Case Study 2: From Guidelines to Groceries, p. 194
c. Case Study 3: Worksite Health Promotion Program, p. 269
d. Case Study 4: The Child Nutrition Program, p. 379

Important Note: Students may choose to work in pairs on this assignment (note: that means in groups of 2—no larger). If you choose this option, you may turn in one paper with both names (that both students have contributed to), or you may turn in two different papers (separate write ups based on discussing the information together). Either way, if you partner with someone else, you will BOTH receive the identical grade—regardless of whether there is an individual or a combined write-up.

Assignment 2. Legislative Assignment (25 pts) Due 4/23
For this assignment you are expected to learn about (the) nutrition policy process, take an action to influence it, then write up your research and experience in a 2–3 page typed paper using the following questions as your guide.

a. Complete elected official handout (3 points)
b. Describe (in your own words) one current nutrition-related bill that you support. (2) What does the bill aim to do? (2) Who is the target population and what is its significance to that population? (2) How will it affect the profession of dietetics, the nutritional status of Californians or Americans? (2) What is the cost (if any) associated with the bill (if none, indicate)? (2) When was the bill first introduced? (2) By whom? (1) What is its current status? (1)
c. Write a letter (suitable to mail, using the correct format) to your senator or assemblyperson in support of the bill OR write a letter to the editor of the local newspaper in support of this issue (8 points)

Assignment 3. Community Project (100 pts) Write up due 5/14
For this assignment, you will choose a project from the list provided. All projects must be finalized by Friday Feb 2nd. Students will perform 20—25 hrs of service learning associated with their project. In addition, all students will complete all forms associated with service learning (including a reflective piece). The final write up is due 5/14/06. *NO late write-ups will be accepted. Student will not receive credit for project in the absence of forms/write-up.*

Appendix B

Student Evaluation of Community Placement

Semester _____ Year _____ Instructor _____

Personal Data (optional)
Age _____ Gender: Male _____ Female _____
Academic Year: Fr _____ Soph _____ Jr _____ Sr _____
Race _____

Service Placement

1. My service placement was with _____

    (organization)

    in _____

    (city)

2. I contributed approximately _____ hours total to this organization.

3. Briefly describe your service activities. _____

4. Rate your service placement in the following areas (mark only one per row):

	Very Satisfied	Satisfied	Dissatisfied	Very Dissatisfied
a. Helpfulness of agency staff	☐	☐	☐	☐
b. Adequate orientation and training	☐	☐	☐	☐
c. Adequate supervision	☐	☐	☐	☐
d. Meaningful tasks to perform	☐	☐	☐	☐
e. Recognition of my efforts	☐	☐	☐	☐

5. Did your service activities enhance your understanding of course content? Yes ___No ___
    If yes, how? If no, why not?

6. Would you recommend this site to future service-learning students? Yes ___ No ___
    Why? Why not?

7. Do you plan to continue serving with this community program after completing this
    service-learning course? Yes ___ No ___ Why? Why not?

8. Please circle the extent to which you agree with the following:

    a. I feel that I was able to make a meaningful contribution to the community through this service-learning experience.

       Strongly Agree   Agree   Disagree   Strongly Disagree

    b. I feel I would have learned more from this class if more time was spent in the classroom instead of doing service in the community.

       Strongly Agree   Agree   Disagree   Strongly Disagree

    c. I feel more comfortable participating in the community after this class.

       Strongly Agree   Agree   Disagree   Strongly Disagree

9. Would you enroll in another course with a service component? Yes ___ No ___

    Why? Why not?

10. As a result of this course, has your attitude toward community service become (check one):

    More positive? _____ Stayed the same? _____ More negative? _____

11. Were you given ample opportunity to reflect upon your service experience in writing or during class discussion? Yes _____ No _____

    Please comment on the reflection activities from which you gained the most insight (i.e., classroom discussions, journaling, etc.)

12. What would you do to improve this service-learning course?

13. What was the most valuable thing that came out of your service-learning experience?

    Additional Comments:

Appendix C

Community Nutrition: Service Learning Evaluation and Grading Key

Student Name: Project Name:

A. Objective(s): What were the objectives of your project?

B. Responsibility shown toward project (50 pts)
    • Please indicate the contact information (email, phone) for all people you worked with on this project. The community contact will provide feedback regarding your work, specifically, whether you did what you were supposed to do, came prepared, showed up on time, acted in a responsible fashion, followed directions, etc. You will also be graded on how well you worked with other members of your group (if applicable).
    • Please answer to the following questions
        • Where was I?
        • Who else was there?
        • When did the experience take place?
        • What did I/others do? (Be specific when describing what you did).
        • Why was I/we there? (Be objective; don't interpret here.)
        • What were the key events and features of this experience?
        • How many hours did I spend on this project?

C. Evaluation (50 pts)
    • Using the information below as a guide, provide a reflective piece on what was learned, what you could have done differently, and the overall value of the project to the community.

        1. Identify Relevant Knowledge (5 pts): Examine academic knowledge (from this course or other sources) that might be applicable to your experience:
            • What course work or reading have I done which is relevant to this experience?
            • What principles, concepts, theories, skills, or information have I learned which relate to this experience?

- How does this experience relate to what I have learned elsewhere?
- How is the experience consistent with my academic knowledge?
- How does my academic knowledge help me to organize, understand, make sense of, or develop hypotheses about this experience?
- How does this experience tie in with my academic learning and understanding of community nutrition?

2. Examine the experience on a personal level (10 pts): Consider:
   - How did the experience(s) make me feel (positively and/or negatively)? How did I handle my emotional reactions?
   - What assumptions or expectations did I bring to the situation(s) (including assumptions about other persons involved) and how did they affect my action? To what extent did they prove true? If they did not prove true, why was there a discrepancy?
   - What personal strengths/weaknesses of mine did the situation(s) reveal? What might I do to build on strengths/overcome weaknesses?
   - What personal skills(s) did I draw upon? What personal skill(s) would I like to have had to better handle the situation(s); and how might I develop them?

3. Articulate learning (10 pts): Using the following questions as a guide, discuss what you learned from this experience.
   - What did I learn? (About myself? About others? About the world around me?) Be specific
   - Why does this learning matter? Why is it important? (Of if you didn't learn anything or do not think the learning was important, justify your answers)
   - In what ways will I use this learning to set goals to improve myself and/or the quality of my learning and/or the quality of my future experiences or service?
   - What knowledge, wisdom, or insights did I gain? What skills (if any) did I acquire?

4. Summary (10 pts)
- What did you think about this experience overall? Did you think it was valuable to the community? Why or why not?
- If you had to do it all over again, what would you do differently? What suggestions would you make to improve this learning experience?

D. Journal (10 pts)

Write at least one paragraph (in an electronic journal) each time you participate in the community activity. You can explain your experiences, jobs you did, and how you contributed to the project. You may also talk about your feelings (frustration/joy), what was going well or what was problematic. You can also reflect on your time/project.

E. Clarity of writing (5 pts)

Includes sentence structure, grammar, spelling, format, overall neatness and presentation. You must turn in all service learning forms as well.

13

AFFECTING COMMUNITY WELLNESS WITH TECHNOLOGY AND CROSS-DISCIPLINARY COLLABORATION

Malu Roldan

T his chapter describes a wide-ranging collaboration that aimed to have an impact on community health programs while helping students build knowledge and skills in the use of leading-edge technologies, cross-disciplinary teamwork, and healthy practices. Participation from various departments at San José State University (SJSU), community partners, and industry partners brought about innovations that addressed real community needs. This chapter begins with a history of how this collaboration and its focus came about, followed by a description of the project resulting from the collaboration, and closes with a discussion of outcomes and lessons learned.

History

In 2003 a group of SJSU professors from the departments of Management Information Systems (MIS), Computer Engineering (CmpE), Aviation and Technology (AvT), Academic Technology (AT), and Finance (Fin) received funding from Hewlett-Packard (HP) to develop a series of cross-disciplinary courses in which students use emerging mobile technologies (e.g., tablet PCs, PDAs) to support course work as well as build mobile computing applications for local entrepreneurs and business clients. This effort, known as the

Mobility Project, kicked off with a first set of courses involving MIS, CmpE, and Fin student teams working on projects for nine clients, including a trendy hotel (Santana Row's Hotel Valencia), a local theater chain (Camera Cinemas), and several entrepreneurs working on e-book, grading, and local events calendar innovations. As with most cross-disciplinary efforts, the first semester of the project (fall 2003) was fraught with misunderstanding regarding the role of each discipline, particularly that of MIS, which served as the bridge between technical and nontechnical participants and thus had the most ambiguous and flexible role. Nevertheless, most students and clients found the experience rewarding (Kelley, 2004).

In spring 2004 two events prompted a refocusing of the Mobility Project goals. First, SJSU, with leadership from the university's Center for Service Learning, received a grant from Purdue University's Engineering Projects in Community Service (EPICS) to seed a service-learning program in the College of Engineering. Second, past experiences with applying service learning in MIS courses at SJSU provided encouraging results regarding students' civic engagement even when the service was indirect if it was coupled with reflective activities in the classroom (Roldan, Strage, & David, 2004). Given these developments and an invitation from HP to apply for an extension grant, a subset of the Mobility Project team—involving MIS, CmpE, and AT—and the Center for Service Learning proposed to take the cross-disciplinary model of the Mobility Project and apply it to efforts that address the needs of community-based organizations (CBOs) and their constituents. This community-based innovation proposal was funded in spring 2004.

At a meeting organized by the Center for Service Learning in summer 2004, as Mobility Project director I met Elizabeth Sills, then director of community partnerships for the Health Trust (THT), a CBO devoted to addressing community health issues in the Santa Clara Valley area. Sills and her colleagues at THT immediately grasped the potential of mobile technologies to support the distributed nature of the work they did in the community—particularly in their health fair, flu shots, Meals on Wheels, and community health education programs. THT personnel embraced the technology, using loaner tablet PCs in summer 2004 to gain familiarity with the technology and generate ideas for their use.

Aside from the resources it possessed as a large CBO and the readiness of its managers and staff to embrace technology, THT also allowed the Mobility Project to tap into a large network of individuals and groups working on community health issues in Santa Clara Valley. As director of community partnerships for THT, Sills was already collaborating with individuals who would become key partners of the Mobility Project on endeavors addressing health issues, most significantly the city of San José's Strong Neighborhoods Initiative and the undertakings of SJSU's health science department.

Mobility Project Description

In fall 2004 the Mobility Project involved several teams composed of MIS and CmpE students in the development of the following applications:

- a health survey to collect data on community members taking advantage of health screening services at a health fair organized by THT at a popular open-air flea market in the fall and spring. Tablet PCs were used as data collection tools, mimicking the paper surveys traditionally used to collect this data. Aside from their portability, the tablet PCs had the potential for enabling direct entry of the data into a database in the field, reducing the need for data entry from paper forms into a database back at THT headquarters.
- a Web-based registration system for individuals seeking to volunteer for various positions at the THT health fair. This system running on laptops was also used to check volunteers in and out at the health fair.
- a Meals on Wheels application to facilitate the scheduling of holiday meal deliveries. Holiday schedules affect driver availability as well as the needs of folks receiving meals. THT personnel then scramble to match drivers with meal delivery routes. This application used tablet PCs to guide drivers through their holiday routes—using mapping software to provide directions to delivery points as well as help with finding their way back to their routes should they get lost.
- a Meals on Wheels application that used the tablet PC as a platform for pen pal communications among homebound community members (Meals on Wheels clients) and schoolchildren. Mimicking an existing pen pal program, this application used the multimedia capabilities of the tablet PCs to enable rich media documents (incorporating audio, video, and larger fonts) to be shared among pen pals. Schoolchildren had the opportunity to become familiar with a leading-edge mobile technology to compose their documents. Drivers then

brought the tablet PCs to the homebound clients as part of their meal deliveries, assisting the clients with reading the document and composing a response.

- a community asset mapping application on tablet PCs used by SJSU health science students to collect data and observations on a local community's physical features that encourage or discourage healthy habits. The students were involved in this project as part of a community health class taught by health science chair and professor Kathleen Roe. Students mapped features including the condition of sidewalks, availability of fresh fruits and vegetables, prevalence of fast-food establishments, and proximity to parks and playgrounds. Aside from filling out a structured survey that stored data directly into a database, the students took advantage of the rich media capabilities of various mobile devices, including recording audio journals and handwritten notes on the tablet PCs, taking pictures using digital cameras, and noting their position at a data collection point using GPS receivers. These data were used by the students to create multimedia reports on their findings for presentation to community members and policy makers.

For all of these applications, MIS students took on the role of project managers, developing and overseeing the project schedule and developing a business case for the application. CmpE students assumed the role of developers, building and installing the mobile computing software required by each application. MIS and CmpE students were involved in meetings with THT staff to elicit project requirements and test the applications in the field (e.g., health fair, local community). THT staff included directors and staff of the Meals on Wheels and health fair programs and the community partnerships program. Additionally, teams worked with SJSU AmeriCorps members assigned to work with various programs at THT. These AmeriCorps members served as context experts on health issues and procedures that were pertinent to the applications being built by the Mobility Project teams. For example, an AmeriCorps member attending SJSU's health science master's program provided expertise on questions to included in the community asset mapping application.

Given resource constraints, the mobility team sought to limit the project requirements and scope to *proof-of-concept* efforts. The applications developed by the teams were intended to help the THT identify and test potential uses of mobile technologies. Based on these proof-of-concept efforts, the directors involved could select applications with the most potential and make a case for their funding by the THT management team. These projects undertaken by the mobility team were thus not intended for permanent installation at THT but rather were ways of exploring potential uses of emerging technologies without the initial expense of a pilot. This was an intentional effort by Professor Roldan to manage expectations and work with the realities of emerging technologies and limited resources for supporting applications beyond the one or two semester engagement.

In spring 2005 Mobility Project teams developed second versions of the applications built in fall 2004, incorporating changes to requirements based on the use of the applications in the community. One CmpE student, an AmeriCorps member, continued to work on the online registration system for the health fair, expanding its capabilities and incorporating registration for other THT volunteer opportunities.

Student Outcomes

For every semester the Mobility Project administered measures of student learning. These measures included surveys of student-reported self-efficacy with the skills taught in each course, familiarity with mobile technology, a survey of teamwork skills, and the Member Teach Evaluation Survey (MATES). MATES was developed by SJSU organization and management professor Marlene Turner (2003) and incorporated University of California, Berkeley's Higher Education Service Learning Surveys (Diaz-Gallegos, Furco, & Yamada, 1999). Because the project's first year involved non-service learning activities, we would compare outcomes for this first year with the outcomes for students involved in service learning activities in the second year of the project. Thus, it was possible to test whether service-learning experiences resulted in stronger gains in student learning when compared with non-service-learning experiences. End-of-semester scores of teams working on projects for CBOs were compared with those of teams working on projects for non-CBO partners. The results show significant differences in students' civic engagement and cross-functional teamwork skills—providing support for the proposition that service-learning experiences result in greater gains than non-service-learning experiences.

Figure 13.1 shows the results of comparing end-of-semester scores of students on civic engagement items of the Higher Education Service Learning Surveys (Diaz-Gallegos et al., 1999). The two items are

- Being involved in a program to improve my community is important.
- I feel that I can have a positive impact on local social problems.

Students who worked on service-learning projects for CBOs scored significantly higher than students who worked on for-profit projects for non-CBO partners.

FIGURE 13.1
Student Civic Engagement Scores: Comparison of Students Working With For-Profit Versus CBO Partners

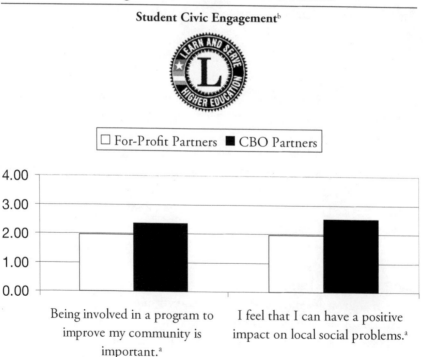

Student Civic Engagement[b]

☐ For-Profit Partners   ■ CBO Partners

Being involved in a program to improve my community is important.[a]

I feel that I can have a positive impact on local social problems.[a]

[a] $p < .01$
[b] Measured using "The higher education service-learning surveys," by D. Diaz-Gallegos, A. Furco, & H. Yamada, 1999, http://www.servicelearning.org/filemanager/download/HEdPostSL_9 9.pdf

Figure 13.2 shows the results of comparing end-of-semester scores of students on team evaluation items from MATES (Turner, 2003). The three items are

- Team goals were clear and specific.
- Team found a solution to its tasks very early.
- Overall, the team performed effectively.

FIGURE 13.2
Cross-Functional Team Skills Scores: Comparison of Students Working With For-Profit Versus CBO Partners

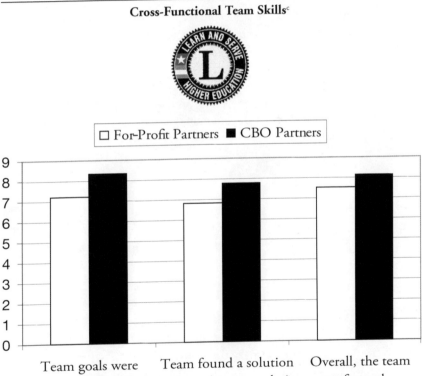

^{a} p < .01
^{b} p < .05
^{c} Measured using *Developing MATES,* by M. Turner, 2003, paper presented at the Celebrating the Scholarship of Teaching and Learning Conference, San José, CA.

Students who worked on service-learning projects for CBOs scored significantly higher than students who worked on for-profit projects for non-CBO partners.

These survey measures were supported by anecdotal evidence from the students. In general, students found the experience challenging but very helpful for learning skills that were essential to their early careers. MIS graduates who took the mobility courses and are now working as IT consultants identify the skills they built working with other disciplines as very helpful in their current positions. Some also reported on personal growth from their experiences, as summed up by this reflection from a student who managed the community asset mapping project in fall 2004:

> Through the community mapping project, I learned a great deal about the local community, especially the Five Wounds/Brookwood Terrace area. I learned about how there is an unusual amount of obese and diabetic community members. . . . These projects have made me aware of my own nutrition issues and my lack of daily exercise. Actually, lack of any exercise. After the end of the school year, I will make exercise and eating well a priority. With my effort for the community mapping projects, I realized I can make a tremendous impact by bringing the tools to create change.

Lessons Learned

Key lessons learned from the Mobility Project are the importance of managing expectations—particularly in the face of success—and the important role that faculty play in keeping a focus on student learning and benefits.

Managing Expectations

As discussed above, a great effort was placed in emphasizing that the projects undertaken by the Mobility Project teams were intended as proof-of-concept efforts. It was challenging to make this point, given the excitement generated by an abundance of new technologies and the opportunity to be creative with technology and work practices. It was therefore necessary to keep repeating the mantra that the projects were only intended to help THT assess whether the applications of mobile technology identified were appropriate for the organization. It was interesting to hear one of the THT participants noting around the beginning of the spring 2005 semester that he "finally understood what 'proof of concept' meant." It was a reminder that, some-times, managing expectations involves an effort at minimizing and/or clearly defining discipline-based jargon, particularly when the collaboration spans multiple disciplines and organizations. Despite best efforts to define collabo-ration parameters up front, there will always be misunderstandings along the way, sometimes because of differences in interpretation of terms that are taken for granted in one discipline (e.g., proof of concept in MIS) but not in another.

Most efforts at managing expectations, such as the proof-of-concept ap-proach, are intended to address potential negative perceptions of results; we were surprised by the effort required to manage positive perceptions of re-sults as well. In many ways, the Mobility Project was a great success, deliver-ing a series of highly visible and well-developed applications. While quite encouraging, this success brought on its own set of issues that had to be managed. Foremost was the large number of new opportunities and partner-ships that cropped up as a result of this success. At one point, it became clear the project leaders were stretched and unable to take on any more of the enticing opportunities that came their way—although this was not before they were already stretched way beyond their capacity. Identifying up front one's level of involvement—for example, proof of concept, long-term en-gagement—in proportion to the resources available can also help with limit-ing the scope of future involvement, as it did with the Mobility Project. Although, granted, figuring out what scope is appropriate given a set of re-sources is not easy. Unfortunately, in the beginning, one generally errs on the side of a larger scope than appropriate; hence the scramble to deliver. Over time one sees the wisdom in "under promising and overdelivering" and making sure that one does not take on tasks that are best left to the responsibility and talents of other participants. This is especially important to keep in mind when working with organizations and individuals who are strapped for resources and eager to get as much help as they can get from partners.

Another aspect of managing expectations is tracking as much as possible the stories that are told about the project. As new partners come into the project, there is a tendency to rewrite history. While it is impossible to track all the stories that emerge from a given project, it is important to make sure to highlight stories that value and recognize appropriately the input of all participants involved. Sometimes this does involve tooting one's own horn and a little bit of luck with finding wise and conscientious storytellers who recognize the dynamics of socially conscious involvement and change. In the end, one hopes to find a balance between telling the story from one's perspective and having others tell stories that bring resources to and advance a project's goals or some higher-order goal: community benefits or student learning.

Faculty Role

Any partnership as wide ranging as the one described here is certain to engender multiple and often conflicting goals among participants. As the professor teaching a service-learning class, it is his or her role to make sure that student learning is foremost among those goals. Students and faculty are vulnerable to being caught up in the exhilaration that comes with doing something good for the community, forgetting that a key purpose for the community involvement is to solidify understanding of course concepts. Community partners have their service-focused organizational mission foremost in mind, and sometimes this may not mesh well with the structure of a university course. For example, students may end up spending too many hours on trying to complete an aspect of the project (e.g., define customer requirements that community partners keep changing) to the detriment of other project requirements (building a business case for the application). Professors sometimes have to play the role of tough cop, refocusing students' priorities to make sure they achieve course objectives. A lot of this is attained through reflections conducted with students, making sure that students continue to make connections between their community service and course goals. It is also part of a continuing conversation with community partners to make sure they understand the full range of priorities encompassed by the course.

Another role faculty can play is identifying auxiliary experiences that provide students with excellent opportunities for growth. For example, the Mobility Project provided many occasions for recognition through events held by THT, HP, and SJSU, as well as interest from the press. Involving students in events, interviews, and photo shoots gives them well-earned recognition for their efforts and provides third-party reinforcement of the importance of community involvement. These occasions are also invaluable for building student confidence and communication skills.

Faculty can also play a role in attaining benefits that are somewhat outside course goals but important at a programmatic level. For example, one of the CmpE students was extremely committed to delivering a product that met community partner needs, accommodating changes up to a few days before the application needed to be delivered despite numerous reminders to freeze requirements early. In the end, though, the successful delivery of the application and the students' commitment to getting the job done were the key learning experiences that helped him get a job as a developer for a local mobile technology startup. Here the faculty's role was to recognize the positive in what was essentially a breakdown of the system and transform it into a beneficial experience for the student.

Conclusion

The outcomes for this project were quite encouraging and show there are benefits to incorporating service learning even when community involvement is not traditionally integral to a field of study. However, as has been often said, the application of service learning in any field is challenging and always takes more coordination and effort than expected. The collaboration described in this chapter was especially ambitious and required a level of support that proved unsustainable. Thus, it has not been institutionalized in the configuration reported on here. Still, its influence can be seen in the establishment of well-attended undergraduate- and graduate-level mobile software development courses in SJSU's CmpE department; a strong appreciation and active interest in mobile technologies in a wide range of disciplines at SJSU including health science; and a rich collaboration on technology innovation to address community needs involving SJSU faculty, HP, Purdue's EPICS program, local entrepreneurs, and the National Collegiate Inventors and Innovators Alliance.

References

Diaz-Gallegos, D., Furco, A., & Yamada, H. (1999). *The higher education service-learning surveys*. Retrieved April 4, 2004, from http://www.servicelearning.org/filemanager/download/HEdPostSL_99.pdf

Kelley, L. A. (2004). *Problem-based learning through mobile technology: External evaluation report on the first year of the Mobility Project* (unpublished report).

Roldan, M., Strage, A., & David, D. (2004). A framework for assessing academic service learning across disciplines. In S. H. Billig & M. Welch (Eds.), *New perspectives in service-learning: Research to advance the field* (pp. 39–60). Charlotte, NC: Information Age Publishing.

Turner, M. (2003, April). *Developing MATES.* Paper presented at the Celebrating the Scholarship of Teaching and Learning Conference, San José, CA.

INDEX

Also available from Stylus

Service Learning for Civic Engagement Series
Series Editor: Gerald Eisman
To stimulate the adaptation of the approaches described in these books, each volume includes an Activity/
Methodology table that summarizes key elements of each example, such as class size, pedagogy, and other
potential disciplinary applications

Race, Poverty, and Social Justice
Multidisciplinary Perspectives through Service Learning
Edited by José Calderón

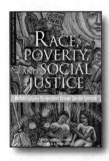

"Calderón compiles a collection designed to advance service learning 'beyond volunteerism (or charity) to a level of civic engagements that advances social justice in
our institutions and a democratic culture in a civil society.' With topics ranging from
day laborer centers and homelessness to preparing the student for life in a diverse
global society, the collection provides practical strategies for achieving transformative learning in multiple contexts."—*Diversity & Democracy (AAC&U)*

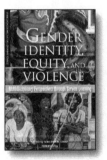

Gender Identity, Equity, and Violence
Multidisciplinary Perspectives through Service Learning
Edited by Geraldine B. Stahly

The authors of the thirteen chapters in this volume bring excitement and innovations to teaching about gender from a wide range of theoretical and discipline perspectives. They exhibit the inclusiveness that is central to feminist
pedagogy—a perspective that centers the educational enterprise in the analysis of the interconnectedness of social categories that have traditionally divided
and given root to inequality and oppression and aims for no less than social
transformation. Empowerment is a core value in gender education and the experiential approach nur-
tures that goal.

Research, Advocacy, and Political Engagement
Multidisciplinary Perspectives through Service Learning
Edited by Sally Cahill Tannenbaum

The chapters in this book describe how teachers in Politics, Education, Urban and
Regional Planning, Business, Communications, Sociology, Mathematics, Economics, and Women's Studies have created effective activities that advance disciplinary
knowledge, develop collaboration with communities, and engage students in the
political process.

Forthcoming:

Social Responsibility and Sustainability
Multidisciplinary Perspectives through Service Learning

Sty/us

22883 Quicksilver Drive
Sterling, VA 20166-2102

Subscribe to our e-mail alerts: www.Styluspub.com